Greenberg's®
Guide to
LGB® TRAINS

By John R. Ottley

**Photographs by Bruce C. Greenberg,
Maury Feinstein, and George Stern**

**Additional photographs through the courtesy of
Lehmann-Gross-Bahn, Nürnberg**

Greenberg Publishing Company
7566 Main Street
Sykesville, MD 21784
(301) 795-7447

Second Edition

Manufactured in the United States of America

Greenberg Publishing Company offers the world's largest selection of Lionel, American Flyer and other toy train publications as well as a selection of books on model and prototype railroading. To receive our current catalogue, send a stamped, self-addressed envelope marked "Catalogue."

Greenberg Publishing Company sponsors the world's largest public model train shows. The shows feature extravagant operating model railroads for N, HO, O, Standard and 1 gauges as well as a huge marketplace for buying and selling nearly all model railroad equipment. The shows also feature a large selection of dollhouse miniatures.

Shows are currently offered in Baltimore, Boston, Cherry Hill in New Jersey, Fort Lauderdale and Tampa, Long Island in New York, Philadelphia, Pittsburgh, and Richmond. To receive our current show listing, please send a stamped, self-addressed envelope marked "Train Show Schedule."

ISBN 0-89778-091-4

Library of Congress Cataloging-in-Publication Data

Ottley, John R.

    Greenberg's Guide to LGB Trains / John R. Ottley. -- 2nd ed.

      p. cm.

    Includes index.

    ISBN 0-89778-091-4

    1. Railroads--Models.   2. Ernst Paul Lehmann (Firm)   I. Title.

TF197.O77   1989

625.1'9'075--dc20   89-32574

Contents

Dedication

In memory of
Alfred E. Lentz
1931-1989
who shared his passion for LGB trains and so inspired us all.

ACKNOWLEDGMENTS

It is with great pleasure that we present the second edition of *Greenberg's Guide to LGB Trains*. This edition provides many new variations, many new color photographs, and a chapter on non-factory production.

John Ottley supervised the Guide's complete re-evaluation; he read and reread each entry, discussed subtle differences in variations, and generally considered each and every listing. **Joe Hylva** provided valuable assistance in specifying variations, reviewing prices, and in making available for photography his sizeable and impressive LGB collection. Both Ottley and Hylva and our panel of reviewers painstakingly reviewed the prices for every listing; a very important task since prices have fluctuated in the past year. In addition, **George Ryall** graciously lent LGB trains and equipment to be photographed.

Friedrich Biggeleben, the translator of the German edition, was more than just a translator. Biggeleben, a very enthusiastic LGB collector, lives in West Germany. When questions arose concerning chronology, subtle variations, or production, he took it upon himself to consult with Rolf Richter at the LGB office in Nuremburg. His methodical and dedicated research are most appreciated.

Special thanks to **Rolf Richter** who worked with Biggeleben and our Sykesville staff to make this second edition as comprehensive and attractive as possible. Richter kindly lent us photographs for the Introduction and patiently answered what I am sure must have seemed like endless questions about LGB production. It was also a great pleasure to meet Rolf, Wolfgang and Johannes Richter on my visit in February, 1988 to the Toy Fair in Nuremberg, and to be given a tour of their most impressive factory. The tour made clear the wonders of computerized technology, assembly line efficiency, and the dedication of the people who work there.

Maury Feinstein, staff photographer, has photographed more trains in three years than most people do in a lifetime. This edition includes a large number of Feinstein's handsome new photographs, particularly of the Hylva and Ryall collections.

Samuel Baum supervised the Guide's production. He also assisted greatly in producing the German version of the book. **Terri Glaser** was responsible for correcting and maintaining both the English and German manuscripts and printing out the final typeset copy. **George Voellmer**, a German-born model railroader, provided invaluable assistance. **Maureen Crum** designed the book's format and presentation, and assisted in sizing photographs. **Donna Price** executed the line drawings in Chapter V and proofread each chapter.

Readers are invited to use the enclosed Addition/Correction sheet to update our records if there is a question about a variation which is not listed. For answers to specific questions, please write to John Ottley at the Greenberg Publishing Company.

Linda F. Greenberg
Publisher
May, 1989

Foreword

PURPOSE

What is LGB? This book will show you. It will help you appreciate your trains, whether you have just a few or a sophisticated collection. It will provide a historical context for most pieces of equipment. It will sensitize you to the factors that affect value. It is not a substitute for experience in the marketplace. But, it will answer the very important question, "Is this particular piece a good value?"

There is NO substitute for experience in the marketplace. *We strongly recommend that novices do not make major purchases without the assistance of friends who have experience in buying and selling trains.*

If you are buying a train and do not know whom to ask about its value, look for the people running the meet or show and discuss with them your need for assistance. Usually they can refer you to an experienced collector who would be willing to examine the piece and offer his opinion.

DETERMINING VALUES

The train values in this book are based on prices obtained at meets throughout the United States and from private transactions reported by our panel of reviewers in 1989. The prices are OBTAINED, rather than asking prices. Obtained prices represent a "ready sale," or a price perceived as a good value by the buyer. They may sometimes appear lower than those seen on trains at meets for two reasons. First, sold items often sell in the first hour of a train meet, and therefore are no longer visible. A good portion of the action at most meets occurs in the first hour. The items that do not sell in the first hour have a higher price tag and this, although not representing the sales price, is the price observed. A related source of discrepancy is the willingness of some sellers to bargain over price.

Toy train values vary for a number of reasons. First, consider the **relative knowledge** of the buyer and seller. A seller may be unaware that he has a rare variation and sell it for the price of a common piece. Another source of price variation is **short-term fluctuation**. If four 2040s are for sale at a small meet, we would expect that supply would quickly outpace demand and lead to a reduction in price. A related source of variation is the **season** of the year. The train market is slower in the summer, and sellers may at this time be more inclined to reduce prices if they really want to

move an item. Another important source of price variation is the relative strength of the seller's **desire to sell** and the buyer's **eagerness to buy**. Clearly a seller in economic distress will be more eager to strike a bargain. A final source of variation are the **personalities** of the seller and buyer. Some sellers like to turn over items quickly and, therefore, price their items to move; others seek a higher price and will bring an item to meet after meet until they find a willing buyer.

Mail order prices for used trains are generally higher than those obtained at train meets. This reflects the cost and effort of producing and distributing a price list and packing and shipping items. Mail order items do sell at prices above those listed in this book. A final source of difference between observed prices and reported prices is region.

If you have trains to sell and you sell them to a person planning to resell them at another train show, you will NOT obtain the prices reported in this book. Rather you may expect to achieve about fifty percent of these prices. Basically, for your items to be of interest to such a buyer, he must buy them for considerably less than the prices listed here.

CONDITION FOR VALUE

EXCELLENT: Item has unblemished factory paint and details, may or may not have box, has signs of light indoor running (i.e. pickup shoes show some wear but are not overly worn and the wheels have minor scuffing). In contrast, MINT means that the item is brand new, absolutely unmarred, is completely original and unused, and is in its original box. GOOD means that the item has blemished paint, has signs of heavy indoor running (i.e., the pickup shoes show considerable wear and the wheels show heavy scuffing). Thus, MINT brings a higher price than EXCELLENT, and EXCELLENT brings a higher price than GOOD.

PRICING CODE

The price when available is for a piece in Excellent Condition. In some cases we do not provide a price, but instead indicate **CP, NRS, or NSS.**

CP — CURRENT PRODUCTION. The item is readily available for purchase from current dealer stocks. The price fluctuates somewhat according to exchange rate, the seller's cost basis, and local competition.

NRS — NO REPORTED SALES. In the few cases where there is insufficient information upon which to determine the value of a given item, we show **NRS** in the price column. Here again we recommend that you rely on your **experience** or on the **assistance** of an experienced collector to determine what price you should pay for any of these items.

NSS — NOT SOLD SEPARATELY. Originally sold as part of a set and not intended for individual sale, however some dealers and/or collectors may have broken up sets.

We include those variations which have been authenticated. In a few cases, where data is missing or doubtful, we ask readers for further information or confirmation. Values are also reported for items which are not available from current dealer stock.

Occasionally there is a request for Reader Confirmation or Confirmation Requested. In this case we are asking you, the reader, to check your collection to substantiate a variation or detail of an item.

Traditionally, in the toy train field, there is a great deal of concern with exterior appearance and less concern with operation. This is somewhat true with LGB, although there has always been more attention given to LGB's running power.

Measurements for all LGB equipment are given in metrics. Both engines and rolling stock are reported in millimeters and reflect the length over buffers. On real railroads, buffers are knob-like protrusions at each end of the car, over or beside the coupler, which serve as powerful shock absorbers. The buffers prevent railroad workers from being squashed between cars while the workers manually couple or uncouple cars.

Letters in parentheses are not part of LGB's car numbering system but have been added by the author to help differentiate between model variations.

NUREMBERG AND NÜRNBERG

There are two spellings of the name Nuremberg which appear in the book. The German spelling "Nürnberg" is used when it refers to specific markings on trains. The American spelling "Nuremberg" is used at all other times.

INTRODUCTION

Although only twenty years have elapsed since Lehmann first began producing trains, numerous changes and continual upgrading have improved the quality of LGB trains while generating many interesting and unusual variations. With LGB's accelerating popularity has also come a greater desire by collectors to understand and decipher the nature and value of this new collectible. These circumstances, coupled with the opportunity to capture all of LGB's rare or little known variations while the product is still new, make this collector's guide both unique and valuable.

However, the information provided here is not just for the "serious" collector; it is also intended to be used on a casual basis to help the sporadic operator discover

LGB trains operate quietly and smoothly year after year.

more about his enjoyable toy and how it happens to be a wise investment in many ways.

LGB, G, AND IIm:
A WORD ON SCALE AND GAUGE

When LGB (Lehmann-Gross-Bahn) trains first began rolling off the assembly lines at the Lehmann factory in Nuremberg, West Germany in 1968, most toy manufacturers considered the 1:22.5 scale toy train too large and awkward to be a practical toy. As we have seen, these early doomsayers were wrong. LGB trains, whose robust qualities allow them to be run either indoors or outside, have experienced an expanding popularity of historic proportion. Not only has LGB been successful, but it has played a major role in rekindling public interest in toy trains and is responsible for creating an industry devoted entirely to large scale trains.

The trains themselves are modeled primarily on European and American narrow gauge prototypes in 1:22.5 scale currently known as G Gauge. The G designation was an imaginative designation utilized to better promote the line and to distinguish it from other large scale trains. In this country, LGB was originally designated by the first United States Distributor, Chas. C. Merzbach Company, as K Gauge to emphasize its king size. However, in the mid-1970s the designation was changed to G to bridge more appropriately the German (gross) and English (giant) language barrier.

These size designations, with the fact that LGB runs on track with the same distance between the rails as 1 Gauge (45 mm), have caused considerable confusion among collectors and modelers as to just what gauge LGB really is. To Europeans, 1:22.5 translates into Gauge II (2). Although LGB trains are made in 1:22.5 scale they run on 45 mm wide track which, coincidentally, happens to be the same width as 1 Gauge track (standard Gauge II track is appoximately 64 mm wide). The reason for the narrow rail span in LGB track is due to the fact that LGB is modeled after narrow gauge prototypes in what is well known to Europeans as Gauge IIm (Gauge II, meter-width narrow gauge).

In the United States, many collectors still refer to LGB as 1 Gauge, while free thinkers have gone so far as to give it a "Gm" Gauge. Despite LGB's popularity, the G designation has not been universally embraced. Indeed, nearly all European manufacturers of 1:22.5 scale trains designate their products as Gauge II. In the name of universal understanding and accuracy, LGB should be called Gauge II as well, with G as a synonym. If and when the G designation receives universal acceptance as a synonym for Gauge II, the "Gm" application would become appropriate. At present, GM is known to our European friends only as an American manufacturer of automobiles!

Wolfgang Richter and John Ottley, Summer 1986.

SOME PERSONAL HISTORY

My first active involvement with LGB happened seven years ago. Although some people may not see any correlation between the change I went through because of my experience with LGB trains, I am sure that Sigmund Freud would find an interesting connection in the story that follows.

In mid-1982, while finishing up the live animal research for my Master's Degree in Herpetology (reptile and amphibian studies), I began looking for a hobby that didn't need to be fed or have its cage cleaned. As I mulled over possible alternatives, I began to remember with very pleasant and positive associations the toy trains I had played with as a child. The seeds planted by Marx windup choo-choos, nurtured by American Flyer and Lionel, suddenly began to sprout! I remembered early train layouts covering sheets of plywood, and rails and trains running all through the house.

These thoughts and memories evoked an idyllic vision of track running from room to room through my home, and of my happiness as I lie on the front room carpet with my children as we all watch the trains whiz by. But, perhaps the best part of this vision was that I could put my hobby away and ignore it when I had finished playing with it! The thought of not having to clean out smelly cages, feed dozens of hungry little mouths, or worry over sick animals further encouraged me.

My father had been collecting and operating several gauges of electric trains for many years. Although I appreciated and enjoyed my dad's trains, I did not feel ready to tackle a multi-gauge train collection. What I needed was a fairly simple and enjoyable toy train that would still offer substantial play value for my children and me. Recalling a visit to my dad's home in 1977, I remembered seeing some large and colorful European trains — that my dad called "LGB" — running, of all places, outside on his lawn and patio. This was my first "close encounter" with "The Big Train."

Bearing all of these memories and circumstances in mind, I took my wife by the hand and set off for the nearest toy store that I thought would most likely carry LGB.

LGB was for me. I would sell my exotic reptile collection and buy trains! A substantial amount of the wind was removed from my sails when we discovered that LGB commanded a rather stiff price: most sets sold for nearly $400 at that time and there was no action without a $40 transformer! A little discouraged but undaunted, we retraced our steps a bit. I recall muttering to myself as we drove home that perhaps my snakes weren't so bad after all and that we could go to K-Mart and pick up a Tyco set on sale for $19.95. My wife, however, whose brilliance is only exceeded by her good looks, offered one of those enlightened suggestions that come when I feel all is lost. She said, "Why not call your dad?"

Somehow, in my exuberance, I had forgotten that the most obvious way to solve our (my) problem was to "ask Dad." I called him immediately and explained my desire to get involved with the electric train hobby, particularly with LGB. His reaction can probably best be compared to the excitement the Old Testament father felt at the return of the prodical son. As my Dad began rattling off names of locomotives and catalogue numbers that he was sure would please, I am sure he was thinking, "At last, my boy has seen the light!" Anyway, the list of LGB items kept getting longer and longer and longer. Dad said he would mail a catalogue and some brochures to me the next day. Before I had hung up the phone, however, he had sold me a slightly used passenger train set, several new freight cars, eight cases of track, and a red 2095 Austrian Diesel Locomotive known as a BoBo, and he had "loaned" me several other items as well. Sure, Dad had exerted filial responsiblity for his son by saving him some money, but I had already spent nearly three times the cost of the train set my wife and I had drooled over at the toy store. We looked at each other thinking, "Good grief, what have we done?"

Within a few days the boxes arrived. They were numerous and big. It was better than opening Christmas presents as we unpacked those brightly colored trains and began running track everywhere. The trains were fantastic and fulfilled my dreams. Our friends were amazed to find that the "crazy snake-man" now had trains running through his house. With my reptiles, most of those good folk just politely smiled and tried to ask questions that would disguise what they really thought or felt. It wasn't long until my friends noticed how elegant LGB looked and what fun the trains were to operate. Suddenly, these same friends all seemed to have only one question, "Where can I get some?"

Seeing an opportunity in the making, I called Dad again. I knew that he had a good working relationship with a fellow who owned a large train shop. I also knew that my dad was usually able to buy LGB at the dealer's cost. Perhaps the train shop would sell me trains. My dad's friend was accommodating as long as I agreed to purchase a minimum of $2,500 in LGB each month for six months. As I remember, that seemed like a very big commitment, but after about four minutes of serious deliberation, I nonetheless jumped in with both feet.

It wasn't too long before some of my friends began expanding their layouts with more trains, extra track, rolling stock, and buildings. Word kept spreading until I could barely keep up with the orders and new inquiries. Before I realized what was happening I was selling more LGB than my dad's buddy could supply. Within six months I was virtually forced to open a retail store; a business generated almost entirely by word of mouth! By now I had sold my reptile collection and had made enough money to purchase the inventory to stock a small store. It seemed as though overnight my new hobby had become a successful, thriving business.

GENESIS OF THE PRICE GUIDE

Once in business and seeing the large amount of LGB that passed through my shop, my trained taxonomic eye began to pick out variations in the equipment. I took great interest in and began discussing and raising questions about these variations with several friends who were considered old-time collectors. Some of these collectors supplied me with early catalogues and occasionally let me see their older LGB items. Their reluctance to share their LGB was not due to their unwillingness to share, but was rather because their collections were usually hidden away to emerge only at Christmas time. As I began to spend more time evaluating my new hobby, it became clear that a study of LGB variations would probably be well received, particularly since this was an unusual opportunity to get a grip on this line as it was being produced. The primary concern voiced by most LGB collectors was that a tremendous amount of variation seemed to appear in the same items from one production run to the next. I realized that occasional minor variations (i.e. the position of a decal or painted marking) could probably be attributed to the artistic license of factory personnel. Factory-sanctioned changes generally took the form of new decals or painted details — black stripes added to the 2060H Locomotive — or an altered color — the 4041 Hopper Car was changed from red to orange. Minor variations in color were most likely caused by a casual mixing of paint,

Outdoor "train gardens" have opened up a new field of train operations.

using different types of paint, or changes in the pigments used to color the plastics.

Bearing all this in mind, I determined that the best way to define "variations" was to focus on consistent and more easily recognizable variables such as whether or not an item was painted, had frame markings, had a particular body type, etc.

After several months of studying, analyzing, and chasing down variations and hard-to-find pieces, I finally assembled a rough but fairly complete manuscript. I mailed copies of the manuscript to several friends and associates in the LGB Model Railroad Club as well as dealers who had been carrying LGB since its early manufacture. To my surprise and delight the guide received very favorable reviews. With the reviews came information on additional variations and refinements. The book was really beginning to take shape and I was getting more and more excited about it every day!

While attending the Fall 1983 TCA meet at York, Pennsylvania, I stopped by the booth of Greenberg Publishing Company and discussed my endeavor with Linda Greenberg. Linda liked LGB and was interested in the book. She asked to see and evaluate the manuscript. I realized at that moment that if the guide had any merit this evaluation would be the test.

As I look back, it doesn't seem like such a hurdle now, but I really thought I would strip my gears while the Greenbergs gave my "whim" the acid test. When I finally heard Linda's voice on the telephone telling me that she and Bruce were very pleased with the rough draft, I breathed a long sigh of relief. What I didn't realize was that lengthy prepublication revisions, changes, and additions, etc., would take about twice the time it took me to assemble and write the original draft. What further complicated matters was that Lehmann was producing a considerable number of new, limited-

Two cars from the 100th Anniversary Set. The car on the left is missing its Jubilee Express lettering over the windows and surrounding gold border. This is an interesting factory error. The car on the right is complete.

run items at the same time I was revising the manuscript. Although it seemed as if something new appeared just as I was getting the guide wrapped up, this circumstance gave me the opportunity to evaluate and catalogue many new items and variations just off the assembly line.

Although I organized and described the trains, had it not been for the help and advice of many good friends and colleagues, I would undoubtedly still be sitting behind a word processor in some darkened room wondering if the guide or myself would ever see the light of day. Avid LGB fans such as Rudi Enners, Robert Cage, Carter Colwell, Hans Kahl, Al Rudman, Joe Hylva, Dave Watts, Robert Schuster, Gary Keck, Howard Banzaff, and Dan Jansen provided me with information and items to help keep me in stride with variations and changes made by Lehmann. Joe Hylva's **LGB Checklist** was a great benefit as well. My dad, Leonard Ottley, whose patience with me is most appreciated and still pretty good, inspired and motivated me to complete this endeavor.

PRICING

The one issue that causes many headaches and will most likely never be completely resolved is pricing. Although most prices reflect genuine values from known sales, many items had to be evaluated according to their relative availability. In other words, some items are rare, but no one we knew had sold any lately, or an engine was hard to find yet no one else seemed to be aware of it. For example, "hot goodies" such as the early solid-color steeple-cabs or ELOKs may fetch well over $1,000. However, the early dark green and black 2050 Tramway or one of the transition orange 2033 Service Locomotives are equally hard to find, but sell for considerably less than a solid green 2035 ELOK. Also, age should not be the primary dictate of value. Many recently produced transition pieces — items produced while a major color or detail change was occurring — are very uncommon. I have seen collectors pass over the rare but newer brown 4010 Low-Sided Gondola with

black and white markings or the orange 2033 Service Engine with gold plating on the manufacturer's plaque for an older yet more common piece.

International currency fluctuations also affect prices. For example, in 1984 the dollar was very strong against the Deutsche Mark, and consequently the price of new merchandise dropped by as much as 40 percent, compared to prices from the previous year. By late 1986 the relationship had changed dramatically. From late 1986 through 1987 the dollar was very weak when compared to the Deutsche Mark, and prices for new LGB rose to an all-time high. Although the 1984 prices dropped, collector prices seemed to hold their own, except for some more common, early pieces and several collector's sets. In 1987 some new merchandise sold for retail prices that were occasionally higher than the prices of some of the older, more collectible items. Under such circumstances, the prices of collector pieces seemed to climb slowly. This augurs well for speculation as long as retail prices remain high. In spite of fluctuating prices, LGB trains have experienced some of the sharpest and quickest increases in values. Under circumstances such as these, LGB trains should be worth more than their purchase price. Most collectors and operators will tell you though that LGB trains are a bargain at any price, owing to Lehmann's attention to beauty and quality — the main ingredients of LGB's success.

Now, LGB's remarkable popularity has brought with it higher quality, stable prices, and finally this new collectors' guide. Most people find that enjoying toy trains has a direct relationship to their self-expression, and LGB has that universal appeal that makes a person's involvement with toy trains a very desirable activity. LGB has cultivated a hobby. It has, as well,

The LGB factory is a very large and modern complex of buildings. The handsomely-painted exterior imitates the red, white, and green color scheme of the LGB box cover.

more simply, brought many would-be train nuts out of the closet. Whether you have a full-blown back yard layout or a circle of track on your family room carpet, you have already added to your vocabulary of fun — a language easily understood by owners of LGB.

INTRODUCTION TO PRIMUS

That Primus trains bear a striking resemblance to LGB is no accident. Manufactured by Lehmann for the Metro Company department store chain of West Germany, Primus was essentially a less detailed, and hence less expensive, version of LGB. Though usually unpainted and not as brightly colored as their LGB counterparts, Primus trains were only produced for a short time and have become highly valued by collectors. Some of the catalogue numbers listed in the Guide or in the Primus Appendix on page 132 may or may not be "official" since Lehmann packaged most Primus pieces in yellow boxes (both the window type and the two-piece box) that lacked any markings or numbers. Individually packaged pieces appear to have had their respective catalogue numbers hand-stamped in ink after leaving the Lehmann factory, perhaps by the Primus distributor; only the box for the Primus train set came with a printed number, similar to the printed numbers on LGB train sets. Primus pieces bear the same embossed identification numbers as their LGB counterparts.

Track and Transformer

LGB track items, track packs, and transformers were also offered with Primus equipment, but the Primus catalogue numbers have not been "officially" recog-

nized by the Lehmann factory and may have been applied to the equipment by those people distributing Primus themselves. All of the track pieces carry the embossed LGB logo and catalogue number on the underside of the plastic crossties.

AN INTERVIEW WITH WOLFGANG RICHTER AT THE LGB FACTORY

By Carter Colwell
Nuremberg, Summer 1986

At the snap of the switch and with much chugging, a large electric model of a steam locomotive comes out of the back wall, its shrill European whistle outlining the curve of the bar before it slows to a stop before me.

"I just use that to bring in drinks when we are having a meeting here," says Wolfgang Richter, co-owner and chief executive officer of the Lehmann Patentwerk. But we are having only a quick cup of coffee as we talk of the company's postwar development and Herr Richter's part in its growth; the open freight wagon is empty today.

Over our heads is a fifteen foot long clear plastic tube with a strange track and on it a low-wheeled mechanism hugs the rails. An experimental model propelled by magnetized track (linear induction), it was developed by Herr Richter's late brother Eberhard in hopes that it might prove to be a marketable item; but analysis showed production costs would be too high. Only the prototype was ever made, a dream that turned out to be impractical.

The walls around us and around the conference table behind us are lined with showcases. Silhouetted against the light-washed wall behind them stand all the current models of the largest mass-produced model trains in the world: LGB, the Lehmann-Gross-Bahn. Tens of thousands are produced at a time, for these are a dream that turned out to be practical indeed.

Perhaps the most famous toy makers in the world, the Lehmann company entered the period of World War II under the direction of Wolfgang Richter's father, Johannes. Already in his sixties when the war began, Johannes Richter refused to turn his toy factory into a war machine, and would not make military supplies. Although production fell radically, he managed to get some tin sheet until 1944 and to continue limited sales through Switzerland. When the Russians swept over Brandenburg, they went through the factory with naive delight, conscripting samples probably to be sent to their children in the USSR.

But though the Russians liked the toys, the East German government did not like the enterprise that made such a private success. Johannes was arrested for having too many employees. Held for four days, he could not be found indictable on any pretext, particularly not for military production, and he was released. But the Brandenburg days of Lehmann were doomed, and in 1948 a writ of expropriation was apologetically delivered by a civil servant who said he could see no legal basis for it. The factory was now "people owned," a Volkseigene Betrieb. Seventy years old, in 1949 Johannes Richter brought his wife and three of his children still behind the Iron Curtain out of East Germany to Nuremberg.

"Nuremberg is the center of the toy industry," Johannes said, and he would consider no other site for a new beginning, although some of his future competitors were not too pleased to have the Lehmann name move into competition, even without capital, equipment, or staff. And as competitors, their fears were justified. Poor but free, Johannes gathered his family to rebuild Lehmann. "These are the best conditions we have ever had," he told his sons. He must have been right.

They started working in the back yard, producing a small string-pull top. Wolfgang and Eberhard sold it from tables in department stores. The repair of a bombed building, the acquisition of a few old foot-operated machines, and after a half year, a 20,000 Deutschmark line of credit, and Lehmann had begun its ascent. The credit was possible because Johannes Richter brought out of East Germany something the government could not expropriate — his good name. A reference from the co-founder of the Nuremberg Toy Fair convinced the local bank to make one of the best investments of the postwar period. The Richter family knew how to turn dreams into profitable realities.

"Make toys," the old man told his sons. "The money comes later."

By the end of the 1950s, with the death at age 74 of Johannes Richter, the company was in the control of his two sons Wolfgang and Eberhard.

The toy business has always been a family activity for the Richters. Wolfgang remembers how as children they would go to the factory with their father on Sundays, and how impressed they were with the big rooms where the toys were assembled. He has written a description of the factory's source of power, transmitted through leather belts to drive all the machinery.

"The showpiece of the entire operation, as well as the main attraction for us, was the 'Lokomobile.' This machine generated the power for the entire factory, making it independent of the city power supply. The black, steam-driven monster behind the windows of the engine house was waited upon by the stoker, Mr. Lorenz, who sometimes let us climb the iron ladders to the various platforms, where we could admire the many polished brass levers, handles, fittings, oilers and the glittering movements of the piston-rods. I will never forget the unique mixed odor of coke, oil, grease and steam! The Lokomobile looked like an immense, walled-in express train locomotive to me. The only difference was that the wheels on this locomotive were on the top rather than the bottom."

At the end of the 1930s, of course, there did not seem much prospect for careers in the toy business. The foreign market was practically gone, the local market not much better. Wolfgang's oldest brother became a doctor, his oldest sister became a dentist, and his other sisters married a banker, a teacher, and a patent attorney. When the war had ended, as his father struggled to keep the factory in Brandenburg, Wolfgang was in Munich, working for the United States Army and taking night classes.

"Elephant-proof" track!

Summertime.

Although the company had solidly re-established itself, in 1963 it seemed stymied in a closed market without room for expansion. As tough and occasionally unscrupulous Oriental competition constantly threatened to undersell with a sometimes inferior, sometimes stolen, but always cheaper toy, Wolfgang turned back to his childhood.

He remembers how as children they were bundled into two train compartments, shared with their parents and piles of luggage, by their governess Nina. (Johannes named a toy for her, a cat catching a mouse.) The occasion was their annual rail pilgrimage to a vacation spot on the Baltic Sea. The steam engines were exciting, and of course Wolfgang had to have a train of his own, a tinplate windup engine, green and black. He wanted to play with it at times in the garden, but dew and damp are bad for tin; and he had to be careful not to step on the tracks.

Perhaps inspired by his toy-building father, Wolfgang loved to build transport models — sometimes a ship or a plane — carved from wood. He designed them himself, working from photographs and plans. His brothers and sisters would play with the finished products.

One he remembers well was an engine, similar to the current LGB 2010. It was an old four-wheeled steamer with a straight stack, and was nearly the same size as the big LGB trains are now. Of course, it had tracks, made of strip wood held to wooden ties by glue and nails. (Wolfgang wanted, even as a child, toys that were sturdy and would last.) There were crossings and buildings and switches — hand-operated, of course. Wheels were a problem for the boy. So Wolfgang went to the factory

during a noon break and without his father's knowledge asked a man in the shipping department, where cases were made of wood, if the cratemaker could help him. He could, and on his lathe turned rimmed wheels to put Wolfgang's childhood dream on the track.

In 1963 Wolfgang was himself a father. His son Rolf, who is with the company now, remembers clearly how Wolfgang designed models of toys for the kids to play with. In 1963 Wolfgang made a cardboard model of what would five years later be an LGB train. Rolf recalls that a nice thing about the big train (the model was redone several times, in wood, then in cut-and-glued plastic) was that you could use other toys with them, compatible for play even though not perhaps exactly to the same scale.

It took Wolfgang two years to convince his brother that a new line of trains, bigger than anything currently on the market, would be good for the company, two years of designing, redesigning, seeking motors, and arguing. Eberhard saw, rightly, that the company would have to expand to handle a complete line of such magnitude, and by consent both brothers had to agree on a line of action before it became company policy. Eventually, he was persuaded. The line would be unique: Marklin and Bing had made No. 1 scale trains until the 1930s, but since then the trend had been toward smaller and smaller trains. First O, whose 1 to 48 scale ratio makes it about half the size of Lehmann's G scale 1 to 22.5, then in 1935 HO scale — "half O" — with its 1 to 87 scale, and since World War II N scale, 1 to 160, and even Marklin's Z scale, 1 to 220. Smaller, smaller, smaller. But LGB would be big.

LGB would be big enough to use with other toys. It would be tough. The trains and cars would be tough enough to run out of doors, unfazed by weather. The material would be tough, a tough plastic fused with fiberglass or rubber, and if the public needed to be educated that these were not cheap oriental plastics, it would be done. The track would be tough, tough enough to stand on. The track would be No. 1 size, a familiar size from prewar years, one that old trains could run on. The track would be narrow gauge, so that engines could run on tight radius curves small enough to use indoors as well as out, and still look realistic. It would, in the German tradition of toy trains, be a complete system, one that could be added to, changed, modified daily if one wished, giving way to shifting fantasies at will. And as that dream of variety is satisfied by the customer, the maker who satisfies the urge to novelty will not have to retool completely. Clever design of standardized parts will see to that.

These considerations convinced Eberhard. The secret was closely guarded when the decision was made in 1965 to produce and market LGB trains. Three years later, in 1968, a prototype engine and two cars were on display at the Nuremberg Toy Fair. On the single-sheet flyer, as on subsequent catalogues in these early years, Rolf and his brothers play happily with the toy trains they tested.

The line is everything the Richter brothers wished. It is tough enough to run in snow; I have run mine in the rain. It is tough enough to run 8,400 hours, the longest presently known and proven endurance run; at the University of Ulm, an LGB locomotive is in the process of running mileage equivalent to a trip around the world, some 40,000 kilometers. The only question is whether the motor will hold up. As for the track, catalogue pictures proudly show not a child, but an elephant standing on it. The tight curves look fine with narrow gauge equipment, the 2040 model of the Rhaetian "Crocodile" locomotive, articulated in two places, looking good even when its twenty-two long inches negotiate twenty-four-inch radius curves. All LGB models, says Wolfgang Richter, even the new two-foot long Swiss passenger car just moving from prototype to production as this is written, will always be designed to operate even on the smallest curves.

And it is variable: not only in the layout flexibility of any sectional track, but also in the variety of equipment Lehmann will continue to offer: a European prototype big, red electric engine featuring a pantograph operated by remote control; the "Frank S," a live steam engine being built by Aster for LGB outdoor gardens; and another Circus Train Starter Set. And to the simultaneous delight and frustration of the avid collector, there are unplanned and unrecorded color variations caused by changes in the colors of plastic pellets and paint, even from the same supplier.

From time to time, models are discontinued. But the original little 0-4-0 locomotives will go on forever. "What if a time comes when there are no plastics, as some predict?" "Then we will do something else," Herr Richter answers. "But there will always be trains and people who love them."

Wolfgang Richter's dream of a toy train has become a practical reality. Automatic molders work twenty-four hours a day making "sleeper bed," tough brown plastic tie strip with wood grain, tie plates, and spikes cast in. 12,000 pieces of curved track (catalogue number 1100) are made each day, all year long. Compressed air hisses from the automatic parts injection molders, as plastic pellets are heated, pressured into the molds, and cooled with water. The recent expansion raised the number of molders from 10 to 40. Although production hours are 7:00 AM to 4:00 PM (to 5:00 PM during overtime runs), the automatic parts injection molders run from 6:00 AM to 10:00 PM.

An occasional metallic clank comes from the shop where a dozen craftsmen work on molds sometimes weighing more than half a ton. Twenty-six pairs of high

quality steel molds will produce the new Swiss passenger car. By a new electric process, "erosion" machines burn small details into the molds with high voltage.

On three parallel tracks, mostly old aluminum rail, stand 74 dark green, colorfully-lettered baggage-mail wagons, ready for inspection. Soon they will be boxed and crated for shipment, pink labels decorated with an open umbrella and a wine glass slapped on each side of the package. The umbrella means "keep dry" and the wine glass means "fragile: this side up."

A worker welds the two red and white parts of a passenger car door together sonically, thereby leaving no surplus glue. Painting is by hand spray, the surplus automotive paint dissipating into a booth the size of a small room, with a foot of water in the bottom.

Each year, the factory makes two to three runs of every one of some 500 items in the LGB line. Among these items are new American prototypes. The "White Pass" Railroad Set with patriotic red, white and blue diesel accompanied by a boxcar in brown and stock car in yellow; and Denver & Rio Grande Western coaches with closed vestibules and bellows are but a few promised for 1989.

The plant itself is a practical dream, a pleasantly asymmetrical group of boxes like a pile of Christmas presents. The Nuremberg city fathers were loath to assent to its bright red- and white-banded colors, but finally agreed. "After all, it is a toy factory," Wolfgang Richter says crisply, walking through the overpass connecting two buildings separated by a street with a quick brisk stride that occasionally shuffles a little as though he is leaning too far forward and must step into the tilt of the earth to keep climbing it. Workers are breaking for lunch, and he exchanges "Mahlzeit" greetings — "have a good lunch" — without pausing. The plant is increasingly automated, "Robert the First" being the latest robot, which as I watched removed a car body from a mold, placed it down beside others, and clipped off the flues by which it had been held. But most of the assembly work is by hand, women's skilled fingers deftly slipping parts and screws together. Occasionally design calls for particular mechanical ability in assembly; Herr Richter thought it inappropriate to tell me what the assembly workers call the clerestory roofs of the 3010, 3011, and 3012 cars, with their recalcitrant roof frames, window sills, and glass panes. These do not go together easily.

But constant improvement is the goal and the practice of the Lehmann Company, and the history of the product is a history of continual betterment. I commented on how ingenious the assembly of the 2010 Locomotive was, and how cleverly parts were used to hold each other together, and Herr Richter replied it was too complicated. Next year, replacing the motor will be much simpler.

Experts, of course, work on the design of cars, locomotives, track, signals, translating the brothers' designs into practical actuality, into things that can be made for a price that can be paid. Every Monday morning the foremen meet with the owner, to suggest procedural improvements. The basic production practices established by Eberhard continue in effect. Recent improvements in production include new mold-making machines and improved printing. Color separations, when masking is necessary, offer a possibility for color bleeding at the mask part-line; but an inspector stands ready, narrow paintbrush in hand, to touch up irregularities — by hand.

Decisions are influenced by the experience of users. When an early polystyrene faded, it was abandoned as a production material. For further color regularity, models are now painted, even though the plastic of which they are made may be the same color. The very first locomotives had spur gears; customer comments on the noise made by 10,000 revolutions per minute led to a change after seven or eight months to the worm gear motors now used. Foremen, customers, all contribute their insights to LGB management decisions, as do those in the sales network. For example, American importer Bill Lamping suggested the popular American caboose, 4065, and the Railway Express car, 4071.

Even the real trains on display outside the factory are subject to playful improvement. Rolf, soon to be joined in the family business by his cousin, Eberhard's son, has installed a smoke maker in the old black and red 0-4-0T locomotive brought here from East Germany. Now its stack smokes and its cylinder blow-down valves leak steam.

Herr Richter considers the decision to start again in Nuremberg their most important decision. Close behind that comes the decision for which he was so much responsible, the decision to produce LGB, now some 93 to 94 percent of their total operation. Important, too, were the decisions to produce in plastic and to sell directly to retailers, still unusual in the German toy industry.

Obviously, these decisions were the right ones. This family product appeals to families. Some say it should be called "Lehmann Gesundheit Bahn" — Lehmann Health Train — for the therapy of its indoor and outdoor play. The backbone of the clientele is fathers in their thirties, their forties, and their fifties. Children love the trains. At adolesence their interest turns elsewhere, but when they start families of their own, they come back to them. Although train toys are traditionally masculine, women like LGB and suggest purchases. And age is no barrier to interest, as is shown by the material sent in to the "LGB Despeche" by an 89 year old New Zealander.

Where does the business sense come from, the practical know-how, that makes such success possible? Wolfgang Richter thinks it came from his experiences in Munich, in part, where he worked in an American Army clothing shop and learned about displays, stockkeeping, and accounting. A good teacher at school (a German high school similar to an American college) taught him much about graphics. The basics of metal work he learned as an apprentice with a manufacturer of sterilizers and household goods who, during the material shortages of the postwar years, made tricycles for his employees out of such primitive materials as tin can covers.

Rolf Richter thinks his father does not adequately credit his own brilliant sense of layout and eye-catching design.

To one of the men who works with him, Wolfgang Richter is a down-to-earth person who wants quality first; the profit goes into tooling and expansion and new lines. (Here Wolfgang surely is his father's son: "The toys first; the profits come later.") Wolfgang Richter, says his staff, makes what is in his heart. And in his heart is a toy train.

PACKAGING
By Donna Price

LGB trains and accessories were originally packed in gray boxes with light red LGB logo and train insignias. In 1971 those boxes were replaced by bright yellow

An early 20301 box lid, a far cry from the vivid colors of the late 1980s.

ones with red and white logos and green train insignias. The bright yellow boxes were used until 1977 when red boxes with green and yellow logos and white train insignias were introduced.

Nearly all of the packaging material, from 1968 until the late 1970s, was composed of a simple two-piece folded and stapled carton and lid.

The one item that sometimes is damaged during delivery is the coupler. A packaging improvement Lehmann introduced at some point was a folded, stapled ring of cardboard, forming a tough cylinder (with squared corners) about one and one/half inches wide, one inch high, and one inch deep to slip over the coupler hook.

In the late 1970s, some pieces, e.g., the Lowenbrau 4032L Beer Car, were packaged in yellow boxes with a plastic display window. Since these window boxes had inserts with wheel slots to keep the cars from moving in the box and end sheets with cutouts for the couplers, the protective cylinder for couplers was no longer needed though still used in most cases. Red boxes with display windows began to appear at about this time too. These window boxes are slightly smaller and are made of lightweight cardboard. More recent versions are of corrugated cardboard and offer considerably more protection than their earlier counterparts.

Some experimental packaging apparently was used in the late 1970s in the form of an all-clear plastic box with opening end tabs within a gray sleeve. Inside the plastic box was a 5/8" high cardboard base with a green stripe around the perimeter. A yellow tab and the Lehmann logo were printed on the stripe. The top of the base was printed in black and white with a picture of track and ballast. The top of the rail was highlighted in yellow. The bottom side of the base was printed in yellow with green and yellow logos. The one-piece base had only one end panel, printed in yellow, with the LGB sticker depicting the contents. (Some early stickers did not depict content; Roth comment.)

The Lehmann Company appears at this time to be switching almost exclusively to the red display window boxes — at least for rolling stock. This red is quite different from the 1977-1980 boxes. This packaging is attractive and promotes in-box display, and with cardboard inserts and supports, in addition to foam padding, it provides more protection than the earlier two-piece box. It also eliminates the staple scratches commonly seen on early pieces. If further strength of packaging is desired, an unlettered, plain gray cardboard sleeve surrounding the window box may be used for shipping.

Several Primus pieces are packaged in all-yellow boxes with display windows and sleeves. The ends have either an orange and white Primus label, or a Primus number stamped directly on the box.

I
TRAIN SETS

See specific sections in text for appropriate and complete descriptions of variations of locomotives, cars, etc. found in each set. Colors may vary somewhat from these cursory descriptions. Other train set combinations may also occur due to manufacturer or dealer substitutions. Most sets were originally packaged with twelve sections of 1100 Curved Track (aluminum indoor track in earliest versions of all early sets), 5016 Track

Power Cable, and a transformer (either 110V or 220V). However, many sets shipped to the United States prior to 1985 had the transformers removed by the dealer/distributor since most had the 220V version not suitable for use with the American 110V standard, and the harder to find 110V transformers did not meet UL approval. In 1984-1985, UL-approved transformers became available for the first time. The larger sets also

The Jubilee or Anniversary Set commemorating Lehmann's 100th anniversary; this very festive set is shown in its most popular version, with the silver boiler front. J. Hylva Collection.

A 1969 20301 Passenger Set with 2020(A) Locomotive and two coaches: a brown 3000 and a green 3010. G. Ryall Collection.

came with the 5041 Station Figures, 1052 Uncoupler, a set of 1150 Track Clips, a catalogue, 0024 Instruction Manual, and a subscription blank for **DEPESCHE** magazine. Copies of **DEPESCHE** have also been included in the packaged train sets from time to time since the early 1970s. Several sets were made specifically for the United States of America and beginning in 1984 some had the letters "US" on the box lids after the set number (i.e. 20401US, 20500US, etc.). The primary difference in the "US" sets is that they have a 110V transformer.

300: 1980-86, railway starter pack with battery-operated 207(C) Steam Locomotive, plastic track, and automatic switching; 4044 short Gondola loaded with barrels; 3041 Summertime Passenger Car with bench seats and grab-handles suitable for use with Playmobil figures.

                                          250

1980BTO: See Chapter XII.

1988BTO: See Chapter XII.

8000: 1977-78, only one Primus set is known to have been manufactured, and it includes a black and dark green 20875 0-4-0T Locomotive, pinkish-red 30800 Coach, and blue 40821 high-sided Gondola. Set contents include 12 pieces of LGB 1100 Curved Track, 5003 (renumbered 50803 or 50806) 220-volt transformer, 5016 Connector Cables, 5040 Figures, etc. Set came packaged in a compartmentalized, styrofoam box with a windowless, yellow lid and the "8000" set number printed on it.   **950**

20087: 1987-88, "American Heritage" or Rio Grande Special American freight train set; has 2117(A) Steam Locomotive with Russian Iron-colored cab, with white stripes and Denver and Rio Grande logo on cab door, 4021 high-sided Gondola in red with Rio Grande markings, and a black 4065(I) Caboose. Set was commissioned by the LGB National Sales Office of Milwaukee, Wisconsin.
(A) 1987, 4021(L) high-sided Gondola painted red.   **300**
(B) 1988, 4021(M) high-sided Gondola painted blue.   **300**

20150: 1985, shown in 1985-86 catalogue and supplement 0011N; anniversary train to commemorate 150 years of German railways; "150 Jahre Deutsche Eisenbahnen" with red 2020DB (2010DB in prototype set) Steam Locomotive and 3150(A) and 3150(B) Coaches; approximately 2500 sets produced. **Note:** Companion car catalogued as 3150(C).   **400**

20277: 1987, two blue and white 3097 and 3098 and one blue 3099 "Orient Express" Passenger Cars. A gray-painted 2072D(C) Steam Locomotive is included.   **750**

20301: 1968- , basic passenger set with 2020 Steam Locomotive, two coaches.
(A) 1968-70, 2020(A) Locomotive, brown 3000(A) and dark green 3010(A) Coaches.   **550**
(B) 1971-74, 2020(B) Locomotive, brown 3000(C), and green 3010(C) Coaches.   **375**
(C) 1975-78, 2020(B) Locomotive, brown 3000(C), and green 3010(C) or (D) Coaches.   **350**
(D) 1977-78, 2020(C) Locomotive, red and white 3011(D), and blue and white 3012(C) Coaches.   **300**
(E) 1979-82, 2020(D) Locomotive, red and white 3011(E), and blue and white 3012(D) or (E) Coaches.   **250**

(F) 1983- , 2020(E) Locomotive, red and white 3011(F), and blue and white 3012(F) Coaches.   **CP**

20301BP: 1984, uncatalogued; Buffalo Pass, Scalplock & Denver Railroad passenger set with red and black 2076BP Steam Locomotive, and two barn red 3006BP Coaches. Only 2000 of these sets were produced and originally sold only in the United States.   **550**

20301BZ: 1982-83, uncatalogued, "The Blue Train" set.
(A) 2020BZ locomotive with silver boiler front.   **600**
(B) 2020BZ locomotive with gold boiler front.   **750**

20301MF: 1984, uncatalogued; Marshall Field & Company passenger set with dark green and black 2010D(G) Steam Locomotive (with "1" on cab) and two dark green 3007MF(A) "Marshall Field" Coaches. These coaches were also boxed and sold separately. Only 500 of these sets were produced in 1984 for the Marshall Field department store based in Chicago, Illinois. Owing to a change of ownership, Marshall Field & Company will no longer offer special sets. Also see 20534.
850

20302: 1971-74, passenger set with green and beige 2034 Steeple-cab Electric Locomotive, green 3008(A) and green 3040(A) or (B) Coaches.
1200

20401: 1968-87, basic freight set with 0-4-0T steam locomotive, gondola, and boxcar.
(A) 1968-75, 2040(A) or 2040(B) Locomotive, straw brown 4020 or green 4021 Gondola, and straw brown 4030(A) Boxcar. Earliest versions have the brown 4020 which was later replaced by a green 4021(A), (B), or (C).   **850**
(B) 1975-76, 2040(B) or 2040(C) Locomotive, green 4021(A) Gondola, and yellow "Chiquita" 4033(A) Boxcar.   **650**
(C) 1977-82, 2010(C) Locomotive, green 4021 Gondola, and yellow "Chiquita" 4033 Boxcar.   **300**
(D) 1983-84, 2010(D) Locomotive, 4021(E), (F), or (G) Gondola, and 4033(D) Boxcar. In late 1984 some of these sets were issued with a 2020(D) Locomotive.   **300**
(E) 1984-85, same as (D), but with dark brown 4021(J) or 4021(K) Gondola.   **275**
(F) 1985-87, same as (E), but has 2020(E) Locomotive.   **250**

20401RZ: 1984, uncatalogued; "The Red Train" (Der Rote Zug), special freight set to promote the Lehmann company; with 2061 Diesel Locomotive, red 4003RZ(A) Container Car, 4069/1RZ Container, and red 4040RZ Tank Car.

TOP SHELF: Set 20301BZ, the "Blaue Zug" (hence "BZ") or "Blue Train", also comes labeled in French. It was one of the first special trains to follow the 1981 anniversary set, issued in 1982-1983, and originally intended for European markets only but was first marketed in the United States by F. A. O. Schwarz. The window frames are red, an unusual color for frames, which matches the red frames and lettering of car 1982 (a supplement to the Lehmann Jubilee Anniversary Set). **CENTER SHELF:** The Pinzga Schenke Set, 20520, is the only limited edition set modeled after an authentic train; it is also the only limited edition passenger set to feature cars of a different color. Note the profile of the two roof vents on the middle car, a diner. The rectangular vent with rounded corners on the cab roof is typical of all 0-4-0T locomotives since the very earliest. Apparently the plaque says "Modellbahn Center", a hobby shop special. **BOTTOM SHELF:** Set 20401RZ. The prototype "Furka" railroad comes by its "Oberalp" name honestly, as it goes over two alpine ranges, passing a glacier en route. "RhB" on the tank car stands for "Rhaetian railway," the larger system to which the FO belongs. The car markings and warnings on the late model tank are typical of the increased lettering of recent LGB productions; very early cars had none at all. A. Rudman Collection.

TOP SHELF: Set 20501(B) (1984-1985), one of several numbers reused by Lehmann after the original item had been out of production a while; this is one of only a few sets with the unique 4042 Crane. Note that the two cars are here coupled hook to hook, which the more flexible newer couplers facilitate; many operators add an extra hook at the loop end, to de-polarize coupling. The bulbous Baldwin stack identifies the locomotive as one of the 2020 Series. CENTER SHELF: The darkly dramatic 380.7030 has two identical 4003P Container Cars sporting the cartoon character "Commander Rom." "Videospiele" is video play or video game. Note the thinness and downward slant of the late model uncoupling pad. BOTTOM: SHELF: Set 20512 is pulled by a 2061FO. The Furka-Oberalp is part of the mountainous Rhaetian network, the largest European narrow gauge system, in southeastern Switzerland. The convivial burghers on the boxcar are, of course, quaffing Cardinal beer. Note the large roof ventilators. The newer angle iron railing on the 4034 brakeman's platform has no side gates. In ordinary service, such cars are operated with the brakeman's platform toward the front.

(A)	2061(B) Diesel Locomotive.	350
(B)	2061(D) Diesel Locomotive.	300
(C)	2061(E) Diesel Locomotive.	300
(D)	2061(F) Diesel Locomotive.	300

20500: 1986-87, three sets were made with this same number.
(A) 1986, Neumann of Berlin train set includes 2020(E) Steam Locomotive, 4010 low-sided Gondola, and 4021 high-sided Gondola. Set has police car load for 4010 (probably added after leaving the factory). Three sets were made with this same number, but only one is factory issued.   200
(B) 1987, non-factory, set has 2020(E) Locomotive and three 3150(C) Coaches; lacks track and transformer.   200
(C) 1987, non-factory, "Euro Zug" train set repainted for the Superscale Company; consists of 2020(E) Locomotive with silver-painted boiler front and "EURO ZUG" in white lettering on each side of cab. Set includes three 4030-type boxcars in different colors, with names and flags of the following European countries: Portugal (yellow), Grossbritanien (white), and Finland (dark blue); lacks track and transformer.   250

20501: 1969-74, 1984-85, two sets were made with this same number.
(A) 1969-74, freight set with 2060 Diesel Locomotive, gray 4001 Flatcar, and green 4010 Gondola. The differences between this set

and 20501L are that at least the earliest of the 20501s came with no light on the 2060 Diesel, and all came with indoor (aluminum) track.
                                                                        450
(B) 1969-74, same as (A), but with green 4011 Flatcar.   450
(C) 1984-85, uncatalogued, Vedes Company limited edition train set; includes standard, non-smoking 2020(F) Steam Locomotive, medium brown 4021(J) Gondola, and yellow 4042 Crane Car.   300
(D) 1985, same as (B), but has 2020(F) Steam Locomotive with factory-installed smoke unit; box has words "Mit Dampf".   300

20501F: 1983, Florsheim Shoe freight set with red 2090(C) Diesel, white 4032F Boxcar, and brownish-red-painted 4065F Caboose. Special "Florsheim" transfer decals were made and applied to these cars by the National Sales Office; only 300 sets produced; 200 additional boxcars and cabooses produced and packaged separately. Sets came packaged in 20401 boxes without transformer, but with Kalamazoo curved track.   350

20501JR: 1976-78, "Junior" freight set with 2060 Diesel Locomotive, brown 4010 Gondola, 4001 Flatcar, and 4011 or 4010 low-sided Gondola, and aluminum (natural or chrome-plated) or brass track. White foam box with "LGB Junior" photo on lid in 1976. See corresponding years of cars in each car section of text for specific variations found in the 20501JR Sets.

(A) 1971-74, 2060Y(B) Diesel Locomotive, gray 4001 Flatcar, and green 4011 low-sided Gondola. **600**

(B) 1975-76, 2060G Diesel Locomotive, gray 4001 Flatcar, and green 4010 low-sided Gondola. Some of these sets came with chrome-plated aluminum track. **700**

(C) 1977-78, 2060Y(C) Diesel Locomotive, gray 4001 Flatcar, and green 4011 low-sided Gondola. **500**

20502: 1982, uncatalogued, Freizeit Hobby Spiel, "FHS" limited edition train set; includes 2075(C) Steam Locomotive, 4003F Container Car (erroneously dubbed 4002/69) with 4069/1F Container, and 4002(A) Cable Car with green spools; 1000 sets produced. **400**

20512: 1983-84, uncatalogued limited edition Furka-Oberalp "Cardinal Beer" freight set with red and black 2061(D) Diesel, yellow 4034(A) Boxcar (with "4031" ID number), and medium brown 4010FO Flatcar. 2500 sets produced. **400**

20513: 1983-84, uncatalogued; Freizeit Hobby Spiel limited edition train set with red and black 2020HS Steam Locomotive, red 3007HS Coach, and red 4031HS Boxcar. 1000 sets produced. **450**

20514: 1983, uncatalogued; "DHS" and "SPIEL & HOBBY" limited edition freight set with 2020(E) Steam Locomotive, 4003D Container Car (has 4069/1D Container), and medium brown 4021(G) high-sided Gondola. 800 sets produced. **400**

20515: 1984, see Chapter XII.

20516: 1983, uncatalogued; Brinkmann Company limited edition train set; includes 2020(E) Locomotive, green 4021(G) Gondola, and 4033B Boxcar. **750**

20518: 1984, uncatalogued, Einkaufsring limited edition train set (also numbered 20518EK); includes red 2061 Diesel, brown 4021(J) Gondola, and orange 4041(F) Hopper Car. **NRS**

20519: 1984, uncatalogued, freight set "Einkaufsgemeinschaft" with 2076D Steam Locomotive, orange 4011 Hinged-hatch Wagon, and orange 4041 Hopper Car. **325**

20520: 1984, uncatalogued; "PINZGA SCHENKE" Austrian railway train set with green and black 2010PB (2010 "Pinzgauer Bahn") Steam Locomotive, dark green 3007PB (3007 "Modellbahn Center Sonderzug") Coach, and dark blue 3013PB Diner (blue 3007 "Pinzga Schenke" Bar Car with 3013 interior). **Note:** Less than 100 sets have been imported into the United States; exact number of sets produced is not known. **500**

20522: 1984, uncatalogued, Freizeit Hobby Spiel "FHS" limited edition train set; includes 2010(E) Steam Locomotive with dark brown cab, 4002(D) Cable Car with green spools, and 4042(E) Crane Car. **300**

20526: 1984, Schmidt Bakery Freight set in dark brown with 2010SB Steam Locomotive, 4003SB (brown "Schmidt / Lebkuchen / aus / Nürnberg") 4003 Container Car with 4069/1SR Container, and 4030SB (brown "Schmidt / Lebkuchen / aus / Nürnberg" Boxcar. One thousand sets were produced, the boxes numbered sequentially, the train items themselves not numbered. **450**

20528: 1985, uncatalogued; "150 JAHRE DEUTSCHE EISENBAHN", Modelleisenbahn Schweiger (Schweiger Model Train Shop) anniversary passenger set to commemorate 150 years of German railways; with 2020SG(A) (gold boiler front) Steam Locomotive and two 3007SG(A) (yellow "150 Jahre Deutsche Eisenbahn" 3007) Coaches; other variations in the yellow 2020SG(A) are non-factory modifications and are listed in Chapter XII. Only 1000 sets produced, numbered on bottom of engine. First 60 sets have 2020SG(A) (black unpainted boilers) Locomotives, a few of which were only available for sale through Modelleisenbahn Schweiger; some of these may have had the boiler fronts painted silver or unpainted black (see Chapter XII). At least 60 percent of these sets were shipped to the United States. **Note:** Companion car for set is catalogued as 3013SG.

(A) 2020SG(A) (gold boiler) Locomotive. **500**

(B) 2020SG (silver boiler) Locomotive (see Chapter XII).

(C) 2020SG (black boiler) Locomotive (see Chapter XII).

Only 300 of the 20501F Florsheim Freight Sets were made with their special "Florsheim" dry transfer decal; an additional 200 boxcars and cabooses were produced and packaged separately. J. Hylva Collection.

TOP SHELF: Red, white, and orange stripes camouflage the staid boxcar lines of this 4030 in Set 20513, proclaiming "Freizeit / Hobby Spiel" (Spare Time / Hobby / Play). The passenger car is one of the 3007 Series most often used by Lehmann in special livery sets. Its wider, squarer windows and medium-arched roof contrast to the narrow windows and low-arched roof of the 3000 Coaches below it. CENTER SHELF: Set 20701DC has its little 2075 Locomotive laden with a railroad name as long as itself, even when abbreviated. The letters stand for Dodge City and Great Western Railroad. The absence of valve rods (added to 2076D), which control steam flow in the prototype cylinders, is theoretically reasonable; many side tank engines carried such rods out of sight between the wheels. BOTTOM SHELF: Set 20301MF, which comes with a 2010D(G) Locomotive, was issued for the famous Chicago Marshall Field department store in a rich green with the company's founding year, the date of set issue, and the company shield in gold. This set shows a 2010D(F) Locomotive, not a 2010D(G). The long vertical funnel right behind the front driver, typical of well-tank engines, represents just that: a funnel for filling the water tank. A. Rudman Collection.

20529: 1986, uncatalogued; green-painted 0-4-0T locomotive and passenger set, includes 2020SG(B) Steam Locomotive, two 3007SG(B) Coaches, and a 3013SG(B) Diner; set sold without track or transformer. **300**

20530: 1986-87, German work train or "Bau-Zug" originally made only for distribution in Germany; consists of a yellow 2090N(B) Diesel Locomotive having white number-boards with black markings, and two medium green, unmarked 4010(G) low-sided Gondolas with tractor loads; the tractors on flatcars were not packaged at the factory, but were added by distributors later; tractors appear to be Playmobile pieces; about 3000 produced. **200**

20531A: See Chapter XII.

20531B: See Chapter XII.

20531CS: See Chapter XII.

20531DV: See Chapter XII.

20531K: See Chapter XII.

20531KT: See Chapter XII.

20531L: See Chapter XII.

20531MC: See Chapter XII.

20531P: See Chapter XII.

20531S: See Chapter XII.

20531SF: See Chapter XII.

20531SLM: See Chapter XII.

20531TS: See Chapter XII.

20531Z: See Chapter XII.

20532: 1985, "Bundesgartenschau-Express"; made for a landscaping show or fair held in West Berlin in 1985, it consists of a green and black 2020(E) Steam Locomotive and two dark blue-painted 3007BE Passenger Coaches (with yellow stripe and "Bundesgartenschau Express-Berlin 1985" markings). Coaches are deep blue with gold line and corner decorations; four windows with orange-yellow window frames and "BUNDESGARTENSCHAU-EXPRESS" over two center windows. "Berlin" and "1985" with child-like flowers between the two. Black chassis. Black filigree brackets; six ribs to roof, three vents on every other section; roof tinted from black at outside to medium gray along most of rooftop. Interior has five sets of medium brown bench seats on a blue floor. It is believed that 1000 sets were supposed to have been made; however, either approximately half of the 3007BE Coaches had misspelled markings and were destroyed, or only 500 sets were originally produced. **500**

20534: 1986, Marshall Field & Company train set with 2010D(G) Steam Locomotive and two 3007MF(B) Coaches. Also see 20301MF. 1000 sets produced, but nearly 150 sets were damaged. **375**

20536L: 1987, "Dortmund Beer" train set commissioned by Lutgenau Train World. Set includes 2020L Steam Locomotive with white cab and boiler front, white 3007L "Thier Pils" Coach, white 4031L "First Bier" Boxcar, and blue 4040L "Kronen" beer Tank Car. These sets had a parchment certificate serially numbered for each set; however, some sets were issued without this certificate (price includes certificate). Set does not include track, transformer, etc. 1000 sets produced. **450**

20575: 1976, "Junior Steam" freight set with 2075 Steam Locomotive, 4001 Flatcar, 4010 low-sided Gondola, and aluminum track. B. Cage Collection. **NRS**

20601: 1974-75, black battery-powered 207 Steam Locomotive, with two bright yellow 4044 high-sided Gondolas. **200**

20601: 1979-82, goods train basic set with 2075(C) Steam Locomotive and two 4043 Tipping Bucket Cars. **180**

20601B: 1974-78, battery-driven goods train set with 207(B) or (C) Steam Locomotive and two orange-brown 4044 high-sided Gondolas. **NRS**

20601L: 1975-76, same as 20601; but with people for Playmobil. **NRS**

20601T: 1977-78, same as 20601; but with transformer. **NRS**

20602: 1983-84, Platelayer's starter set with 2075(C) Steam Locomotive.

(A) 3041(B), (C), or (D) Passenger (excursion) Car and red 4043(D) Tipping Bucket Car. **125**

(B) 3041(C) or (D) Passenger (excursion) Car and yellow 4044(D) Gondola (ore car). **155**

20675: 1975, "The Big Ore Drag" freight set with 2075 Steam Locomotive and aluminum track. Advertised by LGB distributors in 1982 and 1983, authenticity of this set is questionable. **NRS**

20701: 1979-82, passenger train basic set with 2075 Locomotive and two red and white 3041 Passenger (excursion) Cars. **225**

20701DC: 1982, uncatalogued; Dodge City and Great Western Railroad set made for the LGB National Sales Distributor in Milwaukee, Wisconsin. Set comes with 2075DC Steam Locomotive and two yellow 3006 Coaches in first and second class. Because some of these coaches had 3000 identification numbers they were wrongly dubbed by some collectors as 3000DC; however, the factory designated these coaches 3006. 2000 sets produced.

(A) 2075DC(A) with red drivers; 3006(A) and 3006(D) Coaches. **500**

(B) 2075DC(B) with black drivers; 3006(B) and 3006(E) Coaches. **500**

20701T: 1977-78, same as 20701 above, but in earlier packaging. **300**

TOP SHELF: Set 20526 is a railroad jubilee set for the E. Otto Schmidt Bakery in Nuremberg. The red Schmidt logo, a heart with some of the castle-like towers of Nuremberg on top, appears on the chocolate brown container just left of "Schmidt-Lebkuchen". "Lebkuchen" is a German variety of spice cake. The set's boxes are numbered from one to 1000; collectors disagree as to how important the numbering is. **CENTER SHELF:** Black and orange Set 20519 is only one of many dramatic color combinations possible with LGB. The little 0-4-0T, a 2076D, carries its water in side tanks (the square boxes beside the boiler) instead of in a well-tank underneath the boiler, like the other two engines, above and below it. **BOTTOM SHELF:** Set 20514 pulls a high-sided gondola used for more general purposes in Europe than here and a 4003D Flatcar with a container labeled "DHS" and "Spiel & Hobby".

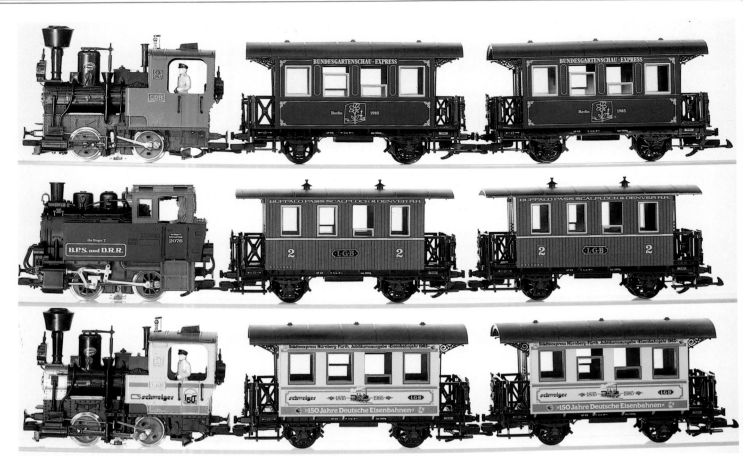

TOP SHELF: In Set 20532 the most distinctive feature of this livery, celebrating a Berlin landscaping company, is the casual irregularity of the child-like flower drawings. Contrast the minimal profile of the three roof vents with the sharp spindle profiles of the paired vents in the set below; both kinds are typical of recent issues of their respective car types (3007, 3000/3006). **CENTER SHELF:** Set 20301BP clearly appeals to an American market, both buffalo and scalplocks being European rarities. Cars with simulated wood sides (3000/3006), rather than the simulated metal of 3007, were probably chosen for the same reason. Not sold in Europe. **BOTTOM SHELF:** As a model train shop in Nuremberg, Schweiger had Set 20528 issued to celebrate the one hundred fiftieth anniversary of railroads in Germany. The cars feature the old locomotive "Der Adler" ("The Eagle"), Germany's first, between the Jubilee year dates. On the engine cab door, the clever "150" logo of the railroad exposition, which was held in Nuremberg, is arranged to suggest a steam locomotive with long stack. A. Rudman Collection.

21401: 1988- , Basic Freight starter set, replaces Set 20401. Set includes 2020(E), orange 4010(H) low-sided Gondola carrying green Mercedes Unimog truck, and 4042(E) Crane Car. Includes track and transformer (110V in 21401US and 220V in 21401). **CP**

21980B: 1981, green, battery-powered 207(C) Steam Locomotive, with one pinkish-red 3041(C) Passenger (excursion) Car and one orange-brown 4044(B) high-sided Gondola with pale blue Aral barrels **250**

21981: 1981, the LGB "Jubilee Train" set to commemorate the 100th anniversary of Lehmann Patenwerk; version (A) is shown in the 1984-85 catalogue with the anniversary cars. Sets included a 2010LJ Steam Locomotive, 3007LJ Coach, and 3010LJ Diner, and were packaged in specially marked, dark red boxes with gold graphics. The set was not catalogued until three years after it was produced and appears with all the anniversary cars in the 1984-85 catalogue. These sets originally retailed in the United States for less than $150 (about half of the price of the regular passenger set), but have since escalated in value more than any other set; just over 10,000 sets produced. Additional anniversary cars made to go with this set: white 1982, blue and white 1983, blue 1984 Coaches, and blue 1985 Baggage Car.

(A) With 2010LJ(B) Locomotive with red boiler front; has 3013LJ(A), "SPEISEWAGON" in red lettering; less than 400 are believed to have been made. **750**
(B) Same as (A), but has 3013LJ(B), "SPEISEWAGON" in gold lettering. **1000**
(C) With 2010LJ(A) Locomotive with silver boiler front; about 9800 produced. **650**

21988US: 1988- , LGB Circus Train Set in white, red, and blue. Set includes a 2010/88 Steam Locomotive and two 4037 low-sided Gondolas; one carrying a white and blue Mercedes Unimog truck, and the other with a white and red circus animal trailer which can be hitched to the Unimog. Although the low-sided gondolas are depicted in the catalogue with stars on their sides, these cars were produced with red and blue half circles. Packaged in standard box with track and transformer. **CP**

22301US: 1989- , Lake George & Boulder Passenger Set painted in silver- blue (Russian Iron). Set includes 2117(B) Steam Locomotive and two 3106 LG&B Coaches. Comes in standard box with track and transformer. For United States distribution only. **CP**

22401US: 1989- , Lake George & Boulder Freight Set. Includes 2117(B) Steam Locomotive, red 4021(N) high-sided Gondola, and

"Dortmund Beer" train set commissioned by Lutgenau Train World. Some sets came with a serially-numbered certificate; 1000 sets were manufactured. J. Schneider Collection.

The very earliest of Set 20501 had a 2060 Diesel Locomotive with no headlights. The gray 4001 was common to all issues of the set, but the 4010 shown here was sometimes substituted for a green 4011; the 1975-1976 catalogue shows a brown gondola with the set. Although the 1970 catalogue lists 4010 brown, while showing a green car, the downward slant (to the uncoupling pads) means these cars are 1974 or later, and most probably the set was listed in 1975-1976.

black 4065LG&B Caboose. Set comes in standard box and includes track and transformer. For United States distribution only. **CP**

25000: See Chapter XII.

380.7030: 1984, uncatalogued "Commander Rom" limited edition freight set for the Philips Video Game company; with 2060P Diesel Locomotive and two midnight blue 4003PV Container Cars and 4069/1PV Containers with randomly scattered heavenly bodies on the dark background. Box reads "Philips GMBH Videospiele Romzug Komplett"; 4003PV Container Car has space robot figure, with "Commander / Rom" written on white shirt front; blast burst reads, "Videospiele / von Philips". 1000 sets produced. Approximately 150 of these sets were independently repainted with the Pennsylvania (Pennsy) road name in both Tuscan red and Brunswick green versions for the North Coast Distributors, Ohio in 1985. **400**

No Number: 1987, Schweiger Model Train Shop train set in red. **450**

II
STEAM LOCOMOTIVES

The nostalgic appeal of the steam locomotive affects even those who have grown up in the age of diesels and electrics. That popularity is reflected in the much larger number of steam locomotives, compared to the other types, in the Lehmann roster. In the Centennial Catalogue of 1981-1982, for example, eleven standard-run steam locomotives are listed, seven diesels, and five electrics. When the handmade locomotives are added, all of which are steam, the disparity is even greater.

STANDARD PRODUCTION STEAM LOCOMOTIVES

The models of the 0-4-0T (B-h2 and B-n2) conventional tank locomotives are probably the most well known among LGB enthusiasts and are perhaps the engines most responsible for Lehmann's success. Since the water and coal supply of a tank locomotive is not sufficient for long trips, a tender is added when needed with the coal (or wood, as in 2018D) normally stacked in front and the water stored to the sides and rear (as in 2015D).

Note: The German "tenderlokomotive" translates to tank locomotive in English, while a "schlepp-tenderlokomotive" is a locomotive with separate tender. Lehmann's models of these little engines have excellent tractive power, reliability, and versatility.

The earliest versions of these locomotives have a relatively bland appearance when compared to those more recently produced and, owing to their noisy drive mechanisms, have been affectionately dubbed "grind-

An early 2015D(A) sold in 1977 and 1978. Notice the KPEV emblem on the tender.

ers" or "growlers." The "grinders" are noisy because they are driven by the 2100 Motor with a spur-gear on the single drive shaft. However, some locomotives with spur-gears were available as late as 1971 even though subsequent models were changed after the first seven or eight months of production to worm-gear drive mechanisms. The spur-gear motors continued to be available as catalogued replacements up until about 1971 or 1972.

Over the years cosmetic as well as mechanical improvements have been made. Most early versions are entirely unpainted and have less detail than newer versions. Examples are:

1. Early smokebox doors, until about 1971-1972, lack simulated latches on the right side, and the forward portion of the boiler lacks rivet-heads.

2. The steam dome on early models lacks the round side plate and lever as well as the actuating rod along the boiler into the cab. Oval peel-and-stick manufacturer's labels, colored red and gold, are positioned at the base of the sand dome on early versions, but were moved about midway up the sand dome when the round plate and lever were added to the later versions.

3. On later models, beginning about 1974, three additional embossed piping details were added to the side of the boiler.

4. The wheel-shaped latch handle on the smokebox door and the small round valve handles on each side of the boiler, directly beneath the sand dome, are black on locomotives until about 1981. On subsequent models these handles have a gold finish.

5. On early models the small box atop the boiler, directly in front of the steam dome, lacks all detail and has smooth corners. This box on later models (beginning about 1974) has simulated angle irons on the corners, rivet-head details, smokebox rivet detail, and roof detail with square roof vent.

6. The snowplows on early models differ slightly from those of newer models. Newer snowplows are notched to better clear the position of the couplers.

7. The buffers of early models are rectangular. More recently, oval-shaped unpainted buffers replaced the rectangular ones. The latest models have oval-shaped buffers with white edging. The white edging was painted on the prototype buffer borders in later years as a safety feature. It enabled the worker between the cars to see the outline of the buffer plate better at night.

8. The earliest models, from 1968 to perhaps 1971, may totally lack gold finish on the window frames, the embossed numbers, and the "LGB" letters on the cab.

9. Earliest versions from 1968 to 1970 or 1971 have a small round cab vent on the roof. This cab vent was replaced by a slightly larger, square-shaped version on later models.

The large size of the taillight and the white ring around the oval buffer help identify this as a late model steamer. A. Rudman Collection.

10. Very early versions may lack lighting altogether and have only unlit lamp units. The operating head lamps on locomotives produced from 1969 to about 1970 are less than 13 mm in diameter. Later versions have bezels (rings or frames around the lens) with a 20 mm diameter. Concomitant with the change in head lamp bezel diameter was the introduction of a reversing lighting system, one in which the head or tail lamp glows according to the direction of travel.

11. Locomotives with the early 2100 Motors with spur-gears lack 2210 Pickup Shoes as do some of the models up to about 1971.

Note: New lighting sockets for facilitating coach lighting were phased into production in the mid-1970s, first being mentioned in the 1976 catalogue. This is a most important feature and can be helpful in establishing the era of a particular locomotive.

Early locomotives of all series had small loops on their rear couplers, not interchangeable with the present coupler and incompatible with cars having double end hooks, which cannot make a tight turn; the engine hook will jam the car hook inside the small loop.

U-locomotives 0-6-2T (C1-n2t) are modeled by Lehmann after the versions built by Lokomotivfabrik Krauss & Company for 760 mm gauge railways. These versions weighed about 24 tons and could achieve a maximum speed of 35 to 45 km/h.

The LGB models have several minor characteristics that may be used to distinguish early and later models. All early versions (2070, 2071, 2072, 2073) until about 1979 have two staggered steps protruding from the left side of the water tank and cab toward the forward half of the cab. These versions also have four horizontal grates over the rear cab windows, except for the 2070 which has only two because of the placement of the coal bin. Later versions have only the rear step and lack the rear window grates. Steam generators are absent from the earliest versions, but appear on most models as of 1973.

An early 2070 has a red plastic trailing wheel and somewhat low cab roof. Although the lower roof is prototypically accurate, it was modified in response to customer complaints about how it looked with the taller rolling stock. A. Rudman Collection.

Early versions have disc-type drivers and red plastic trailing wheels, although the disc-type drive wheels appear to have been used at least until 1980 or 1981, after the plastic trailing wheels were discontinued and replaced by metal trailing wheels with electrical pickups.

The head lamp bezels on the front of the water tank on the early 1971-1973 models may have been shallower than those of the more recent models. A more definitive observation is requested.

Early versions of the 0-6-2T series have a distinctly shorter cab height than current versions; produced after 1977 since the earlier cab height was shorter than the roof lines of the boxcars and coaches. This change made the locomotives more esthetically appealing at the sacrifice of prototypical accuracy.

To describe railway stock in terms of wheel arrangement, use is made of a code:
- Code 1, 2, 3 signifies the number of idlers.
- Code B, C, D signifies the number of linked drive axles (B = 2, C = 3, D = 4, etc.).
- Apostrophe means such axles are swivel mounted in main frame of locomotive to enable it to master tight curves.
- 0 means the wheelset group has individual drive.

In other countries, designations of wheel arrangements correspond, but in most cases numbers are used. A locomotive with wheel arrangement C'C' would be, for instance, 6/6 in Switzerland, 6-0-6 in France, and 0-6-6-0 in America. In America, the number of wheels is given, not axles. The type 1'B1' is a 2/4 in Switzerland, whereby the number "2" denotes the number of driven axles and the "4" is the total number of axles. In America a 1'C would be 2-6-0.

As an example, consider the C'C-n4vt wheel arrangement designations:
- "C'C" means Steam locomotive with two power units, the first of which is flexibly mounted, with three drive axles each.
- "n4" means saturated steam and four cylinders.
- "v" means compound action between high and low pressure cylinders.
- "T" means fuel and water supplies carried on locomotive. In cases where the "T" is omitted the engine involved always is a tender locomotive, while a "T" means locomotive without a tender. Most of the LGB locomotives will have a "T" following the American wheel classification implying a tank-type locomotive without a tender.

Partly in response to the comments of American Charles S. Small, author of numerous books on narrow gauge lines around the world and of the first "Model Railroader" article on the new scale, Lehmann very early introduced electrical pickup shoes or skates on all its 0-4-0Ts. The shoe, attached by a screw, slides on its rail between the two drive wheels.

The triangular, straight-line coupler hook identifies this 2010D as a non-current model, although the picture appeared in the catalogue as recently as 1985. Comparison of individual pieces of gravel with that in earlier catalogue photos of the same locomotive confirms that this picture was taken — and the locomotive therefore made — by 1979. Curved hooks replaced the triangular one, and plastic web springs replaced the metal coil spring just visible in the photo, circa 1980. Catalogue pictures are not proof the model shown was still being produced in that configuration.

206: 1974-75, see 207(A).

207: 1975-87, 0-4-0T (B-n2) tank locomotive BR 99 5001 of the German State Railway. Battery-powered unit very similar to the 2075 Locomotive; red chassis; drive wheels are cast in red plastic. Engine originally produced in glossy black plastic, red underframe and wheels; no traction tire or traction tire on one rear wheel. In early catalogues, locomotive actually numbered "99 5001" in white; however, there is also a version with a blank boiler front number plate (no embossed numbers).

(A) 1975, engine in glossy black plastic finish. **NRS**

(B) 1976-78, dark green; unpainted boiler and water tanks; black cab. **NRS**

(C) 1979-85, similar to (B), but medium green-painted boiler and water tanks; later versions have more markings (in white). **CP**

(D) 1983-87, same black body as 2075(C). **CP**

2010: 1968-86, 0-4-0T (B-n2) tank locomotive, modeled after an 1898-vintage Austrian locomotive from the Salzkammergut Local Railway SKGLB, Salzburg-Bad Ischl. Straight standard stack, total length equals 250 mm. Painted cab colors may vary slightly, particularly on earlier versions. See comments above for brief history and detail variations.

(A) 1968-70, unpainted black boiler and green cab; cab window frames; embossed "LGB" on sides of cab and framed "1" on sides and back of cab lack gold leaf; dull red chassis, early boiler and cab details (see comments on page 29); black valve and lock handles on boiler;

small head and tail lamp bezels with non-reversing lighting system; engineer in left side of cab; black whistle; rectangular buffers without white edging; early 2100 Spur-Gear Motor, no pickup shoes or traction tires. **250**

(B) 1971-73, same as (A), but with gold-finished cab numbers only; 2200 Worm-drive Motor, pickup shoes. **200**

(C) 1974-76, similar to (B), but with gold-finished cab numbers, window frames, and embossed "LGB" on cab; 2210 Pickup Shoes; traction tires. **175**

(D) 1977-82, same motor and pickup shoes as (C), but with dark brown-painted cab; improved, larger, reversing head and tail lamps, clear front lens, red tail lens; oval buffers with or without white edging; engineer in left side of cab; brass-colored whistle. **150**

(E) 1983-86, same as (D), but with white "Letzte HU. 26.6.79" on front of chassis, brass-colored valve and lock handles on boiler. **125**

2010D: 1969- , though basically similar to the 2010 with a 2010/3 Smokestack, the factory discontinued using the "2010" cab molds in 1985. Consequently currently manufactured 2010Ds have "2020" cabs, but still bear the "2010" number on the engine block and in the catalogue. Also some sets used a locomotive identical to the 2010D(F) with a non-smoking, Baldwin stack; to avoid confusion those locomotives are included here.

(A) 1969-70, same as 2010(A), but with smoking stack. **250**

(B) 1971-73, same as 2010(B), but with smoking stack. **200**

(C) 1974-76, same as 2010(B) or (C), but with smoking stack. **175**

(D) 1977-82, similar to 2010(C) or (D), but with dark green-painted cab. **150**

(E) 1983-86, same as (D), but with white "Letzte HU. 26.6.79" on front of chassis.   **CP**

(F) 1986- , same as (E), but has embossed "2" on cab as seen on the 2020 Locomotives (the non-smoking 2020MF is virtually identical to this except for the smokestack).   **CP**

(G) 1986- , same as (F), but has a non-smoking, Baldwin stack; ID number on motor block may be "2010" or "2020". This version was used in several specialty sets (i.e. 20301MF, 20534). Originally only available with sets.   **NSS**

2010DB: 1985, (see 2020DB), similar to 2010(E), but cab and boiler front are painted red; the embossed "1" and "LGB" and window frames on cab lack gold finish, other cab markings include a "150 Jahre Deutsche Eisenbahn" decal on cab; this version is a pre-production prototype only and never saw regular production.   **NRS**

2010LJ: 1981, tank locomotive for the 100 year anniversary Lehmann Jubilee train set, sold only with the 21981 Set; same basic locomotive as 2010, but has a semi-glossy cranberry-painted cab with gold-painted, draped leaf chain and small "100 Jahre Lehmann" inside gold leaf chain oval on cab door; raised "1" and "LGB" embossed plaques on cab are highlighted in gold; black chassis; Baldwin-type non-smoking stack, oval builder's plaque on sand dome; buffers with white outline.

(A) Silver-painted smokebox door and boiler front beneath smoke-stack; engineer usually in right side of cab. Price for set.   **650**

(B) Red-painted smokebox door and boiler front beneath smokestack (red color is very dark since it is painted over unprimed black plastic); engineer usually in left side of cab; on most pieces the cab color has a more glossy finish than (A). Price for set.   **750**

2010PB: 1984, uncatalogued; Pinzgauer Bahn Austrian, 0-4-0T tank locomotive similar to 2010(E); dark green-painted cab; no gold on cab numbers or "LGB"; small bronze-colored plaque on sides of cab with the words "Pinzgauer Bahn"; sold only with 20520 Set. Price for set.   **500**

2010SB: 1984, uncatalogued; 0-4-0T tank locomotive for the 20526 Schmidt Bakery Freight Set; very similar to 2010(E), but cab is painted a rich chocolate brown; sold only with set. Price for set.   **450**

2015: 1975-76, 0-4-0 (B-h2T2) Royal Prussian locomotive and tender of the KPEV (Royal Prussian Municipal Railway). Unpainted black boiler and cab; unpainted pinkish-red chassis; early non-smoking, funnel stack with spark arrestor; no KPEV eagle emblem or other markings on tender; early drivers; length 385 mm. On later versions both locomotive and tender are powered and can be electrically linked via a wiring loom and small sockets for harmonious running. Early tenders, though lacking the 2200 Motor, have wiring sockets and axle gearing to accommodate it.

(A) Powered tender, brownish-colored coal load in tender, engineer in left side of cab. Early prototype, only one made.   **NRS**

(B) Unpowered tender, black-colored coal load in tender, engineer in right side of cab.   **450**

2015D: 1977- , same locomotive as 2015, but with smoking stack and black coal load in tender; length 450 mm.

(A) 1977-78, locomotive cab and tender in medium green; tender has KPEV eagle emblem; early (disc) drive wheels.   **400**

(B) 1979-82, locomotive cab and tender in black satin finish; tender lacks KPEV eagle emblem; Cooke-type 2015/3 Smokestack; early disc

Looking like a European's idea of an American locomotive, with its European wheel arrangement, cab, and tender, Americanized with its diamond stack and cowcatcher, 2017D nevertheless has an authentic prototype. Appropriately, it is a locomotive made by a German company for export to America. Like the model locomotive, the model tender has its own motor.

The 2018D Locomotive, with its bulbous spark-catching stack and sturdy proportions, was Lehmann's first serious move into American prototype locomotives, although a number of American prototype freight cars (4066 Log Car, 4067 Boxcar, 4068 Cattle Car, and 4064, 4070, and 4074 Reefers) already existed. Demand outran production by over 20 percent in 1985.

or late spoke drive wheels; forward chassis markings "Bw Insterburg" and "Letzte Br. Unt. 10.2.76".   325

(C) 1983-87, similar to (B), but has KPEV eagle emblem and late spoke drive wheels; forward chassis markings "Bw. Muhlenstroht" and "Letzte Br.Unt. 10.2.83".   285

(D) 1983- , same as (C), but with standard 2010/3 Smokestack; late spoke drive wheels.   CP

Note: Both early disc and spoke drive wheels have solid metal wheels with plastic simulators (either spoke or disc) inserted.

2016: 1975-76, Porter-style 0-4-0 locomotive and tender of the United States; locomotive has red cowcatcher, based on early Porter locomotives used in Mexico, Canada, and the United States. Medium green cab and tender with yellow striping; large yellow and black "LGB" on each side of tender; silver-colored boiler front with "6" front number plate; black chassis on locomotive and tender; early non-smoking funnel stack with spark arrestor; locomotive has early black-spoked drive wheels; "2016" on bottom of locomotive between drive wheels; early engines have socket for synchronizing wire plug (cf. 2015(A) above); tender not powered; tender has early red 2010/1 Drive Wheels on non-geared axles; length 480 mm. Although this model is not listed

in any catalogue, the photograph with the 2017 number in the 1977-78 catalogue is actually a 2016. This locomotive may have been designed after a locomotive built in Germany used for German movies depicting the American West or "American Westerns." Although this locomotive only approximates early United States "Porter" locomotive styling, the LGB 2016 and 2017 were modified to appear more "American" in an attempt to satisfy a growing demand for a United States prototype locomotive.   450

2017: 1977-82, United States Porter-style locomotive with tender. Same basic locomotive as the medium green 2016, but with a powered tender with black 2065/1 Drive Wheels; either early (up to about 1979) or late drivers; length with tender 440 mm.   350

2017D: 1983- , similar to 2017 with Cooke-type 2015/1 smoking Smokestack; late drivers.

(A) 1983-84, medium green-painted cab, special coupling hook for tender, plain red head lamp cowl, no painted filigree.   CP

(B) 1984- , same as (A), but has red head lamp cowl with yellow-gold filigree.   CP

2018D: 1984-87, 2-6-0 Mogul tender locomotive similar to the type found on almost all narrow gauge railways in America and used

The 2019S Colorado & Southern Mogul with matching coal tender is handsome and comes with many features: steam, whistle and bell sounds, as well as a glowing, sparking firebox. G. Ryall Collection.

You can almost feel the heat from the firebox as the stoker shovels in coal from the tender.

especially for negotiating tight curves through narrow canyons and river beds. With non-powered eight-wheel tender painted dark green; red cowcatcher; black smoking balloon stack; black boiler front with silver door and yellow "18" on front number plate; red boiler; dark green cab and tender; length 665 mm. Although production was pushed back to 1985, a few pre-production prototype models were displayed in the United States in late 1984. Actually a D. S. P. & P. R. R. model although lettered "D. & R. G. W." in the 1984-85 catalogue (cab and tender were also lighter green than production models). Production models have "D. S. P. & P. R. R." lettering. A decal set was provided to alter the road name on the tender to "Denver Rio Grande" or "D. & R. G. W." plus several engine numbers. When it was discovered that the weight inside the boiler of the first run models was not completely secure, a boiler-weight retaining screw was added through the inside of the cab. Models may have one or two traction tires. At least 10,000 Moguls were built in 1985.

(A) Shown in 1983-84 catalogue, "D. & R. G. W" painted on sides of tender; single screw on outside front of dab. Non-production prototype. **NRS**

(B) 1985, gold "D. S. P. & P. R. R." on sides of tender; no screw in cab front to secure weight and only one drive wheel with traction tire; two screws on outside front of cab. **475**

(C) 1985-88, same as (B), but with screw in inside front of cab to secure weight; traction tires on one or two drive wheels. **475**

(D) 1985, perhaps a dozen or so 2018Ds were repainted black at the Lehmann factory as special test runs. Several of these found their way into private collections. **NRS**

2019S: 1988- , Colorado & Southern 2-6-0 Mogul locomotive painted in satin black with silver boiler front and matching coal tender. Locomotive has straight smoking smokestack, smooth sand and steam domes, operating head lamp with number-boards (tail lamp on tender), simulated metal cowcatcher, and front-mounted knuckle coupler. Locomotive cab has number "6" on each side below windows and tender reads "COLORADO & SOUTHERN" on each side in white. Has steam, whistle and bell sounds, as well as glowing, sparking firebox. **CP**

2020: 1968- , 0-4-0T (B-h2) "Stainz 2" modeled from an 1892-vintage tender locomotive of the Steiermarkischen Landesbahnen. Has Baldwin-type (large spark arrestor) non-smoking stack; length 250 mm.

(A) 1968-70, unpainted black boiler and dark brown cab with embossed "LGB" and framed "2" in gold finish on sides and back of cab; red chassis, black whistle; smokestack lacks rivet-head and other details; small head and tail lamps with reversing lighting system; early disc 2010/1 Drive Wheels, rectangular buffers without white edging; early 2100 Spur-Gear Motor and no pickup shoes. **250**

(B) 1971-73, same as (A), but with gold-finished cab numbers only. **200**

(C) 1974-78, similar to (A), but with gold-finished cab window frames, framed "1" and "LGB"; 2200 Worm-drive Motor, 2210 Pickup Shoes; brass-colored whistle; large head and tail lamps, rivet-head and other details added to smokestack. **175**

(D) 1979-82, same as (C), but with medium green-painted cab; larger improved head and tail lamps with reversing lighting system. **150**

(E) 1983- , same as (D), but with the markings "Letzte HU. 26.6.79" on front of chassis (some may have had "Letzte 10.2.76"); brass-colored valve and lock handles on boiler. **CP**

(F) 1985, same as (E), but has factory-installed 2010/3 Smokestack, sold with limited edition train Sets 20501(C) and 20514, and Set 20501(D). Price for set. **300**

2020BZ: 1982-83, 0-4-0T (B-h2) tank locomotive for the Blue Train, a limited edition set originally made for the European market which was later imported into the United States and gained great popularity; similar to the 2020, but has a royal blue-painted cab, a silver-painted boiler front, and black chassis; Arabic "2" and "LGB" in gold, gold valve vent on side and valve circle on boiler front. A version with a gold boiler front is also reported; see Chapter XII. Originally sold only with Set 20301BZ. **175**

2020DB: 1985, 0-4-0T (B-h2) locomotive produced for the 150th anniversary of German railroading which was sold only with Set 20150. The locomotive has a red-painted cab and boiler front, with embossed number "1" and "LGB" on cab; gold plating on window

Solid drive wheels with holes have been used on 2010 and 2020 Locomotives from 1968 up to the present day, as on this special edition 2020HS Locomotive; but only the earliest 0-6-2T-series locomotives and the earliest 2075 have solid drive wheels rather than the current spoked ones. A. Rudman Collection.

frames; flat black-painted chassis and red 2010/1 Drive Wheels, gold-colored "150 Jahre" and "Deutsche Eisenbahn" below embossed "LGB" on sides of cab; "1835" and "1985" with multicolored heralds

(one is yellow with red and black stripes and a black eagle, the other is white with a green clover in the middle) are on the cab doors. Price for Set 20150 .   400

2020HS: 1984, uncatalogued, this tank locomotive came as part of the "Freizeit Hobby and Spiel" limited edition 20513 Set; has a deep, shiny red-painted cab with orange, red, and white horizontal stripes along each side of cab. Although these were made for Set 20513, some were sold separately in a blank box (distributed by North Coast Distributors, Medina, Ohio).   225

2020L: 1987, uncatalogued, Lutgenau train set tank locomotive. This is a 2020(E) with light gray-painted cab with black-painted embossed cab markings.   Sold only with 20536L Lutgenau "Dortmund" Beer train set. Price for set.   450

2020SG: 1985-87, uncatalogued. Three 2020 Locomotives have been manufactured for the Schweiger Company for Sets 20528 (see version (A)), and 20529 (see version (B)). The first was built in 1985 for Set 20528 and has a black boiler with either a gold-painted forward section (versions with silver or unpainted black boiler fronts are also known; see Chapter XII); gold boiler plate, bumpers with white margins; unpainted yellow cab with typical dark olive green roof with black weathered edges; black vent on roof; embossed "2" and "LGB" plaques, two olive green horizontal stripes across cab (one just below the windows and one at the lower edge of the cab); "Schweiger" in half-red, half-black letters, beneath embossed "LGB" on each side of cab; black "1835 Nürnberg — Furth 1985"; beneath "150" logo on cab doors; flat black-painted chassis and red 2010/1 Drive Wheels.

Manufactured from 1969 to 1985, the earliest 2050 lacked the intricate detail of the later versions. Shown here are the 2050(B) on the top shelf, left, with the whitish-gray roof andblack chassis; the 2050(D), right, with darker roof and additional piping through roof; and on the bottom shelf, the 2050(E) without gold finish on manufacturer's plate and "EG" plaque.

(A) 1985, yellow cab, gold-painted boiler front and smokebox door. Price for set.   **500**
(B) 1986, in Set 20529, green version of 2020SG. Olive green-painted cab on flat black-painted chassis with a silver boiler front and smokebox door; cab has a small, red and white Schweiger logo with "Schweiger" below embossed "2" on each side, "150" and "1835 Nürnberg-Furth 1985" on door. Price for set.   **300**
(C) 1987, in red Schweiger Set, version of 2020SG. Red-painted cab. Price for set.   **450**

2020/88: 1988-   , Circus Train 0-4-0T steam locomotive; white-painted cab and boiler, red chassis and roof, and bright gold bumpers and head lamp bezels; otherwise similar to 2020(E). Originally sold only with Set 21988.   **NSS**

2028D: 1988- , 2-6-0 (C'1) Mogul locomotive (see 2018D also) with black cab, tender, and boiler front; boiler painted Russian Iron color with bronze-colored piping; "brass" on steam and sand domes is not as shiny as 2018D; number "71" on cab, and "71" and "D., S. P. & P. R. R." on tender.   **CP**

2040: 1968-75, 0-4-0T (B-n2) tank locomotive; modeled from a 1923-vintage industrial locomotive of the Siegerland Industrial Railway. Unpainted black boiler and cab, red chassis; earliest versions have small non-working head and tail lamps which were shortly thereafter changed to a non-reversing lighting system; narrow support ring around rim of smokestack; cab has embossed "LGB", "4", and window frame; gold finish, if present, usually on numbers only on sides and back; black whistle; no engineer.
Note: 2040 Steam Locomotive and 2040 Electric Locomotive are two different engines with the same number.

(A) 1968-70, early Spur-drive motor, no pickup shoes; no sticker, no lights, some have a gold rather than black bell, no driver, cab has small, round roof vent.   **450**
(B) 1970, same as (A), but with head and tail lamps with small bezels; reversing lights in some and instant (front and rear) in others. **400**
(C) 1970-71, number "4" on cab in bright silver or gold finish. Both versions in J. Hylva Collection.   **400**
(D) 1971-74, same as (B) or (C), but with 2200 Worm-drive Motor, 2210 Pickup Shoes, traction tire; has reversing lights.   **375**
(E) 1975, same as (D), but with square-shaped vent on roof.   **375**

2050: 1969-85, 0-4-0T (B-n2) tramway tank locomotive; modeled after the locomotive named "Feuriger Elias" of the Oberrheinische-Eisenbahn Gesellschaft (OEG). This unit, although called in America a "steam dummy," is a steam locomotive, but has flat slab-like sides and a gently curved roof so as to present a less menacing appearance to horses which shared city streets with it. The model comes with green sides, a black boiler, black or red chassis, and three head lamps but no tail lamps; length 255 mm. Coach lighting sockets were added to 1974 and newer models. 2100 Spur-Gear Motors were replaced by 2200 Worm-Gear Motors in 1970 or 1971. Discontinued in 1985.
(A) 1969, body sides very dark green, not painted, with black-painted support seams; black chassis and wheel skirts; body has embossed manufacturer's and "OEG" plaques above "102" all in silver finish; roof is painted very light tan and lacks many embossed details found on later versions (i.e. the lack of a ring with rivet-heads at the opening in the roof where the smokestack passes through and a row of rivet-heads across the front of the roof). The roof also lacks all piping detail, including the steam pipe which passes through the roof just anterior to the smokestack as seen on later versions. Window glass is flat and lacks the raised frame edging. Power supplied by the early 2100 Spur-Gear Motor; also lacks 2210 Pickup Shoes and sockets for coach lighting plugs. The 1969-70 catalogue depicts this locomotive with only an "LGB" logo plaque on body sides in place of the above described plaques and numbers. However, the 1969-70 version was probably not produced in that exact form and the piece depicted may only be prototypical. The earliest catalogue rendering of this engine (1969-70) is black and white and of little help in deciphering color or fine details. This version is probably one of the rarest early locomotives. **900**

(B) 1969-70, very similar to (A), but roof is painted whitish-gray and embossed manufacturer's "OEG" and "102" plaques have bright gold finish.   **850**
(C) 1970-71, similar to (B), but body is lighter colored, being unpainted medium green with a black chassis and red wheel skirts; window glass has raised frame edging.   **850**
(D) 1972-74, same as (C), but with red chassis.   **500**
(E) 1974-76, similar to (D), but roof is slightly darker gray and has piping details including steam pipe passing through roof just forward of the smokestack; embossed roof details include ring with rivet-heads around opening in roof for smokestack and a row of rivet-heads across front of roof; 2200 Worm-drive Motor (probably also on some of versions (B) and (C)) and is the first version to have 2210 Pickup Shoes; traction tire.   **475**
(F) 1977-85, similar to (E), but with body sides painted medium green (has a shinier finish than previous versions); some of the piping detail on the boiler is in gold finish; manufacturer's and "OEG" plaques on body sides lack gold finish; only the "102" number has gold finish; brass sockets for coach lighting plugs on the rear body panel. **450**

The square plate above the oval was added in 1972, after two years of production of 2070, the only one of the 0-6-2T locomotives to have no coal bin in front of the left cab window. A. Rudman Collection.

2070: 1971-74, 0-6-2T (C1) tank locomotive, U. 43 Series of the Steiermarkischen Landesbahnen. With Baldwin-type smokestack, coal bin at rear of cab; dull black finish on boiler and cab; one step protrudes from left side of body adjacent to forward portion of cab and two grates are on each rear cab window; no steam generator is present on boiler.
(A) 1971, early version, non-smoking Cooke-type stack with early 2010/1 Drive Wheels, red plastic trailing wheels; oval manufacturer's plaque on sides of water tanks and "U. 43" plate beneath window of cab; lacks snowplow; head lamps mounted at top front of water tanks; engineer in cab, black rectangular buffers; cab lower than cabs of post-1974 models. A. Rudman Collection. Reader comments requested.   **NRS**
(B) 1972-74, similar to (A), but with early 2070/1 Drive Wheels; additional rectangular manufacturer's plaque on water tanks; snowplow may or may not be present; head lamps mounted on lower fronts of water tanks.   **400**

2070D: 1974-78, 1988, similar to 2070, but with 2070/3 Smokestack. Discontinued in 1988.
(A) 1974, low cab and red chassis and drive wheels similar to 2070(B).   **400**
(B) 1974-78, same as (A), but high cab (similar to 2071D). Cage Collection.   **400**
(C) 1988, same low cab as (A), but water tanks and cab are painted satin gray with red pin stripes; chassis and drive wheels are black. Sold separately and with "Orient Express" Set 20277.   **CP**

Early Tank Locomotive 2070(B) without snowplow, top shelf, left; early 2071D Locomotive on right; 2072D with snowplow and red plastic trailing wheels, bottom shelf, left; and 2073(D) with plaque and plastic trailing wheels beneath cab window.

This coal bin at rear distinguished the 2070, first of Lehmann's series of Krauss 0-6-2Ts, from other locomotives in the series. The smoking version, 2070D, was discontinued in 1978. A. Rudman Collection.

Canted lids on the steam chests, above the cylinders, are one of the many European features of this 2070's prototype. On the model, well detailed opening smokebox doors were a feature from its introduction in the 1970 catalogue. A. Rudman Collection.

2071: 1971, 0-6-2T (C1-n2) tank locomotive, U Series of the Zillertal Railway. Baldwin-type non-smoking stack, no steam generator; open coal bin in front of left cab window; dull black finish on boiler and cab; early 2010/1 Drive Wheels; red plastic trailing wheels; manufacturer's plaques on water tank and number plates located on cab; head lamps mounted atop front of water tanks; lacks snowplow. Reader comments requested.   **NRS**

2071D: 1972- , same locomotive as 2071, but with 2070/3 Smokestack; manufacturer's plaques located on cab; length 340 mm.

The two staggered steps on this 2072, one in front of the cab lettering and the other under the closed coal bin, are early characteristics. A. Rudman Collection.

(A) 1972-78, similar to 2071, but with early 2070/1 Drive Wheels; 2070/3 Smokestack; head lamps mounted on lower fronts of water tanks; red chassis.   **350**

(B) 1978-80, similar to (A), but with red pin stripes on water tanks and cab; early type drivers; metal trailing wheels.   **275**

(C) 1981- , same as (B), but with black chassis.   **CP**

2072: 1971-74, 0-6-2T (C1) tank locomotive, U Series of the Steyertalbahn; closed coal bin in front of left cab window; head lamps mounted on lower fronts of water tanks; boiler and cab in dull black finish; standard (straight) non-smoking stack and 2070/1 Drive Wheels only; length 340 mm.

(A) 1971, has markings "ÖBB", "298.53", and additional white numbers also on smokebox door; early type drive wheels; red plastic trailing wheels; rectangular buffers; no snowplow.   **350**

(B) 1972-74, same as (A), but with snowplow; oval buffers; deep head lamp bezels.   **300**

2072D: 1973-78, same as 2072(A) or (B), but with smoking stack; length 340 mm. Metal trailing wheels replaced red plastic trailing wheels in 1974.   **365**

2073: 1973-74, 0-6-2T tank locomotive, U Series "Eurovapor" of the Waldenburg Railway, the only line with a 760 mm gauge in Switzerland, branching off from the Swiss Federal Railways Basel-Olten line from Liestal to Waldenburg, a distance of 13.6 kilometers. Same boiler and cab configuration as 2072, with the addition of a third dummy head lamp above the boiler front and extra boiler details; cab and water tanks painted medium green, black boiler, red chassis; smokestack is the standard (straight), non-smoking variety; 2070/1 Drive Wheels only; length 340 mm.

The colorful 2073D, green, red, and black, has as its prototype a very colorful original preserved on an extremely narrow (760 mm) gauge, short (13.6 km) line, the Waldenburg Railway. On special occasions, the locomotive runs through the placid valley of its Rhine tributary to feed the Swiss main line near Basel. The model's third headlight is a dummy.

(A) 1973, no markings or plaques on body; older drive wheels; red plastic trailing wheels; rectangular buffers; shallow head lamp bezels. Early factory prototype. **NRS**

(B) 1974, water tanks are unpainted light gray; only three pieces are known. C. Colwell Collection. **NRS**

(C) 1973-74, same as (A), but with "298.14" on smokebox door and also on plaque in gold finish with the "Eurovapor" name located beneath cab window; oval buffers; deep head lamp bezels. **350**

The long stacks of the old Lehmann steamers (here, 2072) were not always smokers, but they are always functional: ending in a long bolt, they pass through the boiler, often a lead weight, the chassis, and the front coupler loop to hold the engine together.

The Spreewald, a meter gauge locomotive, with much bright gold trim, was modeled after the engine built in 1917 by the Jung Locomotive Works. G. Ryall Collection.

The husky 2080 was the first steam locomotive to be equipped with sound at the factory, including both chuff and mechanically-triggered electronic bell. Introduced in 1974, the 2080S underwent a few minor variations in lettering. The skull and crossbones on the tank were added in 1978.

2073D: 1973-87, same as 2073 with 2072/3 Smokestack in the following variations:
(A) 1973-78, same as 2073(C).   **350**
(B) 1979-83, similar to (A), but with fine yellow pin stripes on water tanks and cab; older or newer drivers; metal trailing wheels.   **300**
(C) 1983-87, similar to (B), but with slightly heavier yellow pin stripes; late drivers; discontinued in 1987.   **275**

2074D: 1987- , Spreewald 2-6-0T (1'C-n2t) locomotive model of the one built by Jung Locomotive Works in 1917. This is a meter gauge locomotive with dark green-painted cab and water tanks, black boiler, and red chassis and wheels.   **CP**

2075: 1974-84, 0-4-0T (B-n2) locomotive of the East German Railway, type number 99 5001, formerly Spremberg urban railway locomotive 11. Body color generally black, but may vary; open coal bin at rear of cab; non-smoking stack and no lights; length 240 mm.
(A) 1974, body painted in flat black; most detail markings in white, however the embossed letters of the Deutsche Reichsbahn plaque are in gold finish; pinkish-red or red chassis; early 2010/1 Drive Wheels.
                                                                  200
(B) 1975-84, no gold finish on Deutsche Reichsbahn plaque; early or late 2015/1 Drive Wheels; usually with red chassis.   **175**
(C) 1977-78, very dark green body and water tanks; black boiler and cab; reddish-pink chassis; small black and gold "LGB" plaque. This version manufactured for Primus; known as 20785. See Chapter XII.
                                                                  475

2075DC: 1982, same as 2075, but painted with Dodge City and Great Western Railroad logo "D.C. & GR. W. R.R." in white over "LITTLE BILLY" in black on curved yellow panel on tank side and "2075" in white on cab doors. Though originally sold only with Set 20701DC, this locomotive has been sold separately.
(A) Late red 2015/1 Drive Wheels.   **200**
(B) Late black 2017/1 Drive Wheels.   **175**

2076: 1984, same basic locomotive as the 2075, with dual head and tail lamps; brake hoses; extra boiler details; rear coal bins with working, hinged lids; interior light in cab; valve gear rods, with reversing rod and eccentrics; may have had a non-smoking stack. This version was not produced in this exact form; see 2076D.   **NRS**

2076BP: 1984, uncatalogued; similar to 2076D, but with red-painted cab; white-lettered "B. P. S. and D. R. R." and white pin stripes on sides of water tanks; "the Roger T." above "B. P. S. and D. R. R." and "2076" in white on cab doors, "the Roger T." in yellow on water tank and smokebox door; red chassis and cab steps; engineer figure in cab. Sold with Set 20301BP and not originally sold separately.   **200**

2076D: 1983- , same as 2076, but with smoking stack, window glass, window curtains in cab door; has three-position "on-idle-off" switch inside cab.
(A) 1983- , no engineer in cab.   **CP**
(B) 1985, engineer in cab. Sold with Set 20519. Price for set.   **325**

2080: 1974-76, 2-6-2T (1'C1'-h2t) tank locomotive. See 2080D listed below.

2080D: 1974- , 2-6-2T (1'C1'-h2t) tank locomotive, built by the Krupp Company and used by the East German State Railways (Trans-Harz). Boiler and cab in dull black finish; red or pinkish-red chassis; although production models have a smoking stack, the earlier models known as 2080 or prototypes may have been non-smokers; length 410 mm.
(A) 1974, engine number "99 6001" on boiler front and beneath cab windows but only the cab numbers painted white; black cab step, forward step (in front of boiler) a single rectangular unit, steam generator stand is well over half as long as the steam generator itself; red plastic leading and trailing wheels; early 2080/1 Drive Wheels; early factory prototype.   **NRS**
(B) 1975, engine number on boiler in white and additional white markings on saddle tanks and cab; red cab fore-step composed of two rungs; steam generator stand only one-half as long as generator; upper

surfaces of forward deck unpainted pinkish-red; early metal leading and trailing wheels; early 2080/1 Drive Wheels; only two are known to exist of this factory prototype.   **1200**
(C) 1974-76, same as (B), but with upper surfaces of forward deck painted black; may or may not have smoking stack. Some earlier models come in yellow boxes with the "2080" catalogue number, although models were virtually unchanged during these years of manufacture.   **400**
(D) 1977-78, same as (C), with smoking stack; embossed "Deutsche Reichsbahn" in silver or gold finish.   **300**
(E) 1978- , same as (D), but with white skull and crossbones warning on sides of saddle tanks; early or late 2080/1 Drive Wheels. Latest versions have "Deutsche Reichsbahn" in gold finish only.   **CP**

2080S: 1974- , same as 2080 or 2080D, but with electronic synchronized steam, bell, and whistle sounds with the following variations:
(A) 1974-75, same as 2080D(A), but with sound; has mechanical bell.
                                                                  NRS
(B) 1975-76, same as 2080D(B), but with same sound as (A).   **NRS**
(C) 1977-78, same as 2080D(D), but with same sound as (A).   **650**
(D) 1978-84, same as 2080D(E), but with same sound as (A).   **650**
(E) 1984- , same as 2080S(D), but with improved electronic bell sound and additional compressor sounds. Previous versions have a "clacky" mechanical bell while this version has a "clear ringing" bell sound. Compressor sounds are sustained and gradually taper off after power is removed.   **CP**

2085D: 1982- , 0-6-6-0T (C'C-n4vt) Mallet tank locomotive manufactured by AG Hanomag in 1925 for heavy duty use on steeply inclined stretches of track with numerous bends; used in service by the South German Railway Company (SEG). Boiler and cab finished in dull

...iculated steam locomotives with their double-drive mechanisms, known as Mallets after their inventor, are a visual joy in ...ration. Note the large front cylinders, operating in the prototype (preserved at the Blonay-Chamby Museum Railway in ...tzerland) from partially expanded steam that has already been through the rear cylinders of this compound engine. The model ...ges both mechanisms to accommodate the radically tight 1100 curves, whose 600 mm radius barely exceeds the 510 mm length of ...locomotive.

black paint with glossy, dark green saddle tanks; SEG logo and "104" on sides of cab, manufacturer's plaque on sides of saddle tanks, "104" on boiler front and additional markings and ZELL plaque on cab; smoking stack; 2085/1 Drive Wheels.

(A) Early prototype is a composite of two 2071D Locomotives with two 2010/5 Chassis; boiler and water tanks are flat black. Tested at factory for one year. J. Cooley Collection.   **NRS**

(B) 1982, smokestack tilted slightly forward due to problems with early boiler molds; flat black finish on boiler.   **550**

(C) 1983- , smokestack normal, not tilted forward; boiler has flat black finish with lightning bolt warning decals on smokebox door, dome, and rear of cab.   **CP**

2117: 1987- , United States Porter-style 0-4-0 steam locomotive. This model is very similar to the 2016 or 2017 but had no tender and was originally sold only in packaged sets. It also has the non-smoking funnel stack previously used on the 2016 and 2017. Two versions have been produced:

(A) 1987-88, Denver & Rio Grande version; cab is painted a silver-blue color known as Russian Iron, with white stripes, Denver & Rio Grande logo on the cab doors, and "100" painted on steam chests. Originally sold only with Set 20087.   **300**

(B) 1989- , Lake George & Boulder version; similar to (A) but has round LG&B logo (in blue, black, and white) on cab doors and "LGB" on steam chests. Originally sold only with Sets 22301US and 22401US.   **CP**

2119D: 1989- , Lake George & Boulder 2-6-0 Mogul locomotive. Same superstructure as the 2019S but with yellow cab, tender, steam and sand domes, and headlight. Two parallel, black stripes run horizontally along cab and tender. Number "2119" in black on low side

of cab, "Lake George & Boulder" in black on sides of tender; tender chassis and archbar trucks are gray. Has smoking stack and constant lighting. For United States distribution only.   **CP**

2901: 1989- , Jagsttal Railway "Frank S" 0-6-0 live steam locomotive with four-wheel tender. Lehmann commissioned Aster to build this easy-to-operate, live steam model of the original Henschel locomotive manufactured in 1941. Unlike most LGB models the 2901 is almost entirely made of metal and has dummy headlights. Suitable for radio control.   **CP**

20872: 1978, this 0-6-2T steam locomotive is believed to be virtually identical to the LGB 2072D and only differs in having been separately packaged for Primus. Reader comments requested.   **500**

20875: 1977-78, 0-4-0T locomotive similar to the LGB 2075 but has semi-glossy, dark green water tanks with a "LEHMANN" label in the middle on each side, while the rest of the body is flat black. Drivers are the older disc type, LGB 2010/1 Slotted Wheels such as those used on the LGB 2010 or 2020. Known to have been sold with Primus Set 8000, but may have been sold separately as well.   **650**

HANDMADE LOCOMOTIVE SECTION

Brass handmade locomotives were manufactured by C. Hohne in limited numbers, a maximum of 100 each year, for LGB. All of these locomotives require LGB 1600 wide radius track (235 cm) and 1605-1615 switches. All have reversing lighting.

1977: South African Railways, 2-8-4 class 24 locomotive was designed for short line work. It was developed in 1949 from totally new technical concepts since the weight over the axles could not exceed 11 tons. The solution was to cast the frame and cylinders as one piece — a production carried out in Great Britain. Other weight savings were gained by using a Vanderbilt-type tender. One especially fine feature was the oversized firebox which allowed the burning of low grade fuel. Tractive force equals 12,530 kg. Model length is 815 mm, height 154 mm, width 118 mm, and weight 11.8 kg; powered by a Buhler 6-18v motor; locomotive and tender are lighted; number series 3601 to 3700.   **5000**

1978: Caminhas de Ferro Mocambique, 2-6-2 + 2-6-2 Garratt-type locomotive is probably one of the best prototype locomotive designs and was patented in 1907. The two British companies, Beyer Peacock & Company and Kitson & Company, made the greatest advances in this construction concept. This locomotive-type is in operation today in South Africa. Model length is 812 mm, height 157 mm, width 123 mm, and weight 10.7 kg; powered by two Buhler 6-18v motors; locomotive is lighted front and rear; number series 2035 to 2134.   **4500**

1979: Bridal Will Lumbering Company (Bridal Veil) 2-6-6-0 Mallet locomotive is one of the most widely used articulated designs. (Due to mis-translation, this locomotive was mis-lettered "Bridal Will" for the Bridal Veil Company of Oregon.) Over the years it has been refined and is virtually unrivaled for reliability and power. This style was first produced in the United States during the 1880s. In 1904 and later it was also found in South America. This model was operated on a private short line in Brazil and has a cabin tender. Model length is 790 mm, height 162 mm, width 113 mm, and weight 10.8 kg; powered by two Buhler 6-18v motors; locomotive and tender are lighted; number series 201-300.   **5800**

1980: Giradot Railway of Columbia, 2-6-6-2T Kitson Meyer Mallet locomotive is actually a modification of the Garratt. (This type of construction allows coal and water to be stored directly on the engine, concentrating more weight over the driving wheels, thus increasing

traction.) The design also allows the locomotive to operate on tight curves. The engine was very popular in Bolivia, Chile, and Colombia, and most were produced by the British firm, Kitson & Company. Model length is 760 mm, height 135 mm, width 159 mm, and weight 11.2 kg; powered by two Buhler 6-18v motors with lighting front and rear; number series 35 to 134.   **5200**

1981: Argentine State Railroad, 4-8-2 locomotive with condenser tender, was a promising innovation in locomotive design. It allowed operation in areas where water was scarce and greatly improved fuel consumption. This locomotive still operates in southern Africa and South America. The Henschel & Sohn Company is mostly responsible for the development of the condenser system through Dr. Roosen. Model length is 970 mm, width 128 mm, and weight 11.4 kg; powered by a single Buhler 6-18v motor; number series 8001 to 8100.   **4900**

1982: Indian State Railway SR (Southern Region), 2-8-2 Mikado-type locomotive with smoke deflectors and standard tender. Approximately five thousand of these locomotives with various wheel arrangements and pulling capacities were supplied by Krauss-Maffei-Munchen, Henschel-Kassel, North British, and United States companies as part of the Western Alliance Development Aid program. A number were also manufactured in Indian Railway yards under license. Some of these locomotives are still in service today. Model length is 875 mm, height 155 mm, width 140 mm, and weight 7.8 kg; powered by a Buhler 6-18v motor in each tender truck, locomotive and tender are lighted; number series 6801-6900.   **3200**

1983: Tungpu Railway of China, 2-10-0 decapod locomotive which was originally produced by Krupp Locomotive Works in West Germany and in the 1930s was produced in the United States by Lima-Alco. The model is based on the German-built versions supplied to the Schansi province of China. This design was chosen due to small permissible axle load. These locomotives were very reliable and saw service up until the 1950s. Model length is 720 mm and weight 7.5 kg; powered by a single Buhler 6-18v motor; both locomotive and tender are lighted; number series 318-417.   **3000**

III
ELECTRIC LOCOMOTIVES and TROLLEYS

The rapid drop from the Alps to the sea makes hydroelectric power practical in much of Europe, as does the dense population, reducing the distance over which power must be distributed. Even short lines are often electrified. Sometimes, when such lines merge, different electrical systems are maintained. On the Rhaetian Railroad, most of the system operates on single-phase alternating current at 11,000 volts, 16-2/3 cycles. (The Swiss standard gauge lines operate on 15,000 volts.) But the Chur-Arosa line in the Rhaetian network operates on 2,400 volts direct current. On European rails, electric locomotives thus are common and varied.

Lehmann introduced electric locomotives to its line in 1971 with a group of six virtually identical steeple-cab locomotives, differentiated by their color. They were numbered consecutively from 2030 to 2035, although two of those numbers, 2035 and 2033, would be used for quite different electric motors later, when the originals had been discontinued. Only the blue and beige 2030 is still in production today, but changed to a slightly gaudier livery in 1986. 2030, 2032, and 2034 have two-toned finishes, with beige tops and blue, red, and green bottoms respectively; 2031, 2033, and 2035 are solid blue, red, and green. Judging from catalogue photos, the company had in mind the possibility of passenger trains in colors that matched the engines, especially the two-toned ones, and featured such groupings in ads. However, only 2034 was ever issued with a factory set.

The early pantograph engines, 2030-2035, were produced from 1971-1974. They had internal wiring soldered directly to the motor housing, which made them difficult to disassemble. Later, screw contacts were introduced facilitating the removal of the cab from the motor housing, a principle used in other locomotives as well. All originally lacked lighting sockets.

1988: 1988-89, trolley cars "Zwanziger" to commemorate the 20th birthday of LGB trains. Similar to red 2036 and 3600, but with gold-painted trim and lettering "1968-1988" on roof boards, "20" on round number plaques, and colorful caricatures of German pioneers and LGB trains painted over a white background on each side of trolleys. As with the 2035/3500 and 2036/3600, the trolley with the roof-mounted current collector bow is powered pulling a dummy "trailer."
CP

2030: 1971-82, electric "steeple-cab" locomotive AEG E1 1508 of the 10.4 kilometer long Mixnitz-St. Erhard Local Railway; modeled after the Bo class AEG electric locomotives built in 1913 and used mainly to pull a mixture of passenger coaches and goods wagons. Blue and beige body; black chassis with red brake shoes and arms; red grab-irons; dark red pantograph; early versions lack lighting plugs; length 245 mm.
(A) 1971-73, blue portion of body unpainted, white portion painted; no lighting plug receptacle. **350**
(B) 1974-82, blue portion of body painted, white portion painted; has lighting plug receptacle. **250**

2030E: 1983- , same as 2030 with EAV (electronic start delay) system. EAV units allow simultaneous shunting with a second locomotive on the same loop.
(A) 1983-84, same colors as 2030(B); silk-screened white lettering "GEW. Lok 15, t" over "P 10, t" over "Hd 8, t" over "H.-Unt. 0.0. 1984" (this last sequence may vary from run to run) to the left of the cab door; "LuP 5, 09m" to the left of the last of the above listed marking sequences; raised portion of manufacturer's plaque on door same color as body; head lamps same as early models with bulbs protruding from lensless bezels; smooth roof. **200**
(B) 1984- , similar to (A), but with black pin stripes on beige portion of cab; black and white pin stripes on blue body (blue color slightly darker than on earlier version); "H.-Unt. 6.6.84" replaces "H.-Unt. 0.0.

The very appealing "steeple-cab" locomotives in unpainted red and blue, made from 1971-1982. J. Hylva Collection.

1984" of (A); head lamps have lenses which conceal bulbs; textured roof.   **CP**

2031: 1971-74, blue steeple-cab electric, same basic locomotive as 2030(A) of same railway company, but entire body is medium blue.
(A) 1971-73, body is unpainted medium blue.   **1200**
(B) 1974, body is painted medium blue.   **1200**

2032: 1971-74, red and beige steeple-cab electric, same basic locomotive as 2030, white lettering to the right of door reads "Lb. M.—St.E." and to the left of door, "Lup 5.09m / Gew. Lok 15 t / P 10, t / Hd 8. t / H.-Unt. 0.0.1980". Has lighting plug, doors open in, gold-painted horn on left front, engineer inside.
(A) 1971-73, red portion of body is unpainted, beige portion painted.
                                                                          650
(B) 1974, red portion of body is painted, beige portion painted.   **650**

2033: 1971-73, red steeple-cab electric, same locomotive as 2030(A), but body is all red. No lighting socket. The original issue, with no lead weights inside, does not have as good an electrical contact as the later, weighted models (also see 2033 below).
(A) 1973-73, body is unpainted red.   **1000**
(B) 1973, body is painted red.   **1000**

2033: 1977-86, B-class track maintenance electric modeled after the Swiss versions having diesel engines to power the locomotives when catenary systems are damaged. They are used for construction and

repair work as well as branch line and tramway operation and shunting purposes. The LGB model features forward service platforms, large head lamp, small tail lamp, flashing warning lamps on roof; red 2030/3 Pantograph; length 270 mm. Discontinued in 1986.
(A) 1977, unpainted green body; red chassis with yellow and black hazard marks at each corner; green roof insulators; no opening on left side of platform at steps; embossed plain, unpainted manufacturer's plaques and numbers; no tools or barrels on service platform. This version was probably never produced.   **NRS**
(B) 1977-78, similar to (A), but with unpainted medium green body; black roof insulators; open access on left side of platform at steps; embossed manufacturer's plaques with gold finish; embossed "60" on cab painted white; red and white or yellow and black hazard stripes at each corner.   **485**
(C) 1979-81, same as (B), but with medium green-painted body without gold finish on manufacturer's plaques.   **425**
(D) 1983, unpainted orange body; gray chassis; plain embossed manufacturer's plaque and unpainted "60"; EAV system.   **250**
(E) 1983-84, same as (D), but with embossed manufacturer's plaque in gold finish and "60" painted white.   **300**
(F) 1984, same as (D), but without gold finish on manufacturer's plaque; no embossed number.   **250**
(G) 1984-85, same as (F), but without embossed "60" on sides, but rather a silk-screened "2033" with additional white dimension markings at lower position of cab.   **185**

The newer version of the 2033 work motor with platform, its number reassigned from an old steeple-cab, follows the recent Lehmann trend toward electronic sophistication. Body color changed from green to this orange in 1983, and in 1985 the single flashing rooftop light became two, their flash rate independent of engine speed.

(H) 1985-86, dual flashing lights on top, new power switch, slightly heavier than earlier models. This is the last version produced. **185**

2034: 1971-74, green and beige steeple-cab electric, same basic locomotive as 2030, with green and beige body. No lighting socket.
(A) 1971-73, green portion of body unpainted, beige portion painted.
850
(B) 1974, green portion of body painted, beige portion painted. **850**

2035: 1971-74, green steeple-cab electric; same basic locomotive as 2030, but body entirely green; red plastic grab-irons, gold-painted horn on left front side; black roof and black or red pantograph. No lighting socket.
(A) 1971-73, body is unpainted green. **1200**
(B) 1974, body painted green. **1200**

2035 (3500): 1977- , conventional style yellow trolley car with enclosed driver's platforms; common version has yellow- and white-painted body; red 2030/3 Pantograph. Has head and taillights that are directional on all but earliest versions. The 3500 Trolley Trailer has the same basic body as the 2035, but is unpowered, lacks a pantograph, has plastic 3000/1 Wheels, and sells for about 30 percent of the price for the pair; both have two seated figures in illuminated passenger compartments; length 350 mm; listed prices are for both powered 2035 and non-powered 3500 together.
(A) 1977-78, yellow window frames in black supports on sides of body; no red tail lamp. **NRS**

(B) 1978, similar to (A), but with brown window frames without painted black side supports. J. Hylva Collection. **350**
(C) 1979, same body as (A), but painted red with black-painted window frame supports; only 100 of these were produced and all were originally shipped to Austria. Hans Kahl Collection. **850**
(D) 1979- , similar to (B), but has window frame supports painted black; has red tail lamp (earliest versions were non-illuminated).
CP

2036 (3600): 1978-84, old-fashioned red trolley car of the kind used everywhere after the horse-drawn era; with open drivers' platforms; three windows on both sides of car; red- and white-painted body; black current collector bow. Working directional taillights in all but the earliest. The 3600 Trolley Trailer has the same basic body as the 2036, but is unpowered; lacks a pantograph or current collector bow; has plastic 3000/1 Wheels; sells for about 30 percent of the price for the pair; two seated figures in both passenger compartments; both discontinued in 1984; length 350 mm. Listed prices are for both the 2036 and 3600 together unless noted differently.
(A) 1978, red 2030/3 Pantograph on roof of powered unit; yellow window frames; red supports on sides of body; no pin stripes on body. Factory prototype. **NRS**
(B) 1978-84, 2036/3 Current Collector Bow in place of pantograph; brown window frames; yellow pin stripes on body. **350**

2036SC (3600SC): 1976, uncatalogued; a red, non-powered 3600 Trailer only; built for the Suchard Chocolate Company of West Ger-

many; this version is very similar to the standard 3600, but has "Suchard" and "Chocolat" decals on each side of the body below the windows. Less than 200 pieces produced. G. Ermler Collection.
750

2040: 1978- , Ge 6/6 "Crocodile" electric of the Rhaetian Railway (RhB), the largest continuous metric gauge rail network in Europe encompassing almost 400 kilometers. Modeled after the largest standard locomotive series of the RhB, which was used as a heavy universal electric locomotive for goods and passenger traffic over mountain tracks. Although the photos in early catalogues depict the prototype, it is unlikely that a model of the prototype shown was produced. Three-piece articulated body, two motorized sections; length 560 mm; with 2030/3 Pantographs, a dull brown-finished body, and several differences in the side vent and window detail. The following variations are known to exist:
(A) 1978, uncatalogued; has semi-glossy, medium brown finish with light gray roof; silver, unpainted (bare metal) pantographs with only a single contact bar at top (early version of 2040/3); brown roof insulators; all-gray wheels which drive slanted drive rods; black grab-irons on main cab; translucent windows on main body (not windows to engineer's cabins) not blocked out with white color; light gray catwalks at edges of roof. Early catalogue photographs depict the prototype with red 2030/3 Pantographs, but these were not used on production models.   **1200**
(B) 1978-79, same as (A), but wheels that drive slanted drive rods have black-painted centers.   **1200**
(C) 1979-80, similar to (B), but with glossy finish and medium green roof insulators.   **675**

Lehmann introduced its huge 2040 model of the Rhaetian Railway "crocodile" proclaiming its more than 600 parts. As in the prototype, both hoods are articulated to the main body suspended between them, enabling the locomotive to move through tight curves and esses with sinuous ease. A conspicuous variation since its introduction in 1978 has been the color of the roof insulators.

(D) 1980-81, similar to (B), but with red roof insulators.   **600**
(E) 1980-81, uncatalogued; similar to (B), but with combination of red and green roof insulators.   **600**
(F) 1983, body has glossy, bright red finish; red roof insulators. A very small number of these were made by Lehmann as a pre-production test.   **NRS**
(G) 1981-84, same as (E), but with silver-painted pantographs with two contact bars at top (late version of 2040/3); red roof insulators; windows on main body blocked out with white; dark gray catwalks at edge of roof.   **500**

The 2036(B), top left, came with a current collector bow instead of a pantagraph; it is followed on the right by the companion 3600(B) trolley trailer. On the bottom shelf is the "Chocolate Trolley," a 2036(C); one of 1500 manufactured in the late 1970s; to its right is a plainer cousin, a 3600 made in the late 1970s for the Austrian market. J. Hylva Collection.

Electrification of parts of the present Rhaetian Railway, in southeastern Switzerland, occurred in the 1920s. Continuing their series of cars and locomotives from this largest European narrow gauge network, Lehmann introduced in 1986 this old-style boxcab electric with its slanting jackshaft drive. J. Hylva Collection.

(H) 1985, similar to (G), but with yellow grab-irons on main body; yellow detail markings in lower right-hand corner of main body
.   **425**

(I) 1985-87, similar to (H), but body color is orange-brown; lower head lamps have gold bezel rings.   **425**

(J) 1986, body painted dark green, silver-gray-painted roof with black shading and chocolate brown-painted catwalks; all handrails and grab-irons have bright gold finish; only one made for pre-production test.   **NRS**

(K) 1988- , similar to (I), but body color is a semi-glossy light tan-brown with a silver matte finish on roof with light green insulators.
                                                                                                    CP

Note: Two engines were given the same number, the 2040 Steam Locomotive and the 2040 Electric.

2043: 1989- , Swiss Rhaetian Railway Ge 4/4 II electric locomotive with dual pantographs. This attractive red-painted, eight-wheel locomotive is designed so that the pantographs will automatically raise or lower depending upon the direction of travel; can be run from track or catenary power.   **CP**

2045: 1986- , Ge 2/4 (1'B1') passenger electric of the RhB, with slanting drive rod, opening driver's cab door with adjustable sliding windows; numbered "205", shown in 1983-84 catalogue with two silver 2040/3 Pantographs; body is same orange-brown color as 2040(I) Crocodile. The 1983-84 catalogue depicts this locomotive with solid guide wheels; however the l985-86 catalogue version is shown with spoked guide wheels. This later version is apparently the only one produced.

(A) 1986, dark green-painted body; pre-production, factory prototype.
                                                                                                    NRS

The first 2000 of the 2045s have Eberhard Richter's signed initials on opposing side cab doors, a gesture to memorialize his spirit and work in creating LGB. W. Richter comment. J. Hylva Collection.

(B) 1986, brown-painted body with red roof insulators as seen in 1985 and 1986-87 catalogues. The first production run of this locomotive has Eberhard Richter's signed initials on opposing side cab doors, a gesture to memorialize his spirit and work in bringing about LGB; W. Richter comment. Eberhard Richter died December 30, 1984 (see *Depesche* magazine, Spring 1985). 2000 of these locomotives were

produced; models produced afterward will not bear Eberhard Richter's
initials.   **480**
(C) 1987-88, same as (B), but no signature on doors.   **350**
(D) 1988- , same as (C), but with light green roof insulators.   **CP**

2046: 1986- , a red 300 mm long track electric with a silver roof built
as Zahnrad-Ellok HGe 2/2 for the Furka-Oberalpbahn; has 2040/3
Pantograph and three lamps at each end; markings include "FO", "21",
"HGe 2/2", "25t", and silver manufacturer's plaque on each side. This
engine is capable of pulling 25 percent grades. Although production
was originally set for mid-1986, the factory postponed this model until
late 1987. They did not feel that the prototype gear box mechanism
met with their standards and therefore they redesigned it in 1987.
The prototype depicted in the 1987 catalogue and 1986 catalogue
supplement has gray roof insulators and a silver-gray roof, however a
prototype seen by the author has green roof insulators and a bright
silver roof.

(A) 1986, motor block assembly has two cog wheels, one at each end.
Perhaps two or three of these were made, but changed due to problems
with drive mechanism. Did not go into production in this form.
                                                                             2000

(B) 1988- , motor block assembly has one cog wheel, only at forward
end. This is the regular production version.   **CP**
(C) 1988- , similar to (B), but body is painted in beige and red. May
be non-production prototype.   **NRS**

3500(A): Same as 2035(A), except dummy unit.   **NRS**

3500(B): Same as 2035(B), except dummy unit.   **150**

3500(C): Same as 2035(C), except dummy unit.   **850**

3500(D): Same as 2035(D), except dummy unit.   **CP**

3600(A): Same as 2036(A), except dummy unit.   **NRS**

3600(B): Same as 2036(B), except dummy unit.   **150**

IV
DIESEL LOCOMOTIVES
and RAILBUSES

Diesel locomotives bear a German name, and it is not surprising that Lehmann has found attractive prototypes, both large and small. Although American diesels are almost all diesel-electrics, with the diesel engines driving generators which power motors on each engine axle, Lehmann identifies its prototypes as diesel-hydraulics, in which the diesel engine operates a pump or impeller to drive oil against a turbine connected to the axles.

209: 1975-87, Kof diesel-hydraulic shunter and main line diesel with side rods. Battery-powered model similar to 2090, but with medium green body; red plastic drive wheels. **CP**

2051: 1979- , V51 / V52 series B'B' (Bo Bo class) twin-diesel locomotive, modeled after one of the five modern diesel-hydraulic locomotives acquired by the German Federal Railways (DB) in the early 1960s for their narrow gauge lines in Wurttemberg. A white stripe may be found in complete or incomplete configurations (on recent models) or may be altogether absent (on older versions) around the edges of the catwalks on the chassis; length 436 mm.

The horn was added to the yellow 2060 in 1971, a year after the model was catalogued in three colors (yellow, 2060Y; red, 2060; and green, 2060G). 2060H now has a battery recharged by track current to maintain a steady volume of blare regardless of speed.

A red 2060(C) (with air hoses added) is on the top shelf with a 2060G(A) next to it; on the bottom shelf are two seemingly identical
2060s, but the one of the left is a 2060H(B) with its distinguishing screw-heads on each corner of the cab roof; next to it is a 2060Y(A).
J. Hylva Collection.

(A) 1979, dull red finish; red grab-irons, "9252 901-4" on sides of cab
and over radiator grills front and rear; large "DB" logo; early red
2031/1 Drive wheels; hood steps quite pronounced; white horizontal
stripe along sides of body; white stripe on chassis only along lateral
catwalks; may be the prototype.   **NRS**
(B) 1979, similar to (A), but with dull dark red finish; black grab-
irons; numbered "251902-3", a smaller "DB" logo; metal
manufacturer's plaque added to lower center of each side of front hood;
white stripe on body, but none on chassis; has red 2030/1 drive wheels.
                                                                   425
(C) 1980, same as (B), but with black 2035/1 Drive wheels.   **425**
(D) 1981- , similar to (C), but with shiny, lighter red finish; white
stripe on chassis is usually complete around all edges of catwalks, has
dimension markings at chassis ends; may or may not have metal
manufacturer's plaque.   **CP**

2051S: 1981-86, same as 2051(C) or (D); earliest models may have
also been produced in a red color similar to 2051(A). These models
have electronic diesel and horn sounds. Discontinued in 1986.
                                                                   600

2055: 1989- , White Pass & Yukon C'C' DL535E diesel locomotive
built by Montreal Locomotive Works (MLW). LGB model is painted
with W P & Y blue, white and red color scheme with a black roof,
trucks, and chassis. It is powered by two motors, has constant lighting
with mode switch, and a horn.   **CP**

2060: 1969-82, Schoma CFL-150 DH (B-class) industrial diesel engine for main line service and shunting; red body on gray or black
chassis; mock roof horn may be black or dull or shiny "gold"-finished;
hazard markings are red and white or yellow and black; length 270
mm.
(A) 1969-70, red, rather dull finished, unpainted body; may be faded
or pinkish-red on some pieces; without embossed manufacturer's

plaques or numbers; roof horn usually black. May have been the
prototype.   **NRS**
(B) 1970-74, same as (A), but with embossed manufacturer's plaque;
white-painted "60" on cab; red and white hazard markers at each
corner of chassis.   **250**
(C) 1974-76, same as (A), but with gold finish on embossed
manufacturer's plaque; white-painted "60" on cab; red and white
hazard markers at each corner of chassis.   **200**
(D) 1975-82, shiny painted red finish; embossed manufacturer's
plaques; white-painted "60" on cab; red and white hazard markers at
each corner of chassis; roof horn usually black. Has lighting socket.
                                                                   175
(E) 1982, same as (D), but with gold finish on embossed manufacturer's plaques.   **150**

2060G: 1970-75, same basic diesel as the 2060, but with unpainted
medium green body with black grab-irons; red chassis, black horn;
white embossed "60" and gold-finished manufacturer's plaque on cab;
clear windows and engineer in cab. No lighting socket.
(A) Red chassis.   **400**
(B) Black chassis.   **450**

2060H: 1971- , same basic diesel as the 2060, but with semi-glossy
unpainted yellow body; red and white hazard markers on front and
back ends; an electric horn concealed under the body; black air tanks,
grab-irons, light covers at each end; black horn on gray roof; gold rim
on cab and door window panels; gold raised panel with "SCHOEMA"
and more information in two panels; length 270 mm.
(A) 1971-72, horn mechanism inside cab, concealed by opaque, black
windows; roof is screwed on with screw-heads showing at each corner;
white "60"; window frames and embossed gold-finished
manufacturer's plaque; no 2110 Contact Shoes; black chassis. **NRS**
(B) 1973-74, same as (A), but with 2110 Contact Shoes present; red
chassis.   **250**

Although now available as a single unit, 2065 originally was marketed only in pairs. Some American sellers have misnamed these flat-fronted railcars "Galloping Goose," after a famous long-snouted Western railcar. As with the streetcars, the motorman (and here, ticket taker) have magnetized bases and can be moved when direction is reversed; the lights reverse automatically, as on most recent Lehmann locomotives.

(C) 1975-79, horn mechanism inside of front motor hood; cab windows clear; engineer figure inside cab; red chassis.   **175**
(D) 1980-85, same as (C), but with rechargeable battery for horn mechanism.   **165**
(E) 1985- , yellow portion of body is painted bright glossy yellow with black stripes on hoods (of the same design as the 2061); hood vents and other embossed markings are painted black. A black-painted "2060" on cab just below manufacturer's plaque replaces the embossed "60" of the other versions (no gold plating on plaque); other black-painted cab markings include: "Gew. Lok 22t / P 18t", "Br. Gew. / G 15t", "Vmax 30km/h", and "Br. Unt. 1.3.84 AW Nur"; chassis is painted bright red with white dimension markings on each end; black tanks on each side of chassis have the markings, "Kraftstoff 3601".   **CP**

2060P: 1984, same basic diesel as the 2060, but with dark blue-painted body with same two horizontal white stripes on both sides of hood and grills similar to the 2061; white "PHILIPS LOK 1" markings on cab; red chassis with yellow grab-irons; black air tanks and step protrusions on side of chassis. Windows have yellow frames, black shading on charcoal gray roof; gold-colored whistle on roof, black-colored head and taillights at each end of cab; sold only with Set 380.7030. Price for set.   **400**

2060Y: 1970-78, same basic diesel as the 2060H(A) or (B), but without the electric horn mechanism.   **150**
(A) 1970-72, similar externally to 2060H(A); black chassis.   **250**
(B) 1972-74, similar to (A), but without gold finish on embossed manufacturer's plaque; clear windows; red or gray chassis.   **250**
(C) 1976-78, similar to (A), but without gold finish on embossed manufacturer's plaque; clear windows; "LGB Junior" embossed on underside of chassis. Originally sold with Junior Set 20501L.   **NRS**

2061: 1983- , Swiss diesel shunter or light line locomotive of the Furka-Oberalp line (part of the Rhaetian system). Same basic body configuration as the 2060(C); shiny red-painted body with white

The latest in the 2060 series, 2061 wears the livery of the Furka-Oberalp, part of the Swiss Rhaetian network. It has been used in several special uncatalogued sets.

horizontal stripes on both hoods and white radiator grills; some may have "2060" on the underside of chassis rather than the correct "2061"; came with engineer. Some versions have "Letzte HU" over "25.05.84" in white letters on chassis.
(A) 1983, light gray chassis with black grab-irons; white "Furka-Oberalp", over "2061" above "Tm 2/2 SCHLEPP VMAX 45KM T21,8t" all on cab side adjacent to door; lower vent screens (two per side on lower sides of forward hood) are painted black or gray to simulate wire mesh.   **160**
(B) 1983, uncatalogued; same as (A), but with yellow grab-irons; came with or without "FO" on cab doors; issued with Set 20401RZ as well as separately.   **160**
(C)1983, same as (B), but hood screens are red rather than black or gray.   **NRS**
(D) 1983- , same as (A), but with yellow grab-irons; issued with Sets 20512 and 20401RZ and separately; black chassis is the only catalogued version, although also produced with dark gray chassis.   **CP**
(E) 1984, uncatalogued; deep red-painted body, darker than in the above pieces; dark gray chassis, same as 2060; yellow grab-irons; without "2061", "Furka-Oberalp", and other previously described cab markings which are replaced by "Gew. Lok 22t" over "Br. Gew. P 18t / G 15t" over "Vmax 30km/h" over "Br. Unt. 1.3. 84 AW Nur"; lower vent screens same color as body; sold only with Set 20401RZ.   **NSS**
(F) 1984, uncatalogued; same as (D), but with "Furka-Oberalp" across lower portion of cab doors; originally sold only with Set 20401RZ.   **NSS**

2064: 1986- , a red railcar with a silver roof and green and white horizontal stripes around body just beneath windows; this car is essentially the same as a single unit of the 2065 which it now replaces; black-painted flying locomotive wheel on side of body. Production model will have special lighting and sound.   **CP**

2065: 1981-85, Wismar twin-unit railbus "Triebwagen" (also inappropriately dubbed "Galloping Goose") modeled after a second class internal combustion engined railcar. Maximum economy was achieved by equipping passenger coaches with their own drive systems, especially since goods wagons could also be hauled; has two powered units each capable of independent travel; 2206 Motor mounted beneath floor. When used together and joined with wiring junction lead, the head and taillights automatically change with direction. Cars were produced with exact details depicted in the 1981-82, 1983-84, and 1985 catalogues. Discontinued in 1985. All versions come with seated driver and standing hostess; interior lighting; EAV system; 2065/3 Decal Sheet.
(A) 1981-82, light gray roof, unmarked frame, and no markings beneath "winged wheel" on each side of body; has a "VT2065" above window next to forward door.   **500**
(B) 1982-85, similar to (A), but with dark gray roof, "LGB" beneath "winged wheel", "2065 LGB" on frame sides and more markings above window next to forward door.   **450**

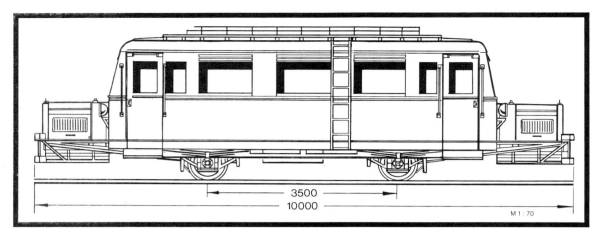

3500
10000

M 1 : 70

If any of the Lehmann railbuses deserves the American soubriquet "Galloping Goose," 2066 is it; but the Germans called these double-ended red and white vehicles "anteater" or "pig's-snout" for their conspicuously protruding motor hoods with baggage racks.

2066: 1981- , Wismar Hannover E "Anteater" railbus of the German Railway Association; model T41-DEV with red and white body, black chassis; automatically reversing head and taillights, interior lighting; comes with seated driver, standing hostess; luggage rack kit; 2065/3 Decal Sheet. Although the photograph of the prototype depicts red radiators, detailed head lamps, and silver handrails, the most recent production models come detailed exactly as depicted in the 1981-82, 1983-84, and 1985-86 catalogues; length 445 mm. **CP**

2090: 1977-85, listed in German 1988-89 catalogue but is actually 2090N(C) (see below). "Kof" diesel-hydraulic shunter and main line locomotive with side rods; similar to locomotives in service on many municipal railways and the North-German Island railway, the Nassau narrow gauge railway, and the Zillertal railway. Has non-working head and taillights; length 240 mm. This diesel was produced in both green and red; the green version appears to be very rare, or a non-production prototype.

Obviously aimed at the lower end of the price market, 2090N's three headlights are non-operating. Its yellow body replaces a common red and a rarer green predecessor.

2096S differs from 2095 in its two-tone livery, which matches Passenger Car 3064, rather than the solid red of 2095 and 3063. And, of course, 2096S has a sound system (motor roar and two-tone horn). The European designation of the two-wheeled power trucks with zero idler wheels is "Bo Bo," by which easily pronounceable name the locomotive is known to many Americans.

(A) 1977-78, unpainted green body; red chassis and running boards; smooth light gray roof without any details or rain gutters; windshields lack wiper blades; cab has a black "LGB" plaque with white heat-stamped lettering above a smaller black plaque with white "2065"; green grab-irons and head lamp bezels, but no light bulbs; no engineer in cab; has early "disc-type" drive wheels; this is a pre-production prototype and was never produced. **NRS**

(B) 1977-78, same as (A), but with black grab-irons; this is also a pre-production prototype and was never produced. **NRS**

(C) 1979-80, similar to (A), but with unpainted red body which may be faded or pinkish-red on some pieces; running boards have gaps and lack "diamond-plate" appearance; gaps in running boards as well as side air tank for use on battery model as well; black bell and black air vent on roof; black grab-irons. **200**

(D) 1980, similar to (C), but roof has distinct rain gutters at lateral edges. J. Hylva Collection. **200**

(E) 1980-81, red body same as (D); gray chassis and running boards; roof with distinct rain gutters at lateral edges, simulated hatches on top and bell; same plaque placement on cab as (A), but upper plaque has "D10" in white figures, the small lower plaque has white "2090"; black grab-irons and head lamp bezels; white detail markings on cab doors; engineer inside cab. **175**

(F) 1982-85, same as (E), but with red-painted body. **175**

2090N: 1983- , similar to 2090(D), but with yellow body; black chassis and running boards; black or white detail markings on cab doors. "Lok Gew 18 Ot" and "Br. Gew 14 5t". Referred to in 1986-87 and 1988-89 catalogues only as 2090.

(A) 1983-86, number plaques on cab are black with white markings. **150**

(B) 1986- , number plaques on cab are white with black markings. Sold separately and with Set 20530. **150**

(C) 1987- , same as (B), but with black, horizontal stripe on each side of cab. **CP**

2095: 1973-85, 1988, B'B' (Bo Bo class) twin-diesel bogie locomotive of the Austrian Federal Railways series 2095.11; has drive rods with exterior counter weights known as Hal cranks; forward and rear heralds embossed and painted silver as are the numbers, numbers on sides of body are similar; red-painted body; gray chassis; length 460 mm. See 2095N.

(A) 1973-78, small pinkish-red plaque with white markings next to cabin doors glued into small depression in body; silver-painted horizontal body molding, actually a composite of three parallel moldings running around the middle of body; only white markings on medium gray chassis consist of fill-level numbers on fuel tank; early red 2030/1 Drive wheels. See LGB *Depesche* 19/20 1973; piece not catalogued until 1974. Early versions lacked coach lighting sockets. **500**

(B) 1979-80, same as (A), but with four additional white detail markings at intervals along sides of chassis just below seam of body and chassis. **475**

(C) 1981-82, same as (A), but with small plaque next to doors molded with body; four additional white detail markings at intervals along sides of chassis just below seam of body and chassis. **450**

(D) 1981-82, uncatalogued; same as (C), but with horizontal mid-body molding painted black. **450**

(E) 1983-84, same as (C), but with black 2035/1 Drive wheels. **400**

(F) 1984-85, same as (E), but with lighter gray-painted chassis.
350

(G) 1988, same as 2095N(B). **CP**

2095N: 1986-87, similar to 2095(F), but lacks embossed heralds and has modern OBB paint scheme; red paint is darker than in the 2095(F), black chassis and white markings reflect changes in OBB logo design: "OBB" on side is smaller, under white builders' plaque with red letters (rather than red with white letters), and bold white logo resembling an "S" replaces winged wheel logo on front; logo also at side rear.

(A) 1986, chassis markings in red and white. **300**

(B) 1987, chassis markings in white only. **300**

2096S: 1983- , B'B' diesel OBB series 2095 in authentic beige and red; other technical data are the same as the 2095(F) Locomotive; comes with an EAV system; two-tone horn and diesel engine sounds in a package containing one 2060/3 Contact Strip to activate horn; black 2035/1 Drive wheels. Aside from its colors the basic external differences between the 2096S and the 2095 are that later versions of

the 2096s have a decal instead of the embossed road name logo on front and rear ends of body and all versions have a beige brake hose on the driver's side of body rather than a black one at both ends. However, the embossed logo on the earlier 2096S may be prototypical and not put into regular production (confirmation requested). Manufacturer's plaque changed from molded-on plastic to an etched brass plaque, glued to side of body.

(A) 1983, embossed road name heralds on front and rear ends beneath windshields; may be prototype model only. **NRS**

(B) 1983- , road name logos on front and rear ends beneath windshields are in the form of decals, not embossed. **CP**

20860: 1977-78, a model of the four-wheel Schoema diesel locomotive, very similar to the LGB 2060(D) but painted. The blue Primus version is known to have been built without gold paint on its embossed cab details (i.e. the manufacturer's plaque, etc.); horn on roof may be black or gold.

(A) With gray chassis. **450**

(B) With black chassis. **450**

V
ROLLING STOCK DESCRIPTIONS

COLORS

Color differences are among the most immediately obvious variations. Since they often arise unintentionally when a manufacturer provides a different shade of plastic or paint under the same number, and because Lehmann often continues prototype photos in the catalogue, many color variations within the same basic hue are uncatalogued. Naming them is often difficult; there have been, for example, several shades of what might be called "yellow" window frames on 300 mm passenger cars, which some describe as "orange," "beige," "light yellow," "bright yellow," "deep yellow," "yellow-orange," etc. If equipment acquired secondhand has an unusual color, it may be sun-faded; the black 4000 may have shifted toward maroon, the green 3050 toward blue, after long exposure. It is important when making color comparisons to remember that adjacent colors and surface texture can distort psychological perception. This list both names colors and identifies some of the specific cars on which they are found.

REDS

There appear to be several variations of red plastic. However, they may all originally have been the same color when produced, but fading may have caused some to turn a pinkish-red.

1. Semi-gloss pinkish-red: early 4065s and 2090.
2. Semi-gloss red: early 4040Es and 4041.

There are five basic red paint shades.

1. Glossy red: 2095, most 3011s, 3063, and 3064 .

2. Glossy cranberry: 2020LJ, some early 3011s, and late 4041s.

3. Dull dark red (almost brick red): early 2051s and 4041 (circa 1980).

4. Glossy barn red (slightly more brown than glossy red): latest 3180, 3181, and 4075 (1988).

5. Glossy boxcar brown-red: latest 4065s.

GREENS

Green plastic variations are more difficult to describe.

1. Dull medium green (very similar to medium green paint): early 4068s and 2050.

2. Dull dark green (very similar to dark green paint): early 4068s (probably second version) and earliest 3019Ns.

3. Dull very dark green: some early 3010s, earliest 3019s, 3020, 2050, and 4047. Some early pieces appear to have a slightly bluish cast and may be a little darker than later pieces.

4. Dull medium-dark green: early 4011s and 4021.

5. Light green: earliest 3010s.

At least two or perhaps three shades of green paint have been used. The most notable deviation from the usual green is on the 3060 coaches (circa 1977) whose paint is slightly lighter than a glossy dark green (medium-dark green).

1. Glossy medium green: latest 2050s and 3010.

2. Glossy dark green: 3070, 3071, and 3007MF.

**The festive scene for one of the first all-color LGB train set box covers; this was for Set 20301.
G. Ryall Collection.**

BLUES

Blue plastic: flat medium blue as seen on the early blue 2031 Steeple-cab Locomotive.

Blue paint: four shades of blue paint have been used, the darker ones more recently; listed in order of increasing darkness.

1. Glossy medium-light (or powder) blue: blue 4040A.

2. Glossy medium blue: 3012, 3015, early 3013s, and 2030.

3. Glossy royal blue: 20301BZ, later, and the 3013.

4. Glossy dark blue (very slightly purplish): 1983, 1984, 1985, and the Set 20517.

5. Russian Iron: although this color could be categorized under blue or gray, we list it here as a somewhat metallic blue-gray. This color was used on the 2028D boiler and on the water tanks and cab of the 2017RG.

ORANGES

Orange paint has not been used on production models; all pieces are in bright, unpainted orange plastic with a semi-gloss finish (i.e. late 4041s, late 4011s, and 2033).

YELLOWS

Yellow plastic appears in several versions.

1. Light lemon-yellow: used on earliest 3510s and the window frames on very early 300 mm coaches.

2. Flat, rich lemon-yellow: 2060H, 2035, 3500, 2090N, and 3510 (circa 1979).

3. Orange-yellow used on window frames on most 300 mm coaches, beginning around 1971.

Lemon-yellow, the only yellow paint used, has been used on only the latest 2060Hs and perhaps the Schweiger Set 20532.

BROWNS

Brown plastic comes in four versions.

1. Straw brown (tan): early 3007s, 4010, 4020, 4029, and 4030.

2. Orange-brown: 4010, 4030, 4035, 4060, and 4067 (SP and latest D. & R. G.).

3. Dark brown (somewhat darker, perhaps less red, than No. 4 painted): early 3000s, 2010, and the ties of most track.

4. Very dark brown, very faintly purplish: 4073.

Variations in brown paint, one of the colors most frequently used by Lehmann, have been very subtle and are hard to describe. The browns most commonly used in major body components have a bright, decidedly orange hue.

1. Tan: 4047 cask, circa 1981.

2. Tan-brown: latest version of 2040 Electric Locomotive.

3. Orange-brown: latest version of 2045 Electric.

4. Brown: 4067 (first D. & R. G. version), 2040 Electric, 3007 (circa 1979), and perhaps some of the early 2010 and 2020 Locomotives.

5. Chocolate brown: Schmidt Bakery Set 20526.

6. Red-brown: latest 4061s.

7. Very dark brown: 2010 (circa 1980).

WHITES AND CREAMS

White plastic has almost the identical tonality as white paint, but its finish is duller.

Whites and creams have been used on two-tone paint schemes on both locomotives and coaches and several freight cars.

White paint usually has a glossy finish, such as on the last version of the 4032L.

Light cream plastic: creamy off-white, clearly more colorful than the whites above: long used on two-tone cars 3011, 3012, and 3064.

Dark cream paint, less white, darker and much yellower than the preceding, over which it is sprayed: latest 3011s, 3012, and 3064.

Beige.

GRAYS

Gray plastic appears in two shades.

1. Dull light gray: early 4045s, 4001, and most early roofs.

2. Dull medium gray: used on some roofs and the 2060-series chassis.

Gray paint to date has only been used as a secondary color, as for roofs.

1. Glossy light gray: used on some early locomotives roofs, 2050.

2. Glossy medium gray: used briefly in the mid-1970s.

3. Glossy greenish-gray: currently used on most roofs.

4. Russian Iron: see BLUES.

BLACK

Black plastic has a glossy finish: it was used on many early 0-4-0 locomotive cabs and currently is used on most 0-4-0 locomotive boilers. It also is seen on early rolling stock chassis and the 4000 Flatcar.

Only one flat black paint has been used on most rolling stock chassis, and on the tank of the latest 4040B.

300 mm FRAME MARKINGS

The earlier four-wheel coaches and freight cars lacked "painted-on" chassis frame markings. The 1979-1980 and 1982-1983 catalogues depicted most four-axle cars in the 300 mm series with the following Type 1 frame markings:

Gew. 5650kg   **LüP 6,75m**   **Rev. 10. 77**

These markings were altered slightly in 1983 as indicated in the 1983-1984 catalogue, and appeared as the Type 2 markings:

Gew. 5650kg   **LüP 6,75**   **Rev 3. 7. 87**

Chassis frame markings were changed again in about mid-1984; these are the Type 3 markings:

←(-)→   LüP 6,75   3,1m   Gew.5650kg   Rev 3. 7. 87

Although these frames have always been manufactured in black plastic the company began to paint the frames in flat black from time to time beginning in 1980. This was most prevalent in anniversary cars and limited production items. In 1984 all rolling stock began routinely to appear with flat black-painted frames.

ROOF TYPES

There are five basic roof styles used on the LGB coaches and boxcars: Low-Arched, Medium-Arched, High-Arched, Clerestory, and Tapered-Arched.

The earliest versions of all these roofs were unpainted light gray. Around 1976 the company began to add shading to the edges of the roof in the form of a swatch of flat black paint giving them a weathered appearance. The next change took place about 1979 with the roofs being painted light, glossy gray with the black edge shading. This color is most common on the larger eight-wheel coaches, the 3060, 3061, 3063, and 3064. In 1982 a medium greenish-gray color with black edge shading was used on most car roofs. This version is currently used today; however, in mid-1984 the company changed the roof molds, adding a textured appearance to many of the roof styles.

Low-Arched: this roof has been produced in six styles and may have a slight rounded arch or two flat pieces with a low-centered ridge.

LA1. This roof is for 300 mm long cars, arched slightly from edge to edge, has six seams across the top, and two roof vents, one each between the second and third and the fourth and fifth seams, used on 3000, 3006, 3013, 3014, 3020, 3150, 4030, 4031, 4032, 4032L, and 4033 Series.

LA2. Similar to LA1, but without seams and vents; surface is lightly textured, used on 4035 and 4036.

LA3. For a 430 mm long boxcar, this version has ten seams

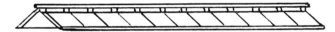

LA4. For 415 mm long cars, this version is not arched but is composed of two flat, pitched portions that peak at the center like a conventional house roof. There is a catwalk down the center and 12 seams across the top; used on 4064, 4067, 4070, 4071, 4072, and 4074.

Medium-Arched: this roof has been produced in eight basic types. It has a Medium-Arch which appears to have three centers of radius forming the curvature of the roof.

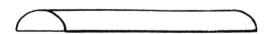

MA1. For 300 mm long cars, completely smooth and lacks seams or bands across top; used on 3007, 3008, 3009, 3019, and 3019N, and 4029, prior to 1971.

MA2. Similar to MA1, but with six seams or bands across top; used on later versions of same cars as well as the 3007LJ and 3013LJ.

MA3. Similar to MA2, but with three very small simulated vents equally spaced; used on 1982, 1983, 1984, 1985, 3007 (1986-1987), 3007BZ, 3007HS, 3007L, 3007LJ, 3007MF, 3007PB, and 3007SG, 3013LJ, and 3036 beginning in 1982.

MA4. For 460 mm long cars, seven seams or bands across top; used on 3063 and 3064 Coaches prior to 1979 and on 3062, 3163, and 3164.

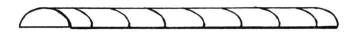

MA5. Similar to MA4, but with three black roof vents; used on 3063 and 3064 coaches beginning about 1979.

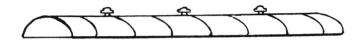

MA6. For 550 mm long cars, ten seams or bands running lengthwise along top and three small vents; used on 3067 beginning in 1986.

MA7. Similar to MA6, but with one large vent added over center of dining area; used on 3068 beginning in 1986.

MA8. For 335 mm long cars; used on 4027, 4028, and the 4029 of 1988.

High-Arched: this roof has been catalogued in three versions and has a single High-Arch.

HA1. This roof is rather strongly arched, for 495 mm long cars and has two vents that are molded with the roof itself; used on 3070, 3071, and 3072.

HA2. Similar to HA1, but has four round vents; used on 3073.

HA3. Only about two-thirds as long as the HA1 version, it lacks vents but has a smokestack, and was to be used on 4075 Service Wagon, which has not yet gone into production.

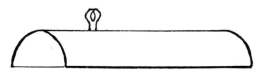

Clerestory: this roof has been produced in five basic versions, with a raised construction atop the roof with windows and/or vents for admitting light and air.

CL1. For 300 mm long cars, roof with short Clerestory that stops about 25 mm from each end of the roof; used on 3010, 3011, and 3012. The Clerestory itself has six small yellow windows and five covered vents on each side.

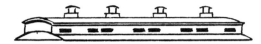

CL2. For 300 mm long cars, flat roof with full Clerestory that extends to the ends of the roof; the Clerestory itself has eight small yellow windows on each side and four vents atop Clerestory; used on 3050 Coach.

CL3. Same basic design as CL1, but for 420 mm long coaches. Low-Arched roof has stove stacks; Clerestory itself has eight small window frames on each side and no obvious vents; used on 3060 and 3061 Coaches.

CL4. For 495 mm long cars, Low-Arched roof with the Clerestory rounded downward at the ends, 12 small windows on each side and stove stacks at opposite corners; used on 3080 and 3081 Coaches. These roofs were painted silver in production units; black shading was added to the edges of later versions and the most recent variation is dark greenish-gray with black edge shading. This roof is known to have had a slight texturing on all variations, with the exception of the

CL5. Similar to CL3, but only 360 mm long; weathered in gray and black. Used on 1988 version of 3020.

Tapered-Arched: this roof has been produced in four versions and used on only two cars.

TA1. For 300 mm cars, a flattened 300 mm roof which is slightly rounded and tapered toward edges and ends; top is completely smooth, without seams; used on 3040 Coach until about 1978.

TA2. Similar to TA1, but with seven seams or bands across top; used on 3040 Coach beginning about 1979.

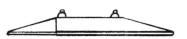

TA3. The basic design is similar to other Tapered Arched roofs but is very short (for 170 mm long cars) with two small, simulated roof vents; used on 3041 Passenger Car.

TA4. Similar to a Medium-Arched roof, but has tapered ends over open platforms; two seams running lengthwise, six thin seams on sides, and nine thick seams across top; used on 3016 Diner.

COUPLERS, TALGOS AND SIDE FRAMES

Interchangeability of parts marks many series, particularly the 300 mm cars, both freight and passenger. These standard parts have their own history, independent of and broader in scope than the histories of individual cars. Often, as with changes in couplers, railings, and wheels, they serve to date an individual car within a long production period.

Couplers

Plastic wheels, a narrow coupling loop, and the thick, untapered hook mark this as an early locomotive.

There are four basic versions of the standard coupler hooking arms and a United States-type knuckle coupler was introduced in 1987. The earliest three versions, from about 1968 to about 1980, have a distinctly triangular-shaped hook and a coiled metal return spring. The first of these is distinguished from the second by its uncoupling pad at the inner end of the hook arm: thick, with a round almost semi-cylindrical bottom when seen in profile, and a horizontal top. After 1972 and by 1974 — probably, that is, sometime during 1973 — the uncoupling pad profile had changed: the top now raked downward from the hook toward the center of the car at about a 40-degree angle, resulting in a thinner total pad. In the mid to late 1970s — definitely before 1979 and perhaps as early as 1977 — a change was made in the

Hooks were riveted in place
up to the mid-1970s, as on this
4040 ET Car.

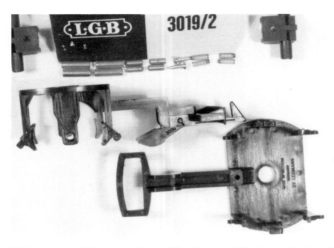

This intermediate coupler, still with the old triangular hook,
has a newer peg pressed into a keyhole slot replacing the
rivet of the older style.

method of hook attachment, which distinguished the
first two versions from the third.

Early versions (from the beginning) were attached
with a horizontal rivet which was inserted, then heated
to permanently secure it. If a hook was broken, the rivet
would have to be cut off and a new one used to re-attach
a new hook. Therefore, a new type of hook and keyhole
mount was designed which was faster to assemble and
cheaper to manufacture.

The hook of this third early version has "ears." They
extend from each side of its shank and snap into key-
hole-shaped openings on the talgos. These variations

The pre-1981 coupler hook has a large pad, and its metal
coiled spring is hidden. Plastic axles were introduced in
1978.

A post-1980 coupler, with its serpentine flat plastic "bedspring," called by upholsterers a "no-sag spring," is clearly
visible on either side of the hook's narrow uncoupling pad.
Notice the marked taper on the hook. These features facilitate depolarized coupling when hooks are installed at both
ends of a car, allowing easy mating and sprung lateral motion. The screw holding the wide coupling loop to the talgo
is a late feature, allowing home installation of a second hook.

The wide coupling loop and the slender, markedly tapered
hook are late features.

can be significant in determining the vintage of some
cars.

The more recent variety, from 1979-1980 on, has a
less angular-shaped hook which is slightly rounded and
has a small "barb" on the inside portion of the hook for
more secure coupling. The uncoupler pad is quite thin,
and curved rather like a comma in profile.

The spring is different as well, being a flat plastic
"bedspring" style which allows better flexibility and

Early talgo trucks have narrow coupling loops permanently
attached.

The four types of truck or bogie, from top to bottom: 3000/3, used on 3060-64; 3080/2, used on 3080-81; 3070/2, used on 3070-71; and 4000/2, used on all freight cars with trucks.

sideways action of the coupler arm. The pivot of the hook arms on the early version is a single plastic rivet which passes horizontally through the arm, permitting only vertical arm movements. From 1979-1980 a plastic rivet passes vertically through the arm, allowing increased side to side movements. The newer loops are wider and have beveled edges, greatly improving coupling on curves. All rolling stock items manufactured and packaged from 1985 have an extra coupler hook provided to accommodate bi-directional operation.

Talgos

The talgos, like the hooking arms, were produced in two basic versions. The earliest of these were produced with the coupler assembly (hooking loop and hooking arm support) molded with the talgo as a single unit. This loop on the hook end has a wider contact surface with a notch to maintain alignment of the hooking arm. The newer versions have the talgo and coupler pieces cast separately with the hooking loops attached with a screw. This change allowed the hooking arms to be attached to either talgo, providing a means for bi-directional coupling and uncoupling.

Side Frames

The side frames used on most rolling stock pieces were cast in black plastic. Around mid-1983 many side frames were cast in a slate gray plastic. This characteristic change is most common in the arch bar-style side frames used on the United States prototype four-axle cars and the 4062, 4063, and 4069 European versions. Late 1985 production shows return to black side frames.

The distinctive heavy metal axle was used on pre-1978 rolling stock.

Trucks (bogies) are of four types, according to the method of springing.

3000/3: leaf springs above the journal boxes, used on Passenger Cars 3060 through 3064.

3080/2: a combination of transverse leaf springs between coil springs; "Commonwealth" trucks, used on 3080 and 3081.

3070/2: leaf springs beneath journal boxes, used on 3070 and 3071.

4000/2: coil springs; arch bar trucks, used on all four-axle freight cars.

WHEEL TYPES

The early wheels (Type E1, spoked 3000/1 or solid 4000/1) have slightly thicker rims and taller flanges than more recently produced wheels. The most distinguishing character of the early wheel sets is the shiny, exposed metal axle which is notably thicker than the later axles. The early wheels were cast separately and slipped onto each end of the one-piece stud axle and are not removable from axle. Type E2 wheels (spoked or solid) have the same basic shapes and dimensions as the E1 wheels, but do not have the thick metal axle exposed

Since 1978 wheels have been mounted on metal axle cores concealed in plastic, which reduces rusting from outdoor use.

between the wheels. The metal axle itself is a slender shaft concealed, except at the ends, by the hollow axle portions cast as part of the wheels.

The Type L wheels (spoked or solid) are very similar to E2 but have shorter flanges. Perhaps the most notable difference between E and L wheels is that during operation the former types will cause the cars to bounce when riding over switches or crossings since the flanges are too tall to clear the frogs!

The E1 wheels were used on rolling stock dating from 1969 to about 1978. E2 wheels first appeared in 1978 and were replaced by L wheels beginning in 1979. L wheels are used on pieces currently produced.

BODY TYPES

Variations in body types for 3000-series 300 mm coaches, 3000, 3006, 3007, 3008, 3009, 3010, 3011, 3012, 3013, 3014, 3015, and 3040, are based mainly on materials represented (either Simulated Wood or Simulated Metal), number of windows, end door arrangement, narrow or squarish window shape, and the presence of vertical and/or horizontal seams. End doors on all these cars open out, but only since about 1981 have they had operating latches. Longer four-axle coach body types are also described here.

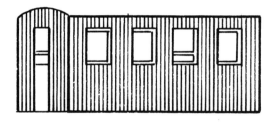

SW1. Simulated Wood; paneled slat-sided body with vertical seams, slightly raised number-boards and logo plaque (if present) on sides, four narrow windows on each side, and centered end doors; used for 3000, 3006, and 3009 cars.

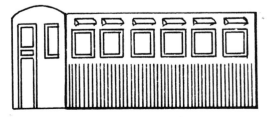

SW2. Similar to SW1, but with six windows on each side and one window and an offset door on ends; used only for 3040.

(A) Tall window openings to accommodate taller window frames, each having a large louvered vent at the top

molded with the frame itself to form a single unit, used for 3040 Coaches from 1971 to 1978.

(B) Short window openings with a louvered vent molded over each window opening as a part of the body; used for 3040 Coaches from 1979 to 1988.

SW3. For 495 mm American-style coaches. Simulated Wood; paneled slat-sided body with narrow, vertical windows and centered end doors. Used on 3080 and 3081.

(A) Nine windows; 3080.

(B) Five windows, baggage compartment door, and a sixth window; 3081.

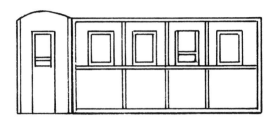

SM1. Simulated Metal body with four narrow windows and centered end doors; five vertical seams (including corners), three horizontal seams — one just below window bases and at upper and lower edges of the body; raised number-boards, used for 3007 (1971-1972), 3008, 3009 (1971- 1973), 3010 (1968-1980), 3011 (1969-1978), and 3012 (1969-1980).

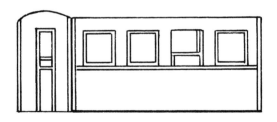

SM2. Simulated Metal body with four squarish windows and centered end doors; corner seams and a single horizontal seam level with window bases.

(A) This car has raised number-boards and logo plaques when used for 3007 series (1974-1982), 3008 (1976-1978), and 3013 (1973-1980).

(B) The sides are smooth without raised number-boards and logo plaques when used for 1982, 1983, 1984, 3007 (1983-   ), 3007BE, 3007BZ, 3007HS, 3007LJ, 3007PB, 3007SG, 3011D, 3013 (1981-   ), 3013LJ, 3013PB, 3013SG, and 3150.

SM3. Simulated Metal body with five vertical seams (including corners) and four horizontal seams, two of the latter closely aligned and just below the bases of the narrow windows; raised number-boards and logo plaques; used for 3010 (1981-), 3011 (1979-), 3012 (1981-), 3014, and 3015.

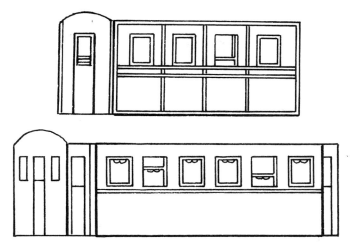

SM4. For 460 mm coaches, Simulated Metal body with six windows and two recessed outside doors on each side, two small windows and centered door on each end; used for 3062, 3063, and 3064.

(A) The door hinge pinions and the pinion holes on the body are small, having a diameter of about 1-1/2 mm. The rectangular recesses at the lower left-hand corner on sides of body if exposed by missing number-board are relatively deep, about 1 mm. If they are not exposed there is a small, plastic rectangular number-board within the depression; used for 3062 (1974-1980), 3063 (1975-1980), and 3064 (1977- 1980).

(B) Same as (A), but rectangular depressions (same position as A) are only superficially expressed, much less than 1 mm. Small plastic rectangular number-boards not used; used on 3062 (1981-), 3097, 3098, and 3099.

(C) The door hinge pinions and the pinion holes on the body are relatively large, having a diameter of more than 2 mm. The rectangular recesses in lower left-hand corner of body are the same as (B); used in 3063 (1981-), 3064 (1981-), 3163, and 3164.

SM5. For 495 mm European coaches. Simulated Metal body with broad operating windows and centered end doors. Used on 3070 and 3071.

(A) Six windows; 3070.

(B) Three windows, a pair of hinged bi-fold operating baggage compartment doors with two very narrow windows, and a fourth broad window; 3071.

CHASSIS TYPES FOR 300 mm ROLLING STOCK

There are basically three versions of chassis frames used on all two-axle, 300 mm long cars. Of these versions there are also early (1968-1970) and late (1971-) variations. The early variety lacks the two square-shaped screw receptacles (for mounting 5005 Track Cleaners) on the cross members adjacent to and between the pivoting truck assemblies. Early frames also

lack holes for the truss rods attached to many of the freight cars. Later versions have both of these features.

Single Brakeman Platform Chassis: This version has two horizontal slots (aproximately 10 mm long x 1 mm high) at only one end of chassis to take the securing tabs for the brakeman platform pieces. This chassis has been used on 3019, 3019N, 3020, 4029, 4030, 4031 Series, 4032 Series, 4033, and 4034.

Dual Brakeman Platform Chassis: This version has two horizontal slots (approximately 10 mm long x 1 mm high) at each end of chassis to take the securing tabs for the brakeman platform pieces. The chassis was used on 3000, 3006 Series, 3007 Series (includes applicable anniversary cars), 3008, 3009, 3010, 3011, 3012, 3013, 3014, 3015, 3040, 3050, all 4040 LT-type Tankers, 4041 and 4041G, and on 4042 produced after 1982.

Full Load Capacity Chassis: This version completely lacks the above described slots. This chassis has been used on 4000, 4001, 4002, 4003 Series, 4010, 4011 (both models), 4020, 4021, 4035, 4036, 4040 ET-type Tankers, 4042 (prior to 1982), and may have been used on the 3050.

Although these chassis applications follow a production purpose, some different combinations may appear due to shortages at the factory or alterations by consumers. For example, 4000 and 4001 Flatcars are known to have been assembled with either type, and 4010 Gondolas could easily take any of the chassis types, but a 3015 Coach can only take a modified dual brakeman platform chassis.

RAILINGS

Platforms (for brakemen) are common on European freight cars as well, of course, as on the early passenger cars without vestibules, commonly found on narrow gauge lines. A very high percentage of LGB rolling stock thus comes with railed platforms. They differ primarily

The SW1 railing, used on freight cars until 1978, has a Solid Wall with triangular gates. A. Rudman Collection.

in solidity (solid wall, solid wall with central aisleway, open frame) and attached fixtures (type of side gate, accordion central gate, relief or separately cast brake hoses and brakewheel shafts).

There are two basic types: solid sheet metal wall, eventually replaced with solid wall with accordion-gated (or otherwise closed) central aisleway; and open frame, usually made of angle iron, occasionally of rods.

Type S. 1968- , solid, includes SW (Solid Wall) and SA (Solid wall with aisleway, usually Accordion-gated).

SW1. 1968-1978, Solid Wall, for freight and postal cars. Simulated metal wall, rounded at corners; two tapered vertical braces cast into exterior of wall; triangular side gates, the slanting member running up toward the car; freestanding brakewheel shaft, with crank handle, attached outside at left of usually the loop end of the car; two low-relief brake pipes, the right one with low-relief hose, cast on outside of wall. Used on 4029, 4030, 4031, 3019, and 3020.

Old passenger cars have this Solid Wall SW2 railing, with rectangular side gates. Both this solid railing and its Accordion-gated successor are prototypical. A. Rudman Collection.

SW2. 1968-1978, Solid Wall, for passenger cars. Similar to SW1, but has rectangular side gates, with "X" struts and a small boss where the struts intersect. Used on 3000, 3008, 3009, 3010, 3011, and 3012.

SW3. 1974- , Solid Wall, for larger old passenger cars. Similar to SW1, but no tapered braces; brakewheel shaft is cast in relief, with separate lever handle; and solid side gates. Used on 3060 and 3061.

Three variations on 4031 have freight railings from different periods. Left is the FA4 Frame of Angle iron, with its vertical tread plate, stiff plastic chain, and no side gates, beginning in 1981; center Solid rail SA1, with Accordion-gated aisleway and triangular gates, 1979-80; and right, the old-style Solid Wall SW1 railing, with triangular side gates. C. Colwell Collection.

SA1. 1979-1980, Solid wall with Accordion-gate, for freight and postal cars. Similar to SW1, but with central portion of wall removed for access between cars, with an accordion-gate attached to the exterior across the opening. Used only on these years' models of 4030, 4032, and 4033.

SA2. 1979- , Solid wall with Accordion-gate, for passenger cars. Similar to SW2, but the same modification as SA1 (central portion of wall removed for access between cars, with an accordion-gate attached to the exterior across the opening). Differs from SA1 in having rectangular rather than triangular side gates. Used on later models of the same cars as SW2 and newer cars of similar type.

Newer, short tank LT-type tankers have this frame of Angle iron railing. The vertical tread plate is immovable on the model, but on the prototype lowers for access between cars.

Type F. Open Frame, used on hoppers, late tank cars, recent freight and postal cars, and American cars. Components are simulated Angle iron (Type FA) or simulated metal Rod (Type FR).

FA. Frame made of simulated Angle iron.

FA1. Frame of Angle iron, used on 4041. Two horizontal and three vertical members, the middle one off-center to the left; the lower horizontal angle does not extend as far as the left vertical. Two brake pipes, the right one with hose attached. Grab-irons on outer vertical members. Two versions:

(A) Until circa 1979-1982, the brake pipes and hose are in the plane of the railing, and rather slender. Also used on 4041G.

(B) Since circa 1979-1982, the right-hand brake pipes and hoses, still vertical, are oriented at right angles to the plane of the railing, as a separate molding. Angle iron is slightly heavier than in (A).

FA2. 1979- , frame of Angle iron, used on 4040 series tank cars with short tanks (type LT), at the platform end. Two narrow vertical rectangles of simulated Angle Iron, joined by a raised immovable tread plate, each with one cross member. No chain across gap. Free-standing brake pipe and hose.

FA3. Frame of Angle iron, used on cars with brakeman's hut. A partial railing, with half free-standing and the other half cast in relief on the hut. Including the relief portion, consists of three vertical and two horizontal members. Brakewheel shaft cast in low relief on hut; housing for brakeshaft handle projects from wall. Grab-iron on each outer vertical. Used on 4062 and 4063. Two types:

(A) Up to circa 1979-1982, brake pipe and hose cast in low relief on hut wall.

(B) After circa 1979-1982, brake pipe and hose free-standing.

FA4. 1981- , for freight and postal cars. Somewhat similar to FA2, but wider, to match frame width; slightly thinner members; medial cross member is positioned higher; and chain across walkway joins the two sides. Unlike earlier freight railings, SW1 and SA1, FA4 has no side gates. Used on such cars as 4030, 3031, 4032, 4033, 4034, and 3019.

FR. Frame made of simulated metal Rods. Used on American-style cars.

FR1. Frame of Rods, used on 4065. Two inverted "U"s, joined by a chain. Brakeshaft and wheel in left part; roof ladder in right part at hook end (rear) of car.

FR2. Frame of Rods, used on 3080 and 3081. Two inverted "U"s, each with an additional vertical member, joined across the walkway by a chain, each with an outward bulge near the bottom of the outer vertical, as a grab-handle at the steps. Brakeshaft and wheel in the left half.

VI PASSENGER COACHES and BAGGAGE CARS

Although the larger cars are impressive, the small 300 mm passenger cars, representing prototypes approximately 22 feet long, have a powerful diminutive appeal. A single man may switch such a car without an engine, simply putting his weight against a handrail and leaning on it until it begins to roll slowly.

Note: For a more detailed description of body and roof types please refer to Chapter V — Rolling Stock Descriptions.

Passenger coach designations are as follows:

- A, B, C — first, second, third class
- D, Pw — Luggage van
- K — Narrow gauge vehicle (DB)
- Post — Post (Mail) van
- i — with open gangway between coaches
- 0 — with covered gangway between coaches
- p — Express coach with central gangway
- /s — Narrow gauge of the OBB (Austrian railway)
- 4 — Bogie wagon with four axles (of the OBB)

Designating and additional letters denote the type of passenger wagon, e.g. Ci/s is a third class, narrow gauge passenger coach with open gangway, of the OBB.

All 300 mm passenger cars with platforms have SW2 railings (Solid Wall with square side gates) if produced through 1978, and SA2 railings (Solid Wall with Accordion-gated aisleway and square side gates) if produced from 1979 to 1986.

Window frames have been produced in yellow, brown, and red. The earliest produced yellow frames are a light lemon-yellow (1969-1970) but later changed (around 1971) to a deeper orange-yellow color which is still currently used.

Some of the 3000, 3007, 3010, 3011, 3012, and 3013 coaches had beveled glass windows from about 1974-

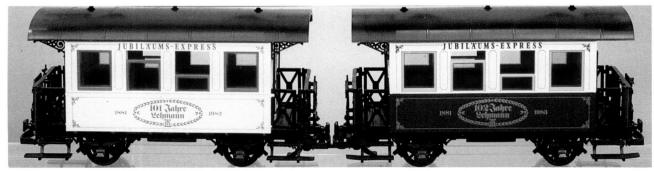

101st and 102nd Anniversary Coaches for 1982 and 1983 to accompany the 21981 Jubilee Train Set.

Often misidentified as the 3000 from which it is derived, 3006 retains its European
air in spite of its American label, "DODGE CITY & GREAT WESTERN RAILROAD".

1977. Use of beveled glass appears to be a random occurrence and its use was probably experimental.

Anniversary cars commemorate the four years subsequent to the 100 year anniversary of the Lehmann Company. All have an embossed 3007 as identification. The cars were sold for use with the 1981 Red Jubilee Train Set 20801 (or the Blue Train 20301BZ). All are 300 mm long.

Anniversary Cars: For each year from 1982 to 1985 Lehmann built anniversary coaches to go along with the 100 year Jubilee Train Set 21980. The 1982 is the most common car, while the 1983 and 1984 coaches appear to be in short supply and consequently command a higher price. The 1985 car is still available through some dealers at the time of this writing.

1982: 1982, 101st anniversary four-wheel coach, with unpainted light cream Simulated Metal SM2(B) body (four squarish windows on each side, vertical corner seams, and horizontal window sill seam); red silk-screened details and lettering; red window frames; Medium-Arched MA3 roof (six seams, three vents); filigree roof supports; Type 2 frame markings. **125**

1983: 1983, 102nd anniversary four-wheel coach, with two-tone light cream and dark blue Simulated Metal SM2(B) body, same as 1982 (four squarish windows on each side, vertical corner seams, and horizontal window sill seam); gold silk-screened details and lettering on the blue lower portion and blue lettering on the cream upper portion; Medium-Arched MA3 roof, same as 1982 (six seams, three vents); filigree roof supports; orange-yellow window frames; Type 2 frame markings. **225**

1984: 1984, 103rd anniversary four-wheel coach, with a completely dark blue Simulated Metal SM2(B) body (four squarish windows on each side, vertical corner seams, and horizontal window sill seam), same type as 1981 and 1982; orange-yellow window frames; Medium-Arched MA3 roof, same as 1981 and 1982 (six seams, three vents); filigree roof supports; body markings and lettering silk-screened in gold; Type 3 frame markings. **225**

1985: 1985, 104th anniversary four-wheel car, a painted dark blue 3019 Postal Wagon with markings which most closely match 3019(E), but markings and window grill edges have gold finish. On the false doors toward end of car opposite brakeman's platform is an "1881-

1985" filigree logo. The car has 3019/1 Metal Wheels; 3031 Tail Lamps; wiring outlets at each end; same Medium-Arched MA3 roof as the preceding cars in this series (six seams, three vents); filigree roof supports; Type 3 frame markings. Came with extra coupler, 2040/2, in 1985. **125**

3000: 1968-81, Bi/s four-wheel second or third class coach of the Lower Austrian Railway (Niederosterreichischen Landesbahn). Unpainted brown or painted red Simulated Wood-paneled SW1 body (four windows on each side); other colors exist: yellow, see 3006; dark red with yellow stripes and markings, see 3006BP; unpainted red or green, made for Primus, see 30800. Most came with a Low-Arched LA1 roof (six seams, two vents); but some may have been sold with a Clerestory CL1 roof (six windows, five vents), B. Cage Collection; glued on metal "LGB" plaque on each side; listed in catalogue from 1968 to 1982; length 300 mm.
(A) 1968-70, dark brown unpainted body with light lemon-yellow window frames; second or third class; no markings on chassis frames; light gray (without shading), Low-Arched LA1 roof (six seams, two vents); 2 and 2 or 3 and 3; Solid Wall SW2 railing. **225**
(B) 1971-77, same as (A), but with orange-yellow window frames; with or without roof shading. **175**
(C) 1978-79, body painted red-brown over brown plastic; SA2 railing (Solid wall with Accordion-gated aisleway); second or third class; no markings on chassis frames; light gray (with shading), Low-Arched LA1 roof (six seams, two black vents). **150**
(D) 1980-81, same as (C), but with improved paint job; Type 1 frame markings. **125**

Note: Two colors were specially produced for Primus; painted bright red or green; B. Cage comment.
(E) 1979-80, same as (C), but body painted red; second or third class in Arabic numerals; made for LGB or Primus. **200**
(F) 1979-80, same as (C), but body painted green; second or third class in Arabic numerals; made for LGB or Primus. **225**

3006: 1982-88, four-wheel passenger coach of the "DODGE CITY & GREAT WESTERN RAILROAD". Similar to 3000, yellow Simulated Wood-paneled SW1 body (four windows) with "3000" or "3006" ID number; green and red trim; brown window frames; painted and shaded Low-Arched LA1 roof (six seams, two vents); no markings on chassis frames; length 300 mm; introduced in 1982 as part of Set 20701DC, but first pictured in 1983-84 catalogue; version (C) is the only one sold separately. Discontinued in 1988. Also see 3006PB and 3106LG&B.

(A) 1982, first class; "3000" ID number; smooth, untextured roof; sold separately and with 20701DC.   **100**
(B) 1982, same as (A), but with "3006" ID number; sold with 20701DC.
                                                                         NSS
(C) 1982-88, similar to (B), but has textured roof.   **85**
(D) 1982, similar to (A), but second class, sold with 20701DC. **NSS**
(E) 1982, similar to (B), but second class, sold with 20701DC. **NSS**

3006BP: 1984, four-wheel second class passenger coach of the "BUF-FALO PASS SCALPLOCK & DENVER RAILROAD" Set 20301BP (also see 3006). Same style coach as 3000, Simulated Wood-paneled SW1 body (four windows); orange-yellow frames; yellow "2" on sides of body; yellow horizontal stripe along body just beneath window sills; yellow road name along body above windows; slightly-raised brass-

colored "LGB" logo plaque on each side; Low-Arched LA1 roof (six seams, two vents); Type 3 frame markings. Price for set.   **550**

3007: 1971-88, BCi/s four-wheel coach issued in first, first/second, second, or second/third class versions of the Zillertal Railway. Body various shades of brown with light lemon-yellow or orange-yellow window frames (all versions have "3007" ID number); hand-painted Simulated Metal SM1 and SM2(A) or (B) bodies (four windows each side) with deep yellow window panels, three horizontal bars over lower glass of door windows; Medium-Arched roofs. Most pieces lack filigree roof supports which are generally turned towards inside of coach, often turned around later by store or purchaser; but the original had no filigree, and Eberhard Richter did not like shipping the standard mold end with empty slots, and so filled them with the reversed filigree.

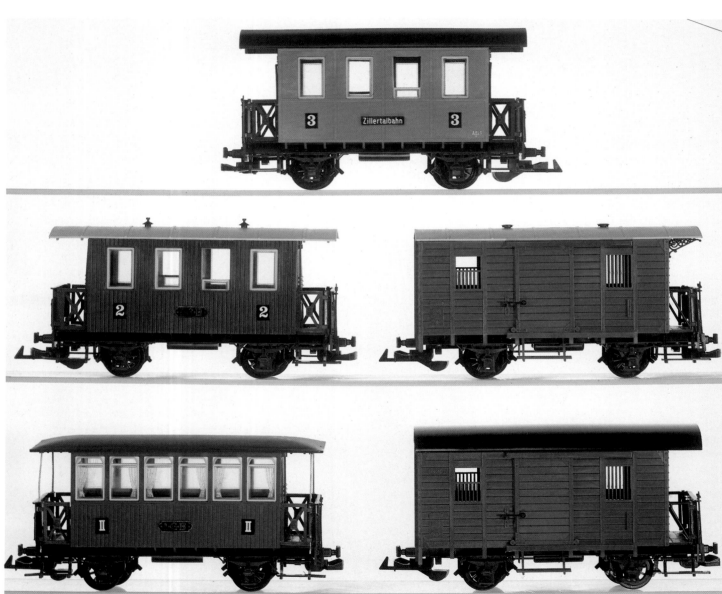

A group of Lehmann passenger classics: at top, 3007(B), still with the tall narrow windows of the first version, in contrast to the squarish windows that typify the car in its many liveries over the last dozen years; middle left, the original dark brown livery of the vertically paneled 3000; lower left, a 3040 whose seamless roof and yellow upper window shade/vents were superceded in 1979. Middle right and lower right, two restfully unlettered baggage wagons, 3020 and 3019, distinguished by their respectively Low-Arched and Medium-Arched roofs. Notice the absence of roof-edge shading from the two gray roofs, suggesting a date before 1976. C. Colwell Collection.

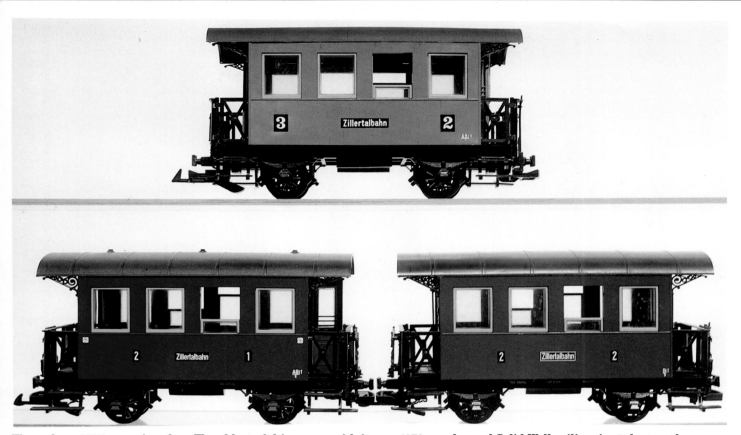

These three 3007s vary in color. The oldest of this group, with its pre-1979 coupler and Solid Wall railing, is at the top; the newer issue is at bottom left. Note that the classes are different on all three. For the very earliest version of this car, compare these wide-windowed versions, the only issue since 1975 and the basis of most passenger cars in limited edition sets, to the narrow-windowed version in the photo found on page 68. C. Colwell Collection.

Also see 1982, 1983, 1984, 3007BE, 3007BZ, 3007HS, 3007L, 3007LJ, 3007MF, 3007PB, 3007SG, 3013PB, 3013SG, 3107, and 3150.

(A) 1971-72, third class with Roman numerals on raised number-boards; unpainted straw-colored Simulated Metal SM1 body (five vertical and three horizontal seams, tall narrow windows); no frame markings; white "Zillertalbahn" logo on black plaque nearly the length of two windows; Medium-Arched MA1 roof (no seams).   **175**

(B) 1972-73, same as (A), but with Arabic numbers; either first, second, or third class.   **175**

(C) 1974-76, first, second, or third class with Arabic numbers on raised number-boards; straw-colored Simulated Metal SM2(A) body (four squarish windows, vertical corner seams, and one horizontal window sill seam); smaller white "Zillertalbahn" logo on raised black plaque; "ABi/S 1" in right side corners of body; no frame markings; Medium-Arched MA1 roof (no seams) or MA2 (six seams).   **150**

(D) 1977-78, same as (C), but painted a deep caramel color; no white detail markings in right side corners of body; no frame markings.   **125**

(E) 1979-83, second class with Arabic numbers reduced in size; painted-on, black "Zillertalbahn" on raised plaque with white border, "Bi 1/S" replaces earlier markings in right side corners of Simulated Metal SM2(A) body (raised boards or plaques; four squarish windows, vertical corner seams, horizontal window sill seam); Type 1 frame markings.   **100**

(F) 1983-85, same as (E), but SM2(B) body (unraised number-boards/logo plaques; vertical corner seams and one horizontal seam).   **CP**

(G) 1986-88, first and second class; decidedly reddish-brown; smaller unraised "Zillertalbahn" plaque with no white outline, tiny "no smok-

ing" emblems (red "X" over cigarette) at side corners. Medium-Arched MA3 roof (six seams, three vents).   **CP**

3007BE: 1985, a four-wheel coach for the "BUNDESGARTEN-SCHAU-EXPRESS" train set made for the landscaping company from West Berlin bearing the same name. This car has a Simulated Metal SM2(B) body (unraised boards or plaques; vertical corner seams and one horizontal seam; also has a "3007" ID number), painted navy blue with orange-yellow window frames and late frame markings. The body markings are all in gold paint (gold filigree markings are the same as on the 1984 anniversary car) and include "BUN-DESGARTENSCHAU EXPRESS" just below roof line. The company's logo, a childlike flower, is in the center of each side of the body below the windows with the markings "Berlin" and "1985" to its left and right respectively. Medium-Arched MA3 roof (six seams, three vents); interior has five sets of medium brown bench seats on a blue floor. Price for set.   **450**

3007BTO: See Chapter XII.

3007BZ: 1982-83, similar to the 3007 (has "3007" ID number), but with painted royal blue Simulated Metal SM2(B) body (unraised boards or plaques; vertical corner seams and one horizontal seam); red trim and lettering; red window frames; originally sold with the Blue Train Set 20301BZ; Medium-Arched MA3 roof (six seams, three vents); gold "DER BLAUE ZUG • THE BLUE TRAIN • LE TRAIN BLEU" over windows, blue "LGB" with gold-painted logo shape centered under windows.   **100**

3007D: 1983, four-wheel coach built to commemorate the 1100 year history of Duisburg, West Germany. This coach has a red-painted Simulated Metal SM2(B) body (3007 identification number), orange-yellow window frames, Medium-Arched roof and Type 2 frame markings (at least on the prototype). All body markings are in gold paint and the following markings appear on one side of the coach: "Jubilaums-Express" above windows; an eagle and castle herald at center of panel below windows; "1100 Jahre Duisburg 833-1983" to the right of herald and the signatures "Josef Krings" and "Herbert Kramer" above their printed names and titles ("Oberbergermeister" and "Oberstadtdirecktur" respectively) to the left. On the other side of the coach, the markings advertise the "Roskothen Co." Only 100 of these coaches were produced as commissioned by the Roskothen Company of West Germany.   **500**

3007HS: 1984, similar to the 3007 (has "3007" ID number), but with painted red smooth-sided Simulated Metal SM2(B) body (unraised boards or plaques; vertical corner seams and one horizontal seam); orange-yellow window frames; an orange, red, and white horizontal stripe along side about 38 mm below window; no other markings on body; Medium-Arched MA3 roof (six seams, three vents); and the usual SA2 railing (Solid wall with Accordion-gated aisleway; operating square side gates); sold with "Freizeit Hobby Spiel" Set 20513. Price for set.   **450**

3007L: 1983 & 1987, two separate versions of this car have been made.
(A) 1983, anniversary car for the 100th year jubilee of Lutgenau Hobby and Train company of West Germany. Simulated Metal SM2(B) body painted beige (unraised boards or plaques; corner seams and one horizontal seam), with "3007" ID number, red window frames; Type 2 frame markings; Medium-Arched charcoal gray MA2 roof (six seams) or MA3 roof (six seams, three vents) with darker shading; very similar to the 1982 101st anniversary LGB car, but blue striping and graphics with "100 Jahre" and "Lutgenau" rather than Lehmann inside wreath; date at left of wreath is "1876" with "1986" to the right. Only 100 produced.   **600**
(B) 1987, body is painted white with "THIER PILS" and company logos on each side below windows; lacks embossed ID number on end. Sold separately and with Set 20536.   **100**

3007LJ: 1981, similar to the 3007(F) (has "3007" ID number), but with painted cranberry body with gold trim and jubilee lettering; sold with the 100 Anniversary Jubilee Red Train Set 21980; Medium-Arched MA3 roof (six seams, three vents). Price for set.   **600**

3007MF: 1984, 1986, uncatalogued; Marshall Field & Company four-wheel coach. Two versions, similar to 3007(F), but with body painted dark green with gold pin stripes and graphics; Type 3 frame markings.
(A) 1984, "MARSHALL FIELD & COMPANY" above orange-yellow window frames; "1852", "1984" at center side of body below windows with company herald in between; "3007" embossed ID number; Medium-Arched MA3 roof (six seams, three vents); filigree roof supports. Sold with Set 20301MF, but boxed separately in a 3007MF window box as well; less than 1200 made.   **250**
(B) 1986, similar to (A), but has "1986" in place of "1984" on side of body; also lacks embossed ID number. Sold only with Set 20534, originally not available separately. Price for set.   **350**

3007MS: 1985-86, four-wheel coach of the limited production commemorative set for Modelleisenbahn Schweiger of West Germany.
(A) 1985, yellow-painted Simulated Metal SM2(B) body (unraised boards or plaques; corner seams and one horizontal seam), with "3007" identification number, red window frames; Medium-Arched gray MA3 roof (six seams, three vents), with black shading; filigree roof supports; SA2 railing (accordion-gates); black "Stadteexpress Nürnberg-Furth, Jubilaumsausgabe (Eisenbahnjahr 1985)" along roof line on both sides of body with an olive green horizontal stripe just below it (stripe has heralds at each end); body panel below windows is decorated with horizontal olive green stripes along with "Schweiger" (in red and black) and "LGB" logos in black. "1835", "1935", and a figure of the Adler locomotive are lithographed at the lower center of each side. "(150 Jahre Deutsche Eisenbahnen)" and heralds are on an olive green stripe at lower edge of each body side; Type 3 frame markings.   **NSS**
(B) 1986, olive green SM2(B) body.   **NSS**

3007PB: 1984, uncatalogued; a four-wheel 3007-series coach (has "3007" ID number) with Simulated Metal SM2(B) body (unraised boards or plaques; corner seams and one horizontal seam), painted in dark green (same color as 3007MF or 3070, etc.); orange-yellow window frames; body markings include a white painted-on plaque with "MC Modellbahn-Center Sonderzug" above "Zell a. See-Krimml" all in black lettering; two small, square-shaped no smoking signs in white, red, and black on each side next to boarding gates; left lower corner markings are : "(— 8,10m —)" above "6,4t 28Pl Av-P5t" above "Bi/S 3850"; right lower corner markings are :

2M	1	2	3	4	5	6	7	8	9	10	11	12		REV	Z	22	8	82
					:									NR			8	84

MA3 roof (six seams, three vents); Type 3 frame markings. Sold only with Set 20520. Price for set.   **500**

3007SG: 1985-87, four-wheel coach of the limited production commemorative set for Modelleisenbahn Schweiger of West Germany. At least three versions were produced.
(A) 1985, yellow-painted Simulated Metal SM2(B) body (unraised boards or plaques; corner seams and one horizontal seam), with "3007" identification number, red window frames; Medium-Arched gray MA3 roof (six seams, three vents), with black shading; filigree roof supports; SA2 railing (accordion gates); black "Stadteexpress Nürnberg-Furth, Jubilaumsausgabe (Eisenbahnjahr 1985)" along roof line on both sides of body with an olive green horizontal stripe just below it (stripe has heralds at each end); body panel below windows is decorated with horizontal olive green stripes along with "schweiger" (in red and black) and "LGB" (in black) logos. "1835", "1985", and a figure of the Adler locomotive are lithographed at the lower center of each side. "(150 Jahre Deutsche Eisenbahnen)" and heralds are on an olive green stripe at lower edge of each body side; Type 3 frame markings. Price for set.   **550**
(B) 1986, olive green Simulated Metal SM2(B) body with yellow stripe above windows in addition to the words "Stadteexpress Nürnberg-Furth, Jubilaumsausgabe Eisenbahnjahr 1985" with the Nuremberg and Furth heralds at each end; below windows on body sides is an Adler locomotive herald with "1835" and "1985" to its left and right, and the words "150 Jahre Deutsche Eisenbahnen"; sold with Set 20529. Price for set.   **300**
(C) 1987, red-painted Simulated Metal SM2(B) body; price for set.
                                                                300

This early 3008 is based on an Austrian prototype. Discontinued about 1978, the latest models were issued with accordion end gates (SA2 railing) and late (L1) wheels. A. Rudman Collection.

3008: 1971-78, second or third class BCi/s Austrian railway coach (Landesbahnen). Painted medium green lower body with white upper body; orange-yellow window frames.
(A) 1971-74, Simulated Metal SM1 body (five vertical and three horizontal seams); LGB logo on raised brass plaque on each side; no

markings on frames; usually second class with Roman numerals; Medium-Arched MA1 roof (no seams); E1 wheels; SW2 railings. **300**
(B) 1975-76, same as (A), but second or third class with Arabic numerals. **300**
(C) 1976-77, second or third class with Arabic numerals on raised number-boards; Simulated Metal SM2(A) body (raised plaques; corner seams and one horizontal seam); plaques are black plastic and have no lettering; no frame markings; Medium-Arched MA2 roof (six seams, no vents). **300**
(D) 1978, same as (C), but with Type 1 frame markings. **300**
(E) 1978, Simulated Metal SM3 body (five vertical, four horizontal seams; raised plaques); Medium-Arched MA2 roof (six seams, no vents); E2 or L wheels. V. Winn Collection. **300**

3009 was only produced for three years, 1971-1973. It has a seamless, Medium-Arched MA1 roof. A. Rudman Collection.

3009: 1971-73, four-wheel second or third class BCi/S passenger coach of the Murtalbahn Railway. Medium-Arched charcoal gray-painted (slightly shaded) MA1 roof (no seams); same basic coach as 3008(A), except in solid unpainted dark or medium green; orange yellow framed windows in SM1 body (five vertical, three horizontal seams); metal axles; the usual black filigree roof supports; length 300 mm.
(A) Dark green body, usually with Roman numerals. **425**
(B) Medium green body, usually with Arabic numbers. **425**

3010: 1968- , first, second, or third class Ci/S Salzkammergut Local Railway coach. Green-painted body; light lemon-yellow or orange-yellow window frames; Clerestory CL1 roof (six windows, five vents on each side); filigree supports; length 300 mm.
(A) 1968-69, second or third class with Roman numerals on raised number-boards, unpainted dark green SM1 body; light lemon-yellow window frames in Simulated Metal SM1 body (five vertical, three horizontal seams); no detail lettering on frames; raised brass "LGB" plaque on each side. **225**
(B) 1968-70, similar to (A), but body is unpainted medium green. **225**
(C) 1970-73, same as (B), but has orange-yellow window frames. **175**
(D) 1974-77, similar to (C), but with Arabic numbers. **150**
(E) 1978-80, same as (D), but has Type 1 frame markings; medium green-painted body. **125**
(F) 1981-82, first, second, or third class numbers on raised number-boards; Simulated Metal SM3 body (five vertical, four horizontal seams); Type 1 frame markings; "Nichtraucher" signs next to class numbers; detail marking in upper and lower left-hand corner of sides. **100**
(G) 1983-84, same as (F), but Type 2 frame markings. **75**
(H) 1984- , same as (G), but Type 3 frame markings. **CP**

3011: 1969- , second or third class four-wheel coach of the North German Island Railway; two-tone red or cranberry and white, light cream, or dark cream body; Clerestory CL1 roof (six windows, five vents); filigree supports; raised metal "LGB" logo glued to each side; early versions may have had beveled window glass; length 300 mm.
(A) 1969-70, second or third class with Roman numerals on raised number-boards; cranberry and light cream Simulated Metal SM1 body (five vertical, three horizontal seams); light lemon-yellow window frames; no frame markings; no extra marking detail on body other than class designation and raised "LGB" logo. **225**
(B) 1970-71, same as (A), but in red and white. **225**
(C) 1971-74, same as (B), with body painted red and white; with orange-yellow window frames. **125**
(D) 1976-78, same as (B), but second class with Arabic numbers. **150**
(E) 1979-80, same as (D), but third class Arabic numbers; Simulated Metal SM3 body (four horizontal seams), painted red and white; Type 1 frame markings. **125**
(F) 1981- , almost all have second class with Arabic numbers; Simulated Metal SM3 body (four horizontal seams) painted red and white

A descendant of the earliest passenger car in the Lehmann line, 3010 has gone through several color and class variations. Since 1981, it has had four (SM3 body) rather than three (SM1) horizontal seams, but always five vertical seams.

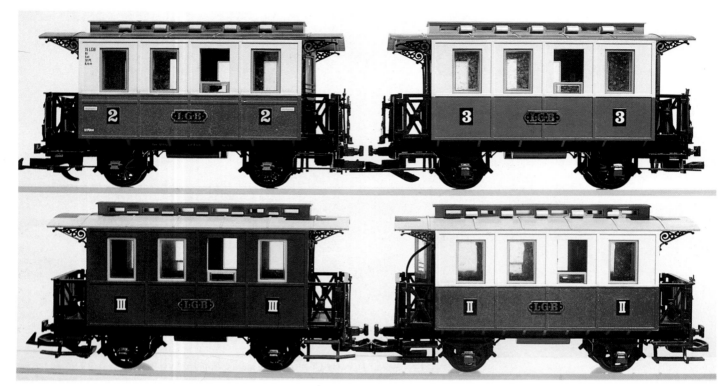

At the top of this group with Clerestory or "Clearstory" roofs, named for the windows in a *story* (level) that *clears* the lower portion of the roof, are the red-bottomed 3011 and the blue-bottomed 3012; they have been in Set 20301, with a recent slight color variation, since 1968, although 3012 is no longer issued separately. Bottom left, is a dark green 3010 (the lighter green of the photo found on page 71), and a darker, cranberry red 3011 at right. Light yellow frames identify the bottom two as quite old, in contrast to the duller and more orange-yellow frames above. C. Colwell Collection.

(1985-86, dark cream); Type 1, 2, or 3 frame markings; body has "Nichtraucher" signs near class numbers, black spec markings in upper left-hand side corner; white spec markings in lower left-hand side corner.   **CP**

3011D: See 3007D on page 69.

3012: 1969- , same basic four-wheel coach as the 3011, but with blue rather than red paint on lower portion of body; Clerestory CL1 roof

(six windows, five vents); filigree roof supports; since 1979, only available with Set 20301; length 300 mm.

(A) 1969-70, second or third class with Roman numerals; Simulated Metal SM1 body (five vertical, three horizontal seams), with light lemon-yellow window frames; painted blue and white or beige; no frame markings.   **225**

(B) 1971-74, similar to (A), but has orange-yellow window frames.

150

Because of its inclusion with 3012 in the basic passenger set, 3011 is one of the most common coaches. For a very small fee, visitors to the Austrian Zillertal Railway can be the engineer on a fare-hauling 0-4-0T pulling this coach and its blue-bottomed mate. The model's striking Clerestory CL1 roof is unpopular at the factory because it is awkward to assemble.

Originally issued with raised plaques, the 3013 authentically diminutive diner has the rather square windows of 3007, unlike the narrower windows of most other 300 mm long passenger cars.

(C) 1975-79, similar to (B) with second or third class with Arabic numbers.   **125**

(D) 1979-80, same as (C), but with Arabic numbers; blue and white rather than beige.   **100**

(E) 1981, similar to (D), but has Simulated Metal SM3 body; Type 1 frame markings.   **75**

(F) 1981- , second or third class with Arabic numbers; Simulated Metal SM3 body (four horizontal seams); black spec markings added to upper left-hand side corner; white dimension markings in lower left-hand side corner; "Nichtraucher" near class numbers; Type 1 or 2 frame markings. This version is sold only with Set 20301. Price for set.   **CP**

3013: 1973- , four-wheel Bi/s dining car of the Steyrtal Railway. Blue-painted Simulated Metal SM2(A) or (B) body; with "3013" ID number; orange-yellow window frames; interior furnishings for restaurant facilities; Low-Arched LA3 roof (six seams, two vents); filigree supports; length 300 mm.

(A) 1973-76, Simulated Metal SM2(A) body (vertical corner seams, one horizontal seam; raised boards/plaques); painted medium blue with yellow-gold markings. Raised "BrauAG" plaque with standing lions on black background is glued into depression on each side of body; no frame markings.   **150**

(B) 1976-78, same as (A), but with larger raised "BrauAG" plaque with painted lettering and plaque lacks black background; Type 1 frame markings.   **125**

(C) 1978-80, body painted darker blue; same body type, color and graphics as (B), but "BrauAG" plaque is larger; Type 1 or 2 frame markings.   **70**

(D) 1981- , like (C), but yellow-gold markings; Simulated Metal SM2(B) body (non-raised, plaque painted on); Type 2 or 3 frame markings.   **CP**

3013LJ: 1981, similar to 3013, but has "3007" ID number on car end; upper half painted white or cream, lower half red (cranberry) with gold trim and jubilee markings; "SPEISEWAGEN" over windows in either red or gold; orange-yellow window and end door panel frames; "1881" and "1981" with gold oval chain with "100 JAHRE/LEHMANN" on side; SM2(B) body (corner seams, one horizontal seam; plaques, if present, not raised); MA3 roof (six seams, three vents); sold only with Set 20801. Two versions exist.

(A) "SPEISEWAGEN" over windows in red. Price for set.   **750**

(B) "SPEISEWAGEN" over windows in gold (rare). Price for set.
1000

3013PB: 1984, uncatalogued; Pinzgauer Bahn Austrian diner. Orange-yellow window frames; "3007" ID number on Simulated Metal

SM2(B) body (unraised boards or plaques, with corner seams and one horizontal seam), which is painted medium blue (about the same as 3007BZ or 3013(D)); the words "PINZGA SCHENKE" in one-half inch tall yellow letters across each side below windows; left lower corner markings are "Barwagen" above "5902" above "Av5t 5,6t above

2M	1	2	3	4	5	6	7	8	9	10	11	12
						:						

right lower corner markings are

REV	Z	22	7	82
NR			7	84

orange-yellow window frames; LA1 roof; Type 3 frame markings. Price for set.   **500**

3013SG: 1986-87, uncatalogued, four-wheel diner for the Schweiger train sets; three different versions were produced for Sets 20528 and 20529.

(A) 1986, yellow Simulated Metal SM2(B) body with "3007" ID number, blue stripes, red and black lettering to compliment the 3007SG(A) Coaches of Set 20528; has 3013 Diner interior. Sold separately. **150**

(B) 1986, olive green "3013" ID number on body, yellow stripes with markings and lettering that are nearly identical to the 3007SG(B) Coaches of Set 20529, but have the words "Restaurant" and "Dining Car" running down posts between the windows; originally sold with Set 20529. Price for set.   **300**

(C) 1987, blue-painted Simulated Metal SM2(B) body, no ID number. Sold only with 1987 Schweiger set; price for set.   **450**

3014: 1979-82, Type C, four-wheel coach of the Suddeutschen Eisenbahngesellschaft, which also runs several lines into North East Germany. Light green Simulated Metal SM3 body (five vertical, four horizontal seams); orange-yellow window frames; raised white flying wheel logo on each side; white dimension markings in upper left-hand side corner; LowArched LA3 roof (six seams, two vents); corner posts from roof to platforms; Type 1 frame markings; length 300 mm.

(A) 1979-80, second or third class with Arabic numbers on raised number-boards; white "nichtraucher" signs.   **100**

(B) 1980-82, second or third class with Arabic numbers on raised number-boards, with red "raucher" signs; double-stacked vents; "32 platze" in lower left corner.   **100**

3015: 1979- , Bavarian second class four-wheel coach of a south German local railway (has "3015" ID number). Low-Arched LA3 roof (six seams, two vents); filigree supports; metal grab-handle supports

Although it is unlikely that a prototype would have both corner posts and filigree brackets to support its roof, Lehmann disovered from their experience with 3007 how popular the brackets are: People who received cars with the filigree turned inward and used simply to fill the slots (the prototype had no such supports), promptly turned them around. 3015, above, displays its unnecessary brackets.

from roof to platforms; blue and white Simulated Metal SM3 body (five vertical, four horizontal seams; raised number-boards and logo plaques); orange-yellow window frames; length 300 mm.
(A) 1979-81, metal "LGB" plaque on each side and class numbers are the only body markings; Type 1 frame markings.   **70**
(B) 1982-83, similar to (A), but with the addition of left-end side detail markings and "Nichtraucher" signs; Type 1 or 2 frame markings.
                                                                                     CP
(C) 1983- , similar to (B), but with winged wheel logo and "LGB 3015" replacing metal side plaque.   **CP**

3016: 1989- , Zillertal Railway Diner of the Zell am Ziller district. This four-wheel car has red- and beige-painted SM2(B) body with "Buffet- Wagen" and district logos on sides. A new roof type, Tapered-Arched (TA4) is introduced on this car, which is basically a Medium-Arch with tapered ends over the open platforms.   **CP**

Note: 3019 Cars built circa 1973 and perhaps earlier had a divider plate on the inside floor of the car just out of the doorway on the blind end. This was used to secure batteries installed in the last versions of the 3019 and perhaps 3020 which lack metal wheels to pick up track power for the three-volt car lighting system used until the introduction of 3019(E) with metal wheel/brush contact. These early cars also have receptacles for 3030 Interior Lighting wires, though they lack metal wheels.

3019 (3019N): 1971- , green-colored, four-wheel parcels/mail van Pw-Post of the former KPEV with luggage space and special compart-ment for mail (all have "3019" ID number). Opening sliding doors; Medium-Arched MA1 or MA2 roofs; typical freight, not passenger, railings — first, Type SW1 (Solid Wall, triangular side gates), then FA4 (Frame of Angle iron, no side gates); as brake van for passenger or goods trains, later models are fitted with 3019/1 Metal Wheel Sets and 3019/3 Current Brushes for tail and internal lighting; earliest edition completely lacked painted detail, markings, or lettering and was not lighted; length 300 mm. A brown version made for Primus also exists; see 30819 on page 132.
(A) 1971-74, 3019; plain very dark unpainted green body; brakeman's platform with SW1 railings (Solid Wall, triangular side gates); no painted numbers, lettering, or decals on body or frame; no lights; Medium-Arched MA1 roof (no seams or vents); Type E1 plastic wheels; small embossed "LGB" logo (on upper right corner of front end and on upper forward window); letter drop slot, envelope plaque, and curled

bugle are all embossed on lower portion of last panel at end of brakeman's platform.   **250**
(B) 1972, 3019; same as (A), in slightly lighter unpainted green.
                                                                                     350
(C) 1975-76, 3019N; same body color as (A), but differs with changes including the addition of a simulated, hinged, non-opening door be-tween the sliding side door and the end opposite the brakeman's platform; Medium-Arched MA2 roof (six seams, no vents); addition of filigree roof supports; 3031 Taillights; 4000/1 plastic Type 2 Wheels; lighting outlet over forward door; lighting current picked up via 3030 Kits, rather than wheels; details on sides include painted orange-yellow window frames; white-lettered "LGB" and "3019N" on sliding doors, covering the height of one slat, KPEV eagle emblem in upper rear corner; printed letter slot reads "Post Nach" and "Briefkasten"; "Post" in white letters on black plaque above non-opening side door, door composed of wood-grain identical to body; "Pw-Post i" above

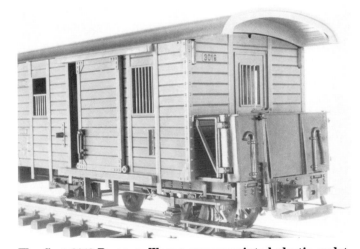

The first 3019 Baggage Wagon was unpainted plastic, unlet-tered but for the embossed ID number and the "LGB" logo. 3019 was produced from 1971 to 1974. Occasionally, as with the 3006, 3007, 3013PB, 3150, 4031, 4032, and 4034, Lehmann has marketed and catalogued a car under a different number from the one stamped on it. A. Rudman Collection.

embossed "LGB" logo in upper forward corner, "Av-P 5.0 t", "Lastgr. 3,1 t", "5,0 t", and "11,2m2" in lower forward corner on fifth through third slots from bottom.   **150**
(D) 1977, 3019N; same as (C), but with 3019/1 Metal Wheels; 3019/3 Current Brushes for lighting.   **150**
(E) 1978, 3019N; slightly lighter green body than (E); "LGB" and "3019N" markings on sliding doors smaller than (C) or (D), covering less than the height of one slat; otherwise very similar to (D).   **115**
(F) 1979-80, 3019; same as (D), but with separate mail section with interior lighting; 3019/1 Metal Wheels with 3019/3 Current Pickups; simulated hinged, non-opening side door smooth, like door to brakeman's platform; SA1 railing to brakeman's platform (Solid wall with Accordion-gated aisleway, triangular gates).   **125**
(G) 1980-81, same as (G), but with Type 1 frame markings.   **100**
(H) 1982-83, 3019; same as (C), but with painted dark green body; FA4 railings (open Frame of Angle iron; no side gates to platform); changes in painted detail include square white computer markings on each corner, level with the fourth slot from bottom, no "N" with "3019" on sliding door, "5,0 t" and "11,2m2" reduced in size and moved up to the seventh and eighth slots from bottom; additional detail includes "3019" in upper forward corner beneath embossed "LGB" logo, "Hz1." in lower forward corner, white detail markings in the lower rear corner and a yellow curled trumpet on hinged, smooth side door.   **75**
(I) 1983- , 3019; same as (E), but with changes in detail on sliding door including two-tone yellow and black "LGB" logo, "Pwgh" added on slot below "3019", and a black "chalkboard" with "von" and "nach" on lower part of door; curled bugle reversed on both sides.   **CP**
(J) 1986, same as (I), but lacks the white computer marks and other white dimensional lettering on one side.   **200**

3020: 1968-74, 1988- , this catalogue number applies to two different cars, an early baggage car and a recent passenger coach.
(A) 1968-73, four-wheel baggage car of the Pinzgau Local Railway. Virtually identical in color and form to the earliest 3019 (see 3019(A) and (B)), but has "3020" ID number; catalogued as having light gray Low-Arched LA1 roof (six seams, two vents) and black filigree roof supports, but some may have left the factory with Medium-Arched (MA1) roofs. Unpainted dark green Simulated Wood body; black frame chassis without markings.   **285**
(B) 1971-74, unpainted slightly lighter green body.   **350**
(C) 1988- , DEV passenger coach Number 9 in third class, compatible with the 2074D "Spreewald" Locomotive. Has four-wheel chassis with solid LGB 4000/1 Wheels. Body painted dark green, black trim, white

Closely resembling the early 3019, 3020 differed primarily in its Low-Arched LA1 roof, rather than the Medium-Arched MA1 roof of 3019. A. Rudman Collection.

window frames. Clerestory CL5 roof weathered in gray and black; length 360 mm.   **CP**

3036: 1987- , circus coach with white-painted body and red roof. Coach has simulated painted balloons around windows, tiger's head etc. on each side; Medium-Arched MA3 (six seams, three vents) roof. Prototype model has "3013" embossed ID number.   **CP**

3040: 1971- , four-wheel Ci/s second or third class passenger coach of the Mixnitz-St. Erhard Railway. Metal corner grab-handles/roof supports from platform steps to roof; off-center aisle separating single seats from double; green hand-painted Simulated Wood-paneled SW2 body (six windows each side, one window, and off-set door on ends — the only instance of this asymmetrical arrangement); orange-yellow window frames; clear tieback curtains incised in windows; length 300 mm.
(A) 1971-73, class numbers in Roman numerals; the usual early passenger SW2 railing (Solid Wall, with square side gates); E1 wheels; SW2(A) body (tall windows split at top by yellow horizontal dividers with yellow louvered shade vents); no frame markings; a flattened seamless Type TA1 roof which is tapered toward edges and ends.   **175**
(B) 1974-77, same as (A), but with second or third class in Arabic numbers; and E2 wheels.   **150**

In 1979 the orange-yellow window frames of 3040 were separated from the vents above them, to which they had always been joined in one casting. Its unique off-center end door and aisle, dividing a row of single seats from a row of double, and its rare tapered roof give this car its distinctive old-fashioned flavor.

A full-length step provides conductor and intrepid passengers access from compartment to compartment while the aisle-less 3050 is in motion. Earlier versions had smaller roof vents and several variations of door handles.

(C) 1974-78, same as (A), but unpainted green body; E2 or L wheels; gold "LGB" on black.   **100**

(D) 1979- , same as (A), but SW2(B) body (shorter windows; panes divided at top, orange-yellow window frames separated from louver-type shade vents which are green and molded with the body); white pin stripes around sides below windows; TA2 roof (tapered like TA1, but seven seams); later wheels; "LB M — St. E." in left lower corner, "C 1" in right lower corner; Type 1, 2, or 3 frame markings; may have second or third class in Arabic numbers.   **CP**

3050: 1971- , third class compartment coach of North German Island Railway (ex-Prussian). Dark green body with both smoking and non-smoking compartments; all compartment doors open; no end platforms or end doors; windows in orange-yellow inset frames; compartment walls with one-piece bench sets; gray Clerestory CL2 roof (eight windows, four vents); length 300 mm. Note the foot plates along the complete length of the body which enable the conductor to enter individual compartments even during the journey.

(A) 1971-73, unpainted dark green grab-irons same color as body; no brake pipes; E1 wheels; step with six supports; white Roman numerals on doors without black background; forward compartment second or third class; cone-shaped roof vents; embossed round plastic green-colored door handles.   **175**

(B) 1974-75, third class only; white Roman numerals on black background; red smoking and white non-smoking signs; embossed round plastic green door handles; grab-irons painted black; cone-shaped roof vents; only five step supports; brake pipe present on end with steps; E2 wheels.   **150**

(C) 1975-78, same as (B), but has round brass- or silver-colored "rivet-head" door handles; no frame markings; painted grab-rails; no brake pipes. D. Weiler Collection.   **130**

(D) 1979-80, same as (B), but painted dark green and has detailed lettering on frames.   **85**

(E) 1981- , same as (C), but with elongated, gold-colored door handles; lettering details on each side include "3050", "KC2", "5,65t", "40

This 3060 lacks the freestanding brake hoses of current 3060s and recent 3061s; instead, its hoses are cast in relief as part of the Solid Wall railing. The triangular coupler hook and slanting uncoupler pad date it circa 1974-1977/8.

Although similar to the Swiss-inspired 3063, 3062 has an Austrian prototype used on several of that country's narrow-gauge feeder lines. Unlike 3063 and 3064, it never has lost its accordion gate to a walk-through bellows.

P1", "6,75m", and "Hbr" in upper left corner and "Nhz" in lower left corner; frame lettering slightly different.   **CP**

3060: 1971-80, 1985-87, Barmer second and third class eight-wheel mountain railway coach. Gray Clerestory CL3 roof (eight windows, no vents, stove stacks), with shading; filigree roof supports; SW3 railings (Solid Wall, solid operating side gates); four pairs of windows on each side and opening centered end doors, either solid 3000/1 or spoked 4000/1 Wheels; length 420 mm.
(A) 1971-73, body is painted dark olive brown with yellow-gold pin stripes on sides; embossed "3060" in upper left-hand corner of body end at platform; etched curtains in windows; gold "II" in panel under first two windows; "III" in panel under last two; no lettering on frames; although early catalogues depict a version with no steam regulator on exterior ends, production models had them.   **250**
(B) 1973-80, similar to (A), but body is painted medium green.   **150**
(C) 1985-87, similar to (B), but has flat black-painted frame with white frame markings.   **100**

3061: 1981-84, 1988- , Barmer Mountain Railway coach, similar to the 3060.

(A) 1973-80, similar to 3060(B), but with dark olive brown body; flat finish (unpainted), light gray roof usually without shading, and "3061" identification on end of body.   **125**
(B) 1980-81, same as (A), but with shiny painted light gray roof with shading.   **100**
(C) 1982, same as (A), but with darker gray-painted roof.   **100**
(D) 1983-84, same as (C), but with white "3061", "BCiP", "14t", "32P1", "9,5m", and "Hbr" in upper left-hand corner of sides; "Abst d Drehz 5.0m", "Achs Unt Bww Mst 7.3.86", "Nhhz", "Einh Dyn Bel", and "N Unt 1.12.88" on frames.   **85**
(E) 1988- , similar to (D), but with new white markings on body.
.   **CP**

3062: 1974- , eight-wheel B4iP/s through-train coach of the Austrian Federal Railways in service on the Pinzgauer Local Railway; similar to the type used on the Maria-Zeller railway, the Murtal railway, the Zillertal railway, and the Steyrtal railway. Simulated Metal SM4(A) or (B) body (six non-sliding windows; two recessed doors open); rigid folding gates across vestibule end doors at both ends; three compartments with interior furnishings. Medium-Arched MA4 roof (seven

A pair of models with recent Rhaetian prototypes, 3063 and its mate have detailed lavatories with operating seat lids. Earlier versions lacked the accordion diaphragms, inoperable on the model, having accordion gates like 3062 instead.

Like its companion car 3063, 3064 is closely modeled on a Swiss prototype, but somewhat shortened. The main changes from version to version have been in lettering, striping, roof vents, and plaques.

seams); restroom has wash basin and hinged toilet seat; length 460 mm. Usually had a set of peel-and-stick decals included.

(A) 1974-75, unpainted all-gray roof; painted dark green SM4(A) body (door hinge pinions and pinion holes are small, 1-1/2 mm in diameter); narrow folding gate and step at ends; window frames same color as body; doors without working handles; limited body markings; "15,ot", "50P1", "Av-Pi3t", "B4ip/S", and "3062" on plaque in a relatively deep depression at lower left-hand side corner of body; frame markings at four intervals along frame directly beneath windows two, three, four, and five.   **150**

(B) 1976, same as (A), but with orange-yellow window frames. **135**

(C) 1976-77, same as (B), but frame markings placed only beneath windows two and five.   **100**

(D) 1977-78, same as (C), but with medium green body.   **100**

(E) 1979-80, similar to (B), but doors with working brass-colored handles; second and third class markings added.   **90**

(F) 1981- , SM4(B) body (door hinge pinions and holes same as (A), but plaque markings in lower left-hand side corner only slightly depressed); body painted dark green; black "Zell am See" over "Krimml" on white rectangle beneath window four; a black-outlined square with detail and lettering beneath window five.   **CP**

3062BTO: See Chapter XII.

3063: 1975-87, Rhaetian (RhB) first/second class eight-wheel express train coach. Basic body composition, Type SM4, same as 3062(A); painted bright red; length 460 mm. Usually had a set of peel-and-stick decals included.

(A) 1975-78, second and third class in Arabic numbers; doors with non-working handles; orange-yellow window frames; Medium-Arched MA4 roof (seven seams, no vents) or MA5 (seven seams, three vents); single white stripe along body beneath bases of windows; body lettering and numbers only on pinkish-red-colored side corner plaque; end doors with gates (no simulated concertina diaphragms for gangways); frame markings, if present, beneath windows two, three, four, and five.
                                                                                   150

(B) 1979-80, same as (A), but with brass-colored working handles on doors; roof may have black shading at edges.   **130**

(C) 1981-84, Simulated Metal SM4(C) body (door hinge pinions and pinion holes relatively large, 2 mm in diameter); doors with working handles; orange stripe designating first class section; simulated concertina gangways; "NICHTRAUCHER" beneath window one, "RAUCHER" sign beneath window six (counting from loop end); white "Chur-St. Moritz" framed in white rectangle beneath window five; "Rh B" at center with "AB 3063" and "44 p1. 25t" beneath it; "6.2m", "1.2m" in lower left side corner, "REV. 7.3.79" in lower right side corner; may or may not have frame markings; medium gray-painted

Medium-Arched MA5 roof (seven seams, three vents), black shading at edges.   **125**

(D) 1984-87, same as (C), but with textured roof; shorter orange stripe designating first class section (only extends over two and one/half windows).   **100**

3063BTO: See Chapter XII.

3064: 1977-87, second class eight-wheel coach of the Rhaetian railway (RhB) in red and white. Basically the same design as 3063; length 460 mm. Usually had a set of peel-and-stick decals included. Discontinued in 1987.

(A) 1977-78, Simulated Metal SM4(A) body (door hinge pinions and holes small); doors with non-working handles; orange-yellow window frames; Medium-Arched MA4 roof (seven seams, no vents); body lettering and numbers only on pinkish-red lower left side corner plaque (in a relatively deep depression); gates across end doors; no simulated concertina gangways; frame markings beneath windows two, four, and five (counting from loop end).   **150**

(B) 1979, same as (A), but with white left side corner plaque with red lettering; more frame markings and sheet of peel-and-stick labels.
                                                                                   125

(C) 1979, Same as (A), but with brass-colored working door handles; white left side corner plaque with black lettering; more frame markings.   **100**

(D) 1980, same body type as (A), but Medium-Arched MA5 roof (seven seams, three vents); brass-colored working door handles; simulated concertina gangways; "2" over "NICHTRAUCHER" beneath windows one and six; white or red "Chur Pontresina" painted beneath window two (counting from loop end); white left side corner plaque; with or without frame markings.   **100**

(E) 1981-87, same as (D), but Simulated Metal SM4(B) body (larger door hinge pinions and holes; slightly indented number-board recess); light-colored portion of body may be white or light or dark cream. **90**

3067: 1986- , Modern Rhaetian Railway (RhB) first or second class coach. Red body with yellow stripe above windows and white stripe below; Medium-Arched silver MA6 roof (ten seams running lengthwise, three small vents); special constant fluorescent lighting system; length 500 mm.

(A) 1986, handmade factory prototype, body is deep red with flat black along window section; bright yellow stripe above window; lighting is operated by wiring hooked up to locomotive lighting sockets. R. Enners Collection.   **NRS**

(B) 1986- , coach body is slightly lighter red with flat gray along window section; orange-yellow stripe above window; constant lighting system receives track current through metal wheels (has on-off switch as well). Truck side frames lack inside support gussets.   **CP**

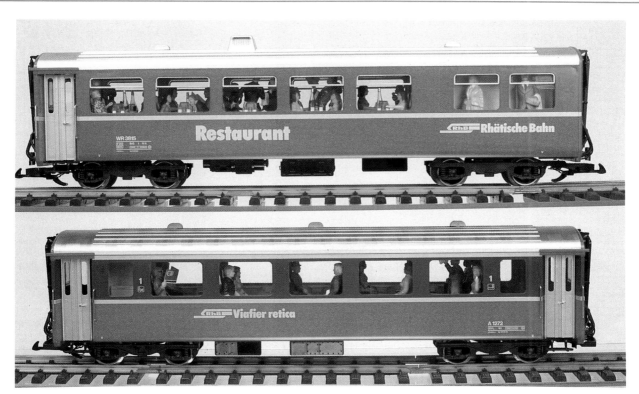

The fully appointed Diner with busy waiters, cooks in the kitchen, and waiting customers is accompanied by a sleek, modern Coach. Roofs are removable. To see how extremely long these cars are, count the ties under the car. G. Ryall Collection.

Lehmann designated 3070, above, and its companion 3071 as "Supermodels" when they were introduced. Windows slide up and down; the tread plate can be lowered to horizontal, for between-car travel; a pair of end gates swings open; and the platform side gates pivot upward at the car end wall, collapsing to a single line.

(C) 1987- , same as (B), but truck side frames have inside support gussets to strengthen the trucks.   **CP**

3068: 1986- , dining car (first pictured in 1985 German catalogue); Medium-Arched MA7 roof (similar to the type MA6 of 3067, but with one large vent added over center of dining area); separate kitchen compartment and dining areas; body is painted red with silver stripes and markings (matches silver roof); length 550 mm; lights on all tables are separately lit. Two factory prototypes, one painted medium green and the other dark red with Rhaetian logo on sides.   **CP**

3070: 1981- , DB second class eight-wheel coach (KB4i-59 class) of German Federal Railways; similar to coaches that saw service on the Mosbach/Mudau secondary railway. Dark green Simulated Metal SM5(A) body (six windows); has 48 seats with overhead luggage racks; all windows adjustable; opening sliding doors; open platforms with SA3 railings (hinged paired aisleway gates, side gates, handrails, and foot plates); High-Arched HA1 roof (two vents); most notable frame marking is "5 Munster"; one version produced; length 495 mm.   **CP**

3071: 1981- , DB second class eight-wheel KBD 4i coach with baggage compartment of the German Federal Railways. A companion car to 3070, but has SM5(B) body (three windows, bifold doors, and a fourth window); only 24 seats with overhead luggage space; baggage compartment with paired two-section folding doors; most notable

frame marking is "AW Karlsruhe"; length 495 mm; one version produced.   **CP**

3072: 1987-88, Wangerooge Island Railway coach of the DB. Same body as 3070, but painted yellow with the words "FLORIDA BOY" (in green), "ORANGE" (in orange), and oranges painted on each side. Fewer frame markings than 3070 and 3071. Discontinued in 1988.   **CP**

3073: 1987- , "Harzquerbahn" coach of the Deutsche Reichsbahn (DR). Second class coach with same body as 3070, but painted tan and red; High-Arched HA2 roof (four round vents); Spoked Wheel Set 3000/1; no frame markings.   **CP**

3080: 1981-87, Denver and Rio Grande Western Railroad (D & R G W) eight-wheel coach, which still operates daily in the summer, used between Durango and Silverton, Colorado. Bright yellow unpainted Simulated Wood SW3(A) body (nine narrow windows); Low-Arched roof with Clerestory CL4 roof (rounded down toward ends, 12 small windows on each side, and black stove stacks at opposite corners); open Frame of Rods FR2 railings (two inverted "U"s with added vertical member, simulated chain); length 495 mm. Discontinued in 1987.
(A) Originally depicted in the German version of the 1981-82 catalogue without any painted details on body and an unpainted gray roof;

3071 has all the movable parts of its companion, 3070, plus a pair of double-hinged baggage compartment doors that open inward like a splitting "W".

Although shortened by three windows, 3080 is a close approximation to its western prototype, well known to American visitors to the Durango-Silverton who ride up the canyon of the Las Animas River in Colorado.

embossed, black-painted grab-irons on ends of body; brown window frames. This car was probably not produced in this form.　　**NRS**
(B) 1981, simulated wooden body; red or brown window frames; black-painted sill beneath nine windows; "3080" at each end painted on sides; black band above windows with yellow "DENVER & RIO GRANDE WESTERN" over windows; embossed, black-painted grab-irons on ends of body; silver-painted roof (as depicted in the English versions of the 1981-82 catalogue).　　**NRS**
(C) 1982, same as (B), but with brass wire grab-irons.　　**125**
(D) 1983, 1986-87, same as (C), but with black shading on roof edges.　　**125**
(E) 1984, same as (C), but plain, without markings. J. Hylva Collection.　　**495**
(F) 1984-85, same as (C), but with dark gray roof with black shading at edges.　　**125**

3080BTO: See Chapter XII.

3080-EO1: 1988, Pennsylvania Railroad Coach with dark green body trimmed in gold pin striping and lettering. "PENNSYLVANIA" in gold lettering on black background above windows; red and gold "PRR" logo on end panel to the right of windows; silver matte clerestory roof. Made only for United States distribution.　　**150**

3081: 1981-87, Denver and Rio Grande Western Railroads (D & R G W) combination coach and baggage car used between Durango and Silverton, Colorado. Same specs as 3080, but with Simulated Wood SW3(B) body (five windows, a baggage compartment door, and then a sixth window). Discontinued in 1987.
(A) Same as 3080(A), but with baggage compartment; this car was probably not produced in this form.　　**NRS**
(B) 1981, same as 3080(B), but with baggage compartment and "3081" numbers on sides; "BAGGAGE / AND / EXPRESS" in small letters on panel between baggage and passenger sections.　　**NRS**
(C) 1982, same as 3080(C), but with baggage compartment.　　**125**
(D) 1983, 1986-87, same as 3080(D), but with baggage compartment.　　**125**
(E) 1984, same as 3080(E), but with baggage compartment. J. Healy Collection.　　**495**
(F) 1984-85, same as 3080(F), but with baggage compartment.　　**100**

3081-EO2: 1988, Pennsylvania Railroad Baggage Combine with dark green body trimmed in gold pin striping and lettering. "PENNSYLVANIA" in gold lettering on black background above windows; red and gold "PRR" logo on end panel to the right of windows, "Baggage and Express" on side panel between windows and sliding side door; silver matte clerestory roof. Made only for USA distribution.　　**150**

Variation in roof shading and the addition of brass grab-irons (embossed in this photo), visible on the end panel of the car body, are the only changes in Baggage Car 3081 and its companion 3080 since their introduction in 1981.

3082: 1989- , Denver & Rio Grande Western closed vestibule coach. Very similar to the 3080 Coach, but has closed end platforms with opening side doors and static end bellows. Silver matte clerestory roof with yellow body and simulated wooden window frames.   **CP**

3083: 1989- , Denver & Rio Grande Western closed vestibule combine. Very similar to the 3081 Combine, but has closed end platforms with opening side doors and static end bellows. Silver matte clerestory roof with yellow body and simulated wooden window frames.   **CP**

3097: 1987, "Orient Express" coach commissioned by the LGB National Sales Office, Milwaukee, Wisconsin and originally offered only in the United States in Set 20277 with 2070D(C) Locomotive and three coaches (3097, 3098, and 3099). This car has the same body as the 3064(E), but is painted dark blue and tan with gold markings and filigree; number "3097" on each side of body. Some early prototypes were displayed in 1985.   **NSS**

3098: 1987, same basic car as 3097, but has number "3098" on each side of body. This is the second of the three cars from Set 20277.   **NSS**

3099: 1987, similar to 3097 and 3098, but entire car is painted blue with "3099" on each side of body. This is the third of three cars from Set 20277.   **NSS**

3106: 1989- , Wuerttemberg Railway Coach with SW1 body similar to the 3006, but painted dark green, black, and white; second class markings (number is white), black and white "LGB" logo and "WN15" in white above section between center windows. LA1 roof, four wheels.   **CP**

3106LG&B: 1989- , Lake George & Boulder four-wheel coach SW1 body type, painted silver-blue (Russian Iron) with white striping. "Lake George & Boulder" in black above windows, "LG&B" three-color logo on center of each side (below windows), and black and white first class designations (white number on black field); yellow window frames. Originally sold only with Set 22301US.   **NSS**

3107: 1989- , Zillertal Railway Coach of the Ramsau and Hippach districts. This four-wheel car has an orange-brown-painted SM2(B) body and markings similar to the 3007(G), but with the Ramsau-Hippach logos on each side in place of one of the class designation numbers; MA3 roof .   **CP**

3150: 1985-86, Anniversary cars to commemorate 150 years of German railways ("Deutsche Eisenbahn"). Three versions of this four-wheel coach were produced for the 20150 Set; all have red-painted Simulated Metal SM2(B) body (corner seams, one horizontal seam, unraised boards/plaques), with four orange-yellow window frames; with "3007" embossed identification number.
(A) 1985, Furth coach. On each side of car on the panel just below the windows there is a lithographed scene of several buildings from Furth, West Germany with the name "Furth" spelled out below it; arched above the scene is "150 Jahre Deutsche Eisenbahn", all in gold

3150(C) supplements the limited edition Set 20150. The shield and lettering on its side panels below the windows are different from those on the two cars provided with the set.

paint. There are two white heralds with a green clover leaf just above each end of worded arch. Sold only with Set 20150.   **NSS**
(B) 1985, Nuremberg coach. Similar to (A), but depicts the city of Nuremberg, West Germany and has the "Nürnberg" name. The two heralds are two-tone black and yellow with an eagle in the center. Sold only with Set 20150.   **NSS**
(C) 1985-86, 150-Year coach. Similar to (A) and (B), but has a painted-on, crossed-flag herald (one red and white, one blue and white) with a yellow-gold crown and wreath (wreath has yellow, blue, and white in the center with a yellow bow at the bottom); flags, wreath, etc. are surrounded by the same colored tassle that is adjacent to the windows. Markings are in gold paint and include "1835" above "Deutsche" and "1985" above "Eisenbahn" to the right and left of the wreath respectively. This is the only version of the 3150 that was sold separately yet still intended to be part of Set 20150.   **85**

3163: 1988- , Zillertal Railway coach in second class. Same SM4 body as 3063(D), but painted royal blue with "Zillertalbahn" and second class markings on each side below windows. Has weathered Medium-Arched MA4 roof (no vents). Length 460 mm.   **CP**

3164: 1988- , Zillertal Railway coach in second class similar to 3163, but painted royal blue and beige. All other details same as 3163.   **CP**

3167: 1989- , Swiss Rhaetian Railway Coach in early green livery with first class designation; has silver matte roof with yellow and silver body trim. Coach has detailed interior with lighting, and opening side doors. Designed to run with the 2040 Crocodile or 2045 Ge 2/4 locomotives.   **CP**

3180: 1988- , Denver, South Park & Pacific Railroad coach. Same body as 3080, but painted red with black trim, and simulated wood window frames. "DENVER, SOUTH PARK & PACIFIC R. R." is printed in white on black background above windows. Roof is painted

The 3180 Denver, South Park & Pacific R.R. coach is another in the growing American roster.

in satin silver without weathering in catalogued versions. Overall length is 495 mm. **CP**

3181: 1988- , Denver, South Park & Pacific Railroad combination coach and baggage car. Same body as 3081, but painted red with black trim and simulated wood window frames. On sides of body between sliding door and window are the words "PACIFIC / EXPRESS / COMPANY" and the word "BAGGAGE" between sliding door and boarding platform. All other details same as 3180. **CP**

30800: 1977-78, unpainted, pinkish-red, Bi/s type, four-wheel coach, with Simulated-Wood slat SW1 body marked with Arabic second or third class numbers similar to the LGB 3000; the "LGB" logo plaque is missing from each side of body and the flat spot for the plaque is bare. This Primus coach is also characterized by an embossed "3000"; LA1 roof, yellow window frames, and no frame markings. Sold separately and with Set 8000.
(A) Pinkish-red molded, second class. **200**
(B) Pinkish-red molded, third class. **200**

30801: 1977-78, similar to the 30800, but painted dark green.
(A) Green-painted, second class. **400**
(B) Green-painted, third class. **400**

30819: 1978, Primus postal and baggage car with unpainted, medium brown body; same body as 3019; ID number and with "3019"; low-arched LA3 roof similar to the LGB 3020; four-wheel chassis. Its few body markings are heat-stamped in white. Has factory-mounted LGB 3019/1 Metal Wheels with LGB 3019/3 Carbon Brush Holders on the trucks and two LGB 3031 Tail Lamps mounted on rear of body, similar to the LGB 3019. Two versions are reported but it is yet unknown which, if either, of the two is rarer.
(A) White, heat-stamped markings are at the same end of car on both sides; the markings will appear to be on the right on one side of the car, and on the left when it is turned around. **250**
(B) White, heat-stamped markings are "kitty-corner" from one another; markings will always appear to be on the left, regardless of which side of car is being viewed. **250**

VII
FLATCARS, GONDOLAS, HOPPERS, CONTAINER CARS, and CABOOSES

A "goods wagon" or, in German, Guterwagen, would be called a "freight car" by an American. Open goods wagons are used for a much wider variety of transport in the short runs common in Europe generally, short at least by continental American standards. Often, goods that in the United States would be shipped in a boxcar are shipped there in open wagons, covered by a tarpaulin. Containers are increasingly common, and of course many cars are special-purpose, such as the side-dumping ballast wagon, Hopper 4041.

One of many cars derived from the original black 4000 and gray 4001 Flatcars, 4002 was introduced with green cable reels in 1979; the spools were lettered in 1982, and have been yellow since 1983. The "KABEL- UNION" sign changed colors in 1984. Such cars are a particularly common sight on electrified roads.

4000: 1968-70, four-wheel flatcar with short bulkheads at each end; no truss rods; used by the Salzkammergut Local Railway. Unpainted black body with no painted markings; length 300 mm. Due to its short production run and uninteresting appearance, few were sold in the United States and consequently it is one of the rarest early cars.

350

4001: 1969-78, same basic car as 4000, but with light gray, simulated wood unpainted body; black frame; one step on each end corner.
(A) 1969-72, early chassis without truss rods; bed also lacks self-tapping screw holes where lower ladder supports would be attached for tank car use (holes are normally on underside of bed). J. Hylva Collection. **NRS**
(B) 1969-72, similar to (A), but has ladder mounting holes on underside of bed; sold separately and with Set 20501I. **100**
(C) 1973-78, late chassis with truss rods. **85**

4002: 1979-87, "Kabel-Union" Reel Car with two removable "Kabel-Union" cable reels as loads; similar to the type used by Messrs. Felten and Guillaume, cable manufacturers in Nuremberg. Car body is essentially the same as the 4000 or 4001, but with the addition of raised restraints for spool supports; small, upright sign on each side reading "KABEL-UNION"; length 300 mm. Frame marking types have considerable overlap from version to version. Discontinued in 1987.
(A) 1979-82, orange-brown body; green reels without painted markings; yellow "KABEL-UNION" sign with black letters; no truss rods.

125

(B) 1982-83, same as (A), but green reels have black and white detail markings. **100**
(C) 1983-84, medium brown body, slightly darker than (A) or (B); yellow reels with black and white detail markings (spool markings vary on later versions). **75**
(D) 1984-87, same as (C), but black "KABEL-UNION" sign with white lettering. **50**

4002/69: This is a non-factory number; see 4003F.

4003: See Container Cars listed on Page 92.

4010 shares with nine other cars the honor of illustration in the very first Lehmann catalogue, and has been available over the years in several greens and browns. Originally brown (companion 4011 was green), the latest version is painted green.

Take a 4010 body, paint it orange, add a pyramidal six-door lid, and you have the "Hilfswagen" or "help-car" with the reassigned number 4011. The super-structure is easily removable. Such a car would be a standard component of a work train.

4010: 1968- , black chassis low-sided gondola used in large quanti-ties by all European narrow gauge railway companies. Four-wheel, with simulated wood exterior and inside flooring; length 300 mm.
(A) 1968-70, unpainted straw brown body; F1 frame without truss rods; no slots in center of gondola sides and ends; no painted markings or detail on body or frame.   **150**
(B) 1971-74, same as (A), but unpainted medium green; with or without truss rods. J. Hylva Collection.   **175**
(C) 1976-78, similar to (A), but with unpainted medium brown body; black F2 frame with truss rods; slots in center of gondola sides only; no end slots; no markings. Sold with Set 20501JR.   **100**

(D) 1973-83, similar to (A), but with Type 1 frame markings; slots both in center of sides and ends.   **40**
(E) 1983, similar to (D), but has white markings which include "4010 x 05" on the left-hand side of center gondola side panels; white- and black-painted side grate screens.   **100**
(F) 1983- , green-painted body exterior with same markings as (E); light blue-gray, whitish-green, or gray-painted interior; Type 1, 2, or 3 frame markings.   **CP**
(G) 1986, similar to (F), but bed is medium green inside and out with no printed or painted markings; originally sold with Set 20530.   **30**

Low-sided ("Niederbordwagen") 4010, brown, beside 4011, green. Below them, high-sided wagon ("Hochbordwagen") 4020 brown, beside a green 4021; this 4021 and the one below it date from the 1980s, differing from that brown 4021(G) in color and from each other in the green interior of (D) and the gray interior of (E). Lettering and color date the 4061 at lower left between 1974 and 1976. A. Rudman Collection.

(H) 1988- , same body as (G), but unpainted orange color same as 4011; came with green Mercedes Unimog truck. Sold only with Set 21401.   **NSS**

4010FO: 1984, same simulated wood exterior and interior flooring, body, and color as 4010(D) or (E), but with white "FO" (Furka-Oberalp), "KK1 4606", and "6.0m" on center of gondola sides; "14,5m" and "10t / 6600Kg" on right-hand gondola side panel. Sold separately and with Set 20512.   **75**

4011: 1968-74, 1979- , this catalogue number applied to two different cars, both of which are listed below in their differing versions.
(A) 1968-74, four-wheel, low-sided gondola similar to 4010, but with dark green unpainted body; no markings on body or frame.   **175**
(B) 1973-74, similar to (A), but unpainted medium brown gondola.
                                                                       NRS
(C) 1979, hinged-hatch service car K "Hilfswagen" of the OEG; auxiliary car for transporting bulk goods sensitive to moisture and for railroad company's own maintenance and auxillary materials; all six hatches can be opened independently; main body same as 4010, but orange-painted body with black markings; Type 1 or 2 frame markings; length 300 mm. Has "Hilfswagen" on side beneath middle hatch; "O.E.G." over "696" on end body panel; apparently a prototype.
                                                                       NRS
(D) 1979- , "Hilfswagen" on side beneath right hatch between fourth and fifth stanchion supports; "OEG" at the side of "4011" between second and third stanchion supports; red and white hazard markings at corners.   **CP**

4011BTO: See Chapter XII.

4011O: See Chapter XII.

4011SD: See Chapter XII.

4020: 1968-74, four-wheel, high-sided gondola Ow. Opening side doors with lift-latch for lock; simulated wooden grain inside and out; unpainted straw brown body; black grab-rails on ends; no markings on body or frame; length 300 mm.   **200**

4021: 1968- , same basic car as 4020, but in green or darker brown than 4020.
(A) 1968-74, unpainted medium green body without markings; no markings on frame.   **175**
(B) 1972-76, unpainted darker green body; no markings on frame.
                                                                       150

(C) 1975-78, unpainted medium green body; white "L.G.B.", "Ow", and "4021" on lower half of second body panel; no frame markings.
                                                                       100
(D) 1977-78, similar to (C), but painted medium green body.   **100**
(E) 1977-78, unpainted blue body, same as (D), produced for Primus as 40821(B) and came with Primus Set 8000.   **275**
(F) 1978-80, unpainted yellow body, same as (D), but has Type 1 frame markings; made for Primus as 40821(A).   **275**
(G) 1979-80, unpainted darker green body than (C) with black chalkboard in lower portion of first body panel, black-painted frame on grate on second body panel; no frame markings.   **75**
(H) 1980-83, similar to (G), but with medium green-painted body; with or without Type 1 frame markings.   **45**
(I) 1983, same as (H), but with gondola interior painted light gray; Type 1 or 2 frame markings.   **45**
(J) 1983-84, medium brown-painted body; light gray-painted interior; white lettering, numerals.   **25**
(K) 1985-87, similar to (I), but with slightly darker brown-painted body.   **CP**
(L) 1987, red-painted body with "Rio Grande" on left-hand portion of each side. Sold with Set 20087; price for set.   **NSS**
(M) 1988, similar to (L), but with blue-painted gondola body. **CP**
(N) 1989- , same red-painted gondola as (L), but has white "Lake George & Boulder" on left and "LG&B" logo on right on each side of body. Sold only with Set 22401 for distribution in the USA.   **NSS**

4023: 1988- , European "X 05" low-sided gondola with brakeman's platform. Gondola body is the same as the 4010, but gray in color. Painted detail markings are also identical to the latest 4010 with the exception that number "4010X05" has been replaced with "4023X05". Total length is 335 mm.   **CP**

4025: 1989- , Swiss Rhaetian Railway Uce Cement-Silo car also known as a "Baby-head." A black four-wheel flatcar with silver-painted silo, tanks, piping, and grab-rails; "Rh B" over "Uce" in black on each side of silo. Frame markings include: "3,50" (with arrows at each side) and "Rh B", all in white.   **CP**

4026: 1988- , high-sided German (DB) gondola with brakeman's platform. Brown gondola bed.   **CP**

4037: 1988- , low-sided gondola for LGB Circus Train; has white-painted gondola and blue chassis. At least three versions with three different loads have been depicted in the catalogues.

The railing of 4041, with its asymmetrical arrangement, is specific to this car. Late versions have the freestanding brake hose; earlier ones had a brake hose cast in the plane of the railing. Older cars were cranberry or red, with a very early gray version 4041G. The hopper doors operate, and can dump plastic pellets on to trackside.

The prototype model 4059 lacks the extensive lettering and large railing plaque of the production model. In this picture, the rear apron is up, in traveling position, while the front apron is down, in loading position: Cars endload, driving on and off the length of the train. Through mountain tunnels, passengers usually stay with the cars.

(A) 1988- , white gondola bed unmarked; load consists of a circus personnel trailer, white with a red roof, blue window shutters and doors, and "CIRCUS" on each side in orange, yellow, and blue letters (as shown in the 1988-89 catalogue). **CP**
(B) 1988- , same as (A), but with multi-colored stars on both sides of the gondola bed (as shown in 1989 "New Items" brochure. **CP**
(C) 1988- , same as (A), but with red and/or blue half-circles on the side of the bed. Carrying either a white and blue Mercedes Unimog truck (colors on truck may vary), or a white circus animal trailer with red roof and blue drawbar with "CIRCUS" on each side in orange, yellow, and blue letters (as shown in 1989 "New Items" brochure). Sold only with Set 21988. **NSS**

4041: 1971-87, OEG four-wheel, 15,000 kg capacity hopper car, based on one of the 1200 cars built by the H. Fuchs Coach Works in Heidelberg, Germany. Manually-operated chute doors on sides to empty loads; beginning about 1977 small bags of multicolored chopped-up bits of plastic were packaged with cars as loads. The asymmetrical FA1 railings composed of frameworks made of simulated Angle iron with off-center vertical and partial horizontal members are unique to the OEG hoppers. Small boarding steps (one at each corner) as well as a portion of the brake piping is cast with these railings in all versions. In most versions hopper color matches that of chute parts, hand-crank wheels, and dispatch boards. Total length 300 mm. Discontinued in 1987.
(A) 1971, semi-glossy, unpainted red hopper (red color may have faded to pinkish-red in cars exposed to the elements) with unpainted black chute doors, and FA1(A) end rails; boarding steps very thick. Hopper body has the following white, heat-stamped markings: robust, oval lettered "O.E.G." above "1200" on center panel to the left center panel, and small markings on dispatch board cast over hopper support. White heat-stamped markings are also on the chassis frame directly above chutes. **275**
(B) 1971-73, very similar to (A), but differs in having unpainted red chute doors. **225**
(C) 1974-78, very similar to (B), but with bright, glossy red-painted hopper and chute parts. **200**
(D) 1979-82, similar to (B), but without heat-stamped markings; lettering and numbers are thinner and more delicate. "OEG" lettering is more rounded than in earlier versions; dispatch boards lack markings. FA1(B) end rails with heavier Angle iron, more delicate boarding steps, and most brake piping separately cast. **175**
(E) 1980, uncatalogued; similar to (D), but hopper and chute parts are painted dark, dull cranberry red. **225**
(F) 1983-87, unpainted orange hopper body and body supports (including chute parts and hand-crank wheels) mounted on flat black-painted chassis. Hopper body markings are black including "OEG" and "737", the latter number replacing the "1200" on all earlier versions (including 4041G); dispatch boards same color as hopper but

covered with black and white decal. Red and white hazard decals on each corner of chassis. **75**

4041G: 1971-74, OEG four-wheel ballast hopper car; similar to 4041(A), but with light gray-colored body. This car was also available as a Primus model, number 40841. **275**

4042: Matra-Frankfurt crane car. See Service Wagon Section on page 110.

4059: 1985-88, automobile transport flatcar with two late model Mercedes 190E Sedans (one red and one dark silver-gray) subcontracted by Lehmann. This is basically an eight-wheel flatcar similar to the 4060 painted black; length 415 mm. Markings: Between first and second stake pockets at left, "Waggon Fabrik" over "1985 14059" over "Talbot" all in an oval, with "6300kg" boxed to the right; between second and third pockets, "LüP 9,3m"; between third and fourth pockets, "LGB"; between fourth and fifth pockets, "4059" (this and the preceding are the most prominent body markings); between fifth and sixth, "Rev 07 90" boxed; to right of sixth pocket, "5.9m" between arrows; plus "LGB Express" in yellow on black background in right-hand guardrails. Although the 1985 catalogue showed this car with gray guardrails, it was produced with yellow/orange ones. The two oval-shaped guardrails per side fit into the first and third, and the fifth and seventh stanchion pockets. There is one yellow- and black-striped flip-up-type loading gate at each end for securing, as well as allowing automobiles to be loaded or unloaded from the bed. A raised ramp covering the center section of the bed has depressions for holding automobile wheels in place. Discontinued in 1988.
(A) 1986, earliest versions; the Mercedes sedans lack the LGB trademark on the plastic underbelly. **100**
(B) 1986-88, Mercedes sedans have LGB trademark on underbelly. **85**

4060: 1971- , American-style eight-wheel narrow gauge flatcar with insertable stanchions; has seven stanchion pockets per side; arch bar trucks; length 415 mm.
(A) 1971-72, unpainted light straw brown color simulated wood bed and four truss rod supports; no numbers or lettering; black plastic stanchions; bed lacks the raised tabs found on subsequent versions for securing 4069/1 Containers; early prototype version. **NRS**
(B) 1973-76, same as (A), but with white "4060" added to each side of bed between fifth and sixth stanchion pockets. **125**
(C) 1977, unpainted orange-brown bed and undercarriage supports; black plastic stanchions; bed has eight raised tabs for securing 4069/1 Containers; "4060" on each side between fifth and sixth stanchion pockets; same car as 4069(A). **150**
(D) 1978-79, same as (C), but with "CAPY 20050" between second and third stanchion pockets, "S. P." placed between third and fourth stanchion pockets, "4060" between fourth and fifth stanchion pockets, "LT WT 14500" between fifth and sixth stanchion pockets, "RPKD OYO" above "38 11 20 39" between sixth and seventh stanchion pockets. **100**

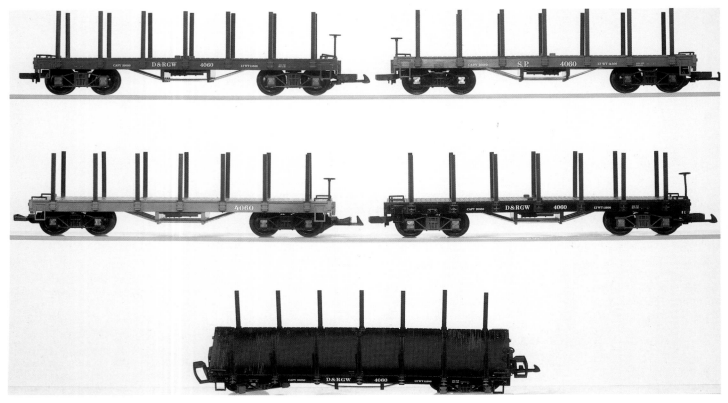

Four versions of 4060, varying in color, road name, and lettering. Top left, 4060(F); top right, 4060(D) or (E) (to tell which you would check the color of the undercarriage supports); middle left, 4060(B), which lacks the raised lugs to hold containers in place on the deck; middle right and bottom, 4060(G). Note that some of the arch bar truck frames are the more recent gray, others are black. A. Rudman Collection.

(E) 1980-82, same as (D), but with black undercarriage supports.
100

(F) 1983-84, medium brown-painted bed with black undercarriage supports; "CAPY 20050" between second and third stanchion pockets, "D & R G W" between fourth and fifth stanchion pockets, "LT WT 11500" between fifth and sixth stanchion pockets, "ALA-6.13" over "BLT-5.88" between sixth and seventh stanchion pockets.   75

(G) 1984, uncatalogued; similar to (F), but with bed partially painted flat black (on sides). Flat black paint finish broke up as it dried into what is known as a "crackle finish".   100

(H) 1984, uncatalogued; similar to (F), but with bed completely painted flat black over orange-brown plastic; same bed markings as (F).   100

(I) 1985- , similar to (F), but bed is unpainted orange-brown.   **CP**
(J) 1987, similar to (F), but bed is unpainted black.   **75**

4061: 1971- , low-sided narrow gauge gondola similar to those used on many American lines; this car also bears a resemblance to gondolas used on the European Hartsfeld Railway, but all LGB models have American-style arch bar trucks. Brakeman's platform with hand brake wheel; no railing; basically the same eight-wheel flatcar as 4060, but black; bed has a four-sided gondola secured by stanchions fitting into pockets; length 415 mm. The best known version of this car has red gondolas; brown gondolas are rare as is the green version produced for Primus as 4081.

(A) 1971-73, no markings or lettering on bed of gondola; no raised tabs for securing 4069/1 containers; black, unpainted bed; reddish-

The low-sided 4061 Gondola has gone through several shades of brown and red, atop what is basically a black 4060 Flatcar. The truss rods, on the prototype, were meant to keep the car's center from sagging under heavy loads, as it aged. If over tightened, to correct sag, they sometimes bowed the center upwards.

Unfamiliar to American eyes are the brakeman's hut and heavy truss beam of open Goods Wagon 4062, a high-sided gondola first modeled in 1973. Changes include the freestanding brake hose replacing the one cast in relief on the hut and changes in color toward this darker, more orange brown. And, as so often, increased lettering.

pink, unpainted gondola without embossed details such as rivet heads on stanchions, rope eyelets or "4061" as seen on more recent models. Not produced in this form. **NRS**

(B) 1974-76, same as (A), but with the following white markings: "CAPY 40000" above "WT 13900K 2 24" between second and third stanchion pockets, "S P" (spaced apart and without periods) between third and fourth stanchion pockets, "4061" ("4" is open at top) between fourth and fifth stanchion pockets, "IL 26" (spaced apart) above "CU FT 269" between fifth and sixth stanchion pockets; embossed details, "LGB" logo and "4061" on reddish-pink gondola sides. **125**

(C) 1976-78, similar to (B), but with unpainted medium brown gondola. May have been made for Primus. **175**

(D) 1978, Primus version, numbered 40861, with unpainted dark green gondola sides; otherwise similar to (E) below. **650**

(E) 1977-81, same as (B), but with raised tabs for securing 4069/1 Containers on bed; gondola sides red-painted over brown plastic; markings between second and third stanchion pockets same as (B) but reduced in size, "S. P." between third and fourth stanchion pockets, "4061" ("4" is closed at top) between fourth and fifth stanchion pockets, "IL 26" (spaced apart) above "CU FT 269" between sixth and seventh stanchion pockets, additional markings "RPKD MINA" over "UP 1832" between sixth and seventh stanchion pockets. **100**

(F) 1982, same as (E), but with flat black-painted bed. **75**

(G) 1983, similar to (E), but "CAPY 40000" (no space between second and third zeroes) above "WT 13900K 224" between second and third stanchion pockets; "IL 26" above "CU FT 269" between fifth and sixth stanchion pockets; "RPKD MINA" above "UP 1732" between sixth and seventh stanchion pockets. M. Richter Collection. **125**

(H) 1983- , similar to (G), but with bed painted flat black; gondola same red color as (G) or slightly darker; notches to clear container securing tabs; most markings are reduced in size as compared to (E), (F), or (G) and differ as follows: "D & R G W" between third and fourth stanchion pockets, "CAPY 40000" (no space between second and third zeroes) above "WT 13900 ALA 12", "ALA-5.12" above "BLT-8.92" between sixth and seventh stanchion pockets. **CP**

4062: 1973- , eight-wheel, high-sided gondola (00m/s class) used by the Pinzgau Local Railway. Eight opening doors on sides of body and a brakeman's cab with opening doors; FA3 railing (Frame of Angle iron, half in relief); arch bar trucks; length 430 mm.

(A) 1973-74, light straw brown body without markings; FA3(A) railing (brakeman's cab has embossed brake hose); no markings on frame. **NRS**

(B) 1974-75, similar to (A), but with white, heat-stamped markings limited to the first two body panels adjacent to the brakeman's platform. **100**

(C) 1975-81, orange-brown body, white heat-stamped markings on first two body panels adjacent to brakeman's platform. **75**

(D) 1982-83, same as (C), but with silk-screened markings which include "4062LGB" over vent gate at center, side of car body; FA3(B) railing (freestanding right-hand brake pipe and hose, not embossed on cab). **60**

(E) 1984- , same as (C), but with silk-screened frame markings spaced at eight intervals; no embossed brake hose on brakeman's cab. **CP**

The cabooses can be dated 1973 left, and 1979-1982, right, by color, uncoupling pads, lettering, and the absence of brass grab-irons. A. Rudman Collection.

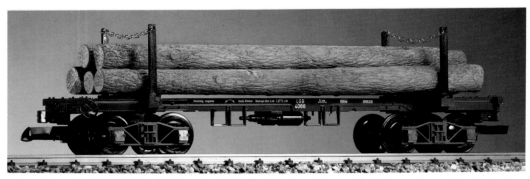

Log Car 4066 has varied little since its introduction in 1973, mostly in lettering and paint color. But the logs have changed several times, now approximating telephone poles more nearly than the richly textured bark of the earliest version.

4065: 1971- , short "bobber" four-wheel caboose of the Denver Rio Grande Western narrow gauge railway; brakeman's platforms at each end; FR1 railings (open Frame of Rods, two inverted "U"s joined by a chain); roof with stove smokestack; centered cupola with roof vent; produced with 3000/1 Spoked Wheels; has European buffers, unlike most American equipment; length 300 mm.

(A) 1971-75, unpainted pinkish-red body without any markings; embossed black-painted grab-irons on body. Nonproduction prototype.
                                                                                                    NRS

(B) 1973-75, same as (A), but with white "4065" on lower center of each side.   **250**

(C) 1974-78, same as (A), but with white "4065" on lower center of each side, "Rio Grande" between side windows of body.   **200**

(D) 1978-79, uncatalogued; pinkish-red body; embossed black-painted grab-irons; round-shaped, white logo placed between "Rio Grande" and "4065" comprised of "RIO GRANDE", "ROYAL / GORGE", "MOFFAT / TUNNEL", and "SCENIC LINE / OF THE / WORLD".   **150**

(E) 1979-82, same as (D), but with reddish-brown-painted body and cupola; white "WT 20300" above "ALA 6-32" added to lower right corner of body. On some pieces the cupola and body color were of a slightly different hue.   **125**

(F) 1982-86, same as (E), but with brass wire grab-irons on body.
                                                                                                    100

(G) 1986, same as (F), but has darker and less glossy brownish-red finish.   **75**

(H) 1986, same as (G), but color has more red in it than (F) or (G).
                                                                                                    CP

(I) 1987- , same body as (H), but painted semi-glossy black with white markings; roof is flat black. Several separately boxed pieces have also been seen with a gray roof with black edging. Originally sold with Set 20087; price for set.   **300**

4065BTO: See Chapter XII.

4065F: See Chapter XII.

4065-GO1: 1988, Colorado & Southern bobber caboose with four wheels and bright yellow painted body. All markings are black and include: "C & S", above C & S logo, above "4065". Tail lanterns have red and clear lenses with a brass wire bail on top. Has European-type 3000/1 spoked wheels. Made only for distribution in the United States.   **135**

4065LG&B: 1989- , Lake George & Boulder bobber caboose with four wheels and black-painted body. Body markings include white "Lake George & Boulder" above white, black, and blue L G & B logo, above "4065". Tail lanterns have red and clear lenses with a brass wire bail on top. Has European-type 3000/1 spoked wheels. Made only for distribution in the United States and originally sold only with Set 22401.   **NSS**

4066: 1973- , lumber car with stanchions and chains and a load of five logs; underside detailed with brake cylinder, piping, and steps; brakeman's wheel on side; has buffers, unlike most American equip-

Container cars are the heart of much modern freight traffic. Like the 4060 Flatcars on which it is based, the car of 4069 varies primarily in lettering. In addition, a variety (more than thirty have been listed) of containers have accompanied it, especially in limited edition sets.

Issued in a much darker brown than its original catalogue photograph, 4073 continues Lehmann's expansion of its line of American prototype models. The trucks of this entirely newly designed body are arch bar, a type characteristic of American freight cars until the development of roller bearings and modern high speed, high capacity trucks.

ment; length 410 mm. The major variations have more to do with the logs than the car itself.

(A) 1973-74, green bed with black stanchions; no white markings on car; very light plastic logs are of varied diameter with thick bark and are quite realistic looking. **150**

(B) 1974-78, same as (A), but with white "N.W.L. Co." above "4066" at center side edge of bed; logs are more uniform in shape and size. **125**

(C) 1979-84, same as (A), but with white "N.W.L. Co." above "4066" at center side edge of bed; logs appearing more like telephone posts; bark is weakly simulated. **100**

(D) 1984-86, similar to (C), but with the following markings on chassis sides: "Vorsichtig rangieren", "Hardy-Bremse Drehzapf. Abst. 5,8m", "LüP 9,25m", "LGB / 4066", "8,35mm", "9500 kg", "REV09.12.85". **75**

(E) 1987- , similar to (D), but painted dark green. **CP**

(F) 1987- , similar to (D), but painted brown. Confirmation requested. **NRS**

4069: 1977- , eight-wheel flatcar with two four-wheel trucks; two removable 4069/1 Containers; bed has eight raised tabs to secure the containers; length 415 mm. The earliest catalogue photograph shows 4060(B) Flatcar with 4069/1(A) Containers; however the first issue was actually the 4060(C) Flatcar. Prices are for flatcar with two containers.

(A) 1977-78, orange-brown bed; with "4060" between fifth and sixth stanchion pockets, same flatcar as 4060(C); this is the earliest version sold and usually had 4069/1(A) Containers. **165**

(B) 1978-80, unpainted black bed; with "4069" between fifth and sixth stanchion pockets; with 4069/1(B) Containers. **125**

(C) 1980-81, same as (B), but with 4069/1(C) Containers. **90**

(D) 1980, same as (B), but with 4069/1(D) Containers. **150**

(E) 1980, same as (B), but with "CAPY 20050" between second and third stanchion pockets, "S.P." between third and fourth stanchion pockets, "4069" between fourth and fifth stanchion pockets, "LT WT 14500" between fifth and sixth stanchion pockets, "RPKD OYO" over "38 11 20 39" between sixth and seventh stanchion pockets, with 4069/1(C) Containers. M. Richter Collection. **115**

(F) 1980, same as (D), but with 4069/1(D) Containers. **175**

(G) 1980-81, same as (B), but with "S.P." between third and fourth stanchion pockets, "4069" between fourth and fifth stanchion pockets, with 4069/1(C) Containers. **80**

(H) 1980-81, same as (G), but with 4069/1(D) Containers. **135**

(I) 1981-82, similar to (G), but with "CAPY 40000" over "WT 13 900K 224" between second and third stanchion pockets, "IL 26" over "CU FT 269" between fifth and sixth stanchion pockets, "RPKD MINA" over "UP 1732" between sixth and seventh stanchion pockets; usually with 4069/1(C) or (E) Containers. **80**

(J) 1983- , European version with bed either unpainted black or painted flat black; "Wagonfabrik Talbot 1965 4069" inside an oval next to "9600kg" between first and second stanchion pockets, "LüP 9,3m"

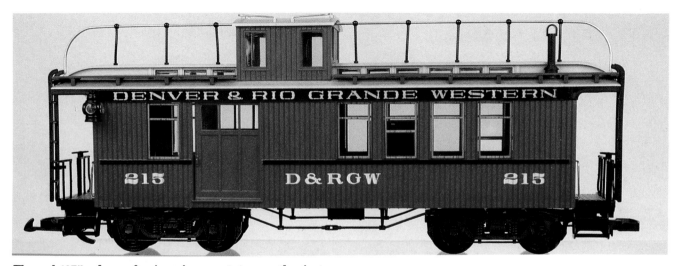

The red 4075 caboose for American prototype enthusiasts.

between second and third stanchion pockets, "LGB" between third and fourth stanchion pockets, "4069" between fourth and fifth stanchion pockets, "REV 03 85" between fifth and sixth stanchion pockets, "5,9m" between sixth and seventh stanchion pockets; packaged with 4069/1(E) or (F), or 4069/1RZ(B) Containers. **CP**

4073: 1985- , eight-wheel, high-sided gondola of the narrow gauge United States rail lines, unpainted maroon-brown with white markings and logos of the Denver and Rio Grande Western Railroad (prototype depicted in 1985-86 catalogue is painted dark brown). Body is composed of simulated wooden plank sides with ten stanchions on each side for support. (This car is not another variation of the 4060 Flatcar.) The grab-irons are cast separately in black plastic and are attached to side and ends; markings (all painted in white) include a round-shaped logo containing the words "D & R G W R R", "ROYAL / GORGE / ROUTE", and "SCENIC / LINE" between the first and second stanchions. "D&R GW 1646" is painted on the sides of the bed between the first and fourth stanchions, "1646" is on the second side plank from the top between the fifth and sixth stanchions, "CAPY 50000 LBS." is on the same plank between the sixth and eighth stanchions, and "WT 20400" above "SAL 10-26" are on the bottom side planks between the seventh and eighth stanchions; "LENGTH INSIDE 30 FT 10 IN" above "WIDTH INSIDE 6 FT 11 IN" above "HEIGHT INSIDE 4 FT 2 IN" are on the bed between the seventh and ninth stanchions; "BUILT 10-82" is on the bed between the ninth and tenth stanchions; "D&RGW" above "1646" is at the upper right-hand corner of each end. **CP**

4073-CO3: 1988, Denver & Rio Grande Western eight-wheel wood-sided gondola painted dark gray with white markings. All markings are the same as those on the 4073. Manufactured for United States distribution only. **125**

4075: 1984- , two cars were catalogued with this number, one of which was never produced.
(A) 1984, European four-axle service car with tool shack and spot lights. This car was catalogued in 1984-85 and 1986-87, but was never produced. See 4075 in Chapter X.
(B) 1988- , D & R G W drovers caboose with sliding side doors, adapted from an eight-wheel combination coach and baggage car as was frequently done by many of the early narrow gauge lines. Body is basically the same as the 3081 or 3181. True to its heritage, the LGB model has a cupola and roof catwalk with handrail. This caboose is painted barn red with black trim, silver roof, and markings include "DENVER & RIO GRANDE WESTERN" in silver letters on black background above windows, and "215" and "D & R G W" in white on both sides. Dummy marker lights with red and clear lenses are attached to the end of car closest to the sliding doors. End doors to boarding platforms hinged and spring-loaded to open and shut. Total length is 495 mm. **CP**

4076: 1988- , East Broad Top hopper car as used by this narrow gauge railroad company which operated in the Appalachian Mountains. This eight-wheel hopper is painted satin black with East Broad Top logo and other markings in white. Overall length is 415 mm. **CP**

4076-DO2: 1988, Santa Fe (A. T. S. F.) eight-wheel hopper car with dark blue hopper body and yellow markings which include "Santa Fe" logo, "A. T. S. F.", "4976", "CAPACITY 60 000", "ORB WT 223000", and "BLT 1.87". Manufactured for United States distribution only. **125**

4076-XO1: 1988, Peabody Short Line eight-wheel hopper car with yellow hopper body and green markings which include "PEABODY" above "SHORT LINE" with red and brown logo between the latter two words above "The Coal Route"; all other markings and lettering also in green. Manufactured for United States distribution only. **135**

4141: 1988- , OEG hopper car very similar to 4041(F), but hopper and chute parts, etc. are painted light gray. Markings are in black and are identical to those on the 4041(F). **CP**

4169: 1988- , D & R G W lumber car based on the brown 4060 Flatcar. This car is virtually identical to 4060(H) with the exception of having the number "4169" substituted for "4060" (except on first

run models; see variations below), as well as having a lumber load added. The car depicted in the 1988 catalogue lacks a number and has a lumber load of real wood boards. Total length is 415 mm.
(A) 1988, has "4060" number on sides of bed. **CP**
(B) 1988- , has "4169" number on sides of bed. **CP**

40821: 1977-78, a high-sided "Ow"-type gondola made for Primus, similar to the four-wheel LGB 4021. Has embossed "4021" and "LGB" but lacks painted detail markings on body.
(A) No painted markings on frame. **275**
(B) Has the following white frame markings below the embossed "LGB": "10,57", "5.8m", "13.4m2", "4340 kg". **275**

40841: 1978, Primus OEG hopper car. Same unpainted gray hopper as LGB 4041G. **275**

40861: 1978, S. P. (Southern Pacific) low-sided gondola on eight-wheel chassis made for Primus. Similar to LGB 4061, but differs in having unpainted, dark green gondola sides. White numbers and dimension markings on black bed the same as LGB 4061(D). This car may also have the Primus catalogue number "40861". See 4061(D).
500

CONTAINER CARS

4003: 1983-87, four-wheel container car with single six meter container; same basic car as the 4002, but produced in black plastic and painted flat black; first sold with 4069/1(G) Container, but has also been seen with other versions; length 300 mm. Price includes car with container. Discontinued in 1987. **40**

4003A: See Chapter XII.

4003B: See Chapter XII.

4003BTO: See Chapter XII.

4003CS: See Chapter XII.

4003CSK: See Chapter XII.

4003D: 1984, uncatalogued; white DHS container car; same as 4003 with white 4069/1D Container with red, black, and green markings; sold with Set 20514 and boxed separately; container held on to black chassis with doubled rubber band from buffer to buffer; black "SPIEL & HOBBY" between pairs of orange and green stripes; 800 produced. **125**

4003DV: See Chapter XII.

4003F: 1982, uncatalogued; Freizeit Hobby Spiel (FHS) container car comprised of an orange-brown-colored 4002 Flatcar and white 4069/1F Container with red, blue, and orange markings; erroneously dubbed 4002/69 by collectors; available only with Set 20502; 800 produced. **150**

4003GB: See Chapter XII.

4003K: See Chapter XII.

4003KT: See Chapter XII.

4003L: See Chapter XII.

4003MC: See Chapter XII.

4003N: See Chapter XII.

4003NF: 1985, Nuremberg Furth 150 Anniversary car, same color as 4003RZ Container Car, but with red and white "150 Nürnberg Furth Anniversary" decal instead of "LGB" logo; with Container 4069/1NF. Price for car and container.
(A) "150th Nürnberg / Furth" decal placed over left side of container stripe. **100**
(B) Same decal, but placed over right side of container stripe. **100**

4003P: See Chapter XII.

4003PH: See Chapter XII.

4003PV: 1984, uncatalogued; "Commander Rom" container car on standard 4003 Flatcar with dark blue 4069/1PV Container; sold only with Philips Video Set 380.7030; price for set. **350**

4003RZ: 1983-84, 1986, uncatalogued; LGB "der Rot Zug" (The Red Train) container car with 4003 Flatcar and red, white, and green 4069/1RZ(A) Container; sold separately and with Set 20401RZ.
(A) 1983-84, also sold separately in a 4003 window box. **75**
(B) 1986, same as (A), but has "150th Nürnberg / Furth" decal placed over right side of green/white stripe. **100**

4003S: See Chapter XII.

4003SB: See Chapter XII.

4003SF: See Chapter XII.

4003SLM: See Chapter XII.

4003SR: 1984, uncatalogued; Spielzeug Ring container car, on standard 4003 Flatcar with white 4069/1SF Container with green and yellow markings; sold separately; 1,000 produced. **75**

4003SSB: See Chapter XII.

4003TS: See Chapter XII.

4003Z: See Chapter XII.

4103: 1988- , P & O container car. Dark blue-painted container with large, white "P & O" on each side below four-color flag; all other markings in white. Container is mounted on same type flatcar used in 4002 and 4003. Overall length is 300 mm. **CP**

CONTAINERS

4069/1: 1977- , models of six-meter transport containers for simplified freight handling for use by rail, road, or sea. Roof pins for securing stacking; doors can be opened; length 170 mm. Sold separately in boxed sets of two (up to 1986) or singly with a 4003 Container Car or in sets of two with a double 4069 Container Car. Listed prices are for a single container only with no box. Boxed sets of two containers may be slightly higher than twice the listed price.
(A) 1977-78, white container with large green and yellow peel-and-stick "LGB" logo on each side. Price for two containers and 4069(A) Container car. **150**
(B) 1978-80, white container with smaller red and yellow logo combined with horizontal stripe just below midline on each side of container; red color of stripe touches outside red outline of logo; "LGB" over "Ht" at top of sixth side panel, two solid black rectangles at bottom of sixth panel; "Eigegewicht" divided between tops of sixth and seventh panels, "00" above "6 252" at top of seventh panel, "5069" above "2360kg" at top of eighth panel, "Gewahr GW", "Behalter 17.7.7", "Anstrich Sp. H.", "20.7.7" and cross-hatching all at the bottom of the eighth panel. Container doors have the following markings: the top of the left door has "LGB" logo; the top of the right door has "LGB 00 5069", "Groptes", "Gesamtgew. 20320 kg", and "Eigengew. 2360 kg". Price for pair only. **50**
(C) 1980-81, same as (B), but with light gray container. **45**
(D) 1980-81, uncatalogued; same as (C), but with green and yellow "LGB" logo and stripe. **100**
(E) 1981-82, same as (C), but markings differ as follows: "Zum Aw" above "12.83 bis 12.85" at bottom of fifth panel; "Eigengewicht" and "Ht 6 252" reduced in size and limited to the top of the sixth panel, "5069" and "2360 kg" at top of seventh panel, "Gewahrl." with Thyssen logo above "Container 12.81" at bottom of seventh panel. More cross-hatching at bottom of eighth panel than in (C), with Thyssen logo; "12.80", "05.81", "12.81" vertically with Thyssen logo; "12.90", "05.81", "12.81", and vertically situated "Besichtigungen". The left door has a solid black rectangle added to the lower portion, the right door is much the same as (C), but markings are reduced in size with "OFFNEN", "OUVRIR", "ABRIR", and "APRIRE" added near the latch. **20**
(F) 1982- , same as (E), but red color of stripe does not touch red outline of "LGB" logo and the symbol "R" for registered trademark is at the top right of the "LGB" logo. Price for pair only. **CP**
(G) 1984-87, white container with blue horizontal stipe on sides; "VEREINSUND WESTBANK HAMBURG" in darker blue letters; usually sold with 4003 Container Car; price for container only. **20**

(H) 1985, uncatalogued; similar to (G), but with a red and yellow stripe; sold with 4003 Container Car; price for both. **50**
(I) 1985- , unpainted white container with same markings as (F). Containers were not available separately after 1986. **CP**

4069/1A: See Chapter XII.

4069/1B: See Chapter XII.

4069/1CS: See Chapter XII.

4069/1BTO: See Chapter XII.

4069/1D: 1984, uncatalogued; DHS white container with red, green, and white diagonal stripe on sides and "SPIEL & HOBBY" as part of stripe; figure of teddy bear is on the doors; sold only with 4003 Container Car in Set 20514 or separately as 4003D. Price for container and car. **150**

4069/1DV: See Chapter XII.

4069/1F: 1982, uncatalogued; FHS container, white with two, two-tone, non-intersecting stripes of red and blue, each of which forms a right angle but does not run parallel to the edges of the container. Beneath the left stripe are the words "Freizeit Hobby Spiel" in black. The right stripe is interrupted by a square logo with rounded corners outlined in blue with an orange-colored line-drawn clown's head inside; originally sold only with 4003F Container Car in Set 20502. Price is for container on 4003 Flatcar. **140**

4069/1GB: See Chapter XII.

4069/1K: See Chapter XII.

4069/1KT: See Chapter XII.

4069/1L: See Chapter XII.

4069/1MC: See Chapter XII.

4069/1P: See Chapter XII.

4069/1PH: See Chapter XII.

4069/1PV: 1984, uncatalogued; Philips Video dark blue-painted container with white-, light blue-, and pink-colored "Commander Rom" video figure emitting an electrical flash from his left hand with the words "Videospiele / Von Philips" inside it; small red and white computerized video bodies and figures cover most of the dark blue background; originally sold on 4003PV Container Car with 380.7030 Train Set. Price includes 4003 Flatcar. **100**

4069/1RZ: 1983-85, uncatalogued; Der Rot Zug (the Red Train) container made as part of a promotional set and as a separate item for the Lehmann Company; two versions:
(A) 1983-84, painted cranberry red or bright red, glossy or at least semi-gloss finish; with a green and white horizontal stripe (green center stripe with white borders) just above the midline on each side of the container; a white and red circle with a red and white LGB logo in its center interrupts the stripe on the left side; originally sold with 4003RZ Container Car in Set 20401RZ. Price is for container and 4003 Flatcar. **75**
(B) 1985, very similar to above, but red color is slightly brighter yet has a flat finish; green and white stripes and markings are somewhat translucent due to a lighter coat of paint; sold in pairs with 4069(D) Container Car and may have also been sold with 4003. Price is for 4069 Flatcar with two containers. **50**

4069/1S: See Chapter XII.

4069/1SB: 1984, uncatalogued; Schmidt Bakery, chocolate brown-painted container with red and white Schmidt Bakery logo on the right side of container; white "hmm... / Schmidt-Lebkuchen / aus Nürnberg" next to logo; sold with 4003 Container Car in Set 20526. Price includes 4003 Flatcar. **150**

4069/1SF: See Chapter XII.

4069/1SR: 1984, uncatalogued; Spielzeug Ring white container with yellow and green horizontal stripes around middle of body; green "DER SPIELZEUG RING" above stripes, "DAS TOLLE DING" below stripes. Price with 4003SR Container Car. **75**

4069/1TS: See Chapter XII.

4069/1Z: See Chapter XII.

VIII
BOXCARS
and REFRIGERATOR CARS

Covered goods wagons, or closed body "box" cars, are the staple in any general purpose railroad's rolling stock. They come in various lengths. Short runs have encouraged European lines to use some shorter wagons than those common in America, where 32-foot boxcars were once common and 40-foot cars are still fairly standard, in contrast to the 22-foot cars of European narrow gauge lines. On both continents, more modern cars are longer.

Lehmann's many 300 mm long freight cars (representing 22-foot prototypes) are closely related in design, and sometimes (e.g. 4032L, 4034), as with passenger cars 3000/3006, a run has been made with a body embossed with a different number from the official one under which the car is catalogued, made, packaged, and sold.

All 300 mm boxcars with platforms have SW1 railings (Solid Wall with triangular side gates) if produced through 1978, and FA4 railings (open Frame of Angle iron, no side gates) if produced from 1981-1985. 300 mm boxcars produced in 1979-1980 have SA1 railings (Solid wall with Accordion-gated aisleway, triangular side gates).

4026: 1989- , Beck's Beer reefer with raised brakeman's shanty, on four-wheel chassis. The reefer body is basically the same as that used on the 4035 Boxcar, but with an added brakeman's platform, raised shanty and ladders, all mounted on a 335 mm chassis. Body is painted tan-beige, with "Beck's" in black-outlined lettering, four-color Beck's logos, and green and red horizontal stripes; roofs on car and shanty are silver matte. **CP**

4027: 1988- , Swiss "MOB" (Montreux-Oberland-Bahn) refrigerator car with brakeman's platform. Brown-painted, simulated wood body

with white and black markings and silver ice hatches and sliding doors. Medium-Arched MA8 roof, painted satin silver without weathering. Chassis has large cylinder to assist braking. Overall length is 335 mm. **CP**

4028: 1988, Kronenbourg Brewery "Gk 509" refrigerator car with brakeman's platform. Commonly used on the Montreux-Overland Railway of Switzerland. Brownish-red-painted simulated metal body with "Kronenbourg" in white lettering below yellow and white coat of arms; all other markings in white or black. Ice hatch and unweathered MA8 roof painted satin silver. Chassis has large cylinder to assist braking. Overall length is 335 mm. Discontinued in 1988. **100**

4029: 1971-74, 1988- , this catalogue number applies to two different four-wheel, European freight cars. The earliest is a boxcar and, more recently, a refrigerator car.
(A) 1971-?, a four-wheel boxcar commonly used on most European railways. Smooth Medium-Arched MA1 roof (no seams) with filigree roof supports. Body has embossed "4029" ID number in upper left-hand corner of body at brakeman's platform, but is otherwise very similar to most of LGB's small boxcars. Has unpainted light brown simulated wood body without markings, with the most distinguishing character of this version being a simulated door on end of body at brakeman's platform. Unpainted chassis without frame markings; overall length is 300 mm. **300**
(B) 1972-74, same "4029" ID number but differs in lacking simulated door on end of body at brakeman's door, and has MA2 roof (with six seams). A version of this car has been found with a seamless, Low-Arched (LA1) roof which is uncatalogued, but it is unknown whether it was assembled this way at the factory. **275**
(C) 1988- , Boissons Riviera "Gk 518" refrigerator car with brakeman's platform. Used on the Montreux-Berner-Oberland Railway (MOB) of Switzerland. Blue-painted simulated metal body with "BOISSONS RIVIERA S.A." lettering on each side above the words "Eaux minerales, bieres" and "MONTREUX — VEVEY"; other markings in white or black. Open ice hatch and unweathered MA8 roof painted satin silver. Chassis lacks large cylinder to assist braking found on 4027 and 4028. Overall length is 335 mm. **CP**

4029: 1971-74, four-wheel boxcar used by most railway companies. Medium-Arched roof, filigree roof supports; unpainted light brown

body without markings; no frame markings; sliding doors open, early versions have simulated door on body end at brakeman's platform; two vents with horizontal grills on each side of body near roof line; embossed "4029" ID number in upper left-hand corner of body at brakeman's platform.
(A) 1971-?, smooth MA1 roof; has simulated door to brakeman's platform. **250**
(B) 1972-74, MA2 roof (six seams); lacks door to brakeman's platform. Has also been seen with Low-Arched LA1 roof (no seams); possibly a post-factory substitution. **225**

An early variant on the original 4030 Boxcar, 4029 was issued as a separately catalogued item, with a Medium-Arched roof initially smooth and then beginning in 1972, seamed in contrast to the Low-Arched roof of 4030.

4030: 1968- , four-wheel boxcar (Gw class) of the Deutsche Reichsbahn. Sliding doors and brakeman's platform railings; body similar to 4029, but lacks simulated door to brakeman's platform; Low-Arched LA1 roof (six seams, two vents); filigree roof supports; "4030" embossed in upper left-hand corner of body end at brakeman's platform; length 300 mm.
(A) 1968-76, unpainted straw brown body; no body or frame markings. **185**
(B) 1977-80, unpainted light brown body; white detail markings on middle of first body panel next to brakeman's platform on slats six through nine; large "DR" heat-stamped above "4030" above "Gw" on sliding doors; Type 1 frame markings or frame markings absent. **125**
(C) 1981-82, same as (B), but with one white, square computer mark at each corner of body. **100**
(D) 1982-83, same as (C), but with "4030" painted on third slat of first panel next to brakeman's platform with markings added to bottom slat and markings at center of first panel reduced in size and limited to slats six, seven, and eight; markings also added to bottom slat of last panel opposite brakeman's platform; Type 1 frame markings. **75**

4030 has as long a production record as any car in the Lehmann line. It was unpainted and unlettered through 1976, but since then markings have slowly increased.

(E) 1983- , same as (D), but with "Deutsche Reichsbahn" on sliding doors in place of "DR"; Type 2 frame markings. **CP**
4030SB: 1984, Schmidt Bakery boxcar with four wheels; rich, chocolate brown boxcar same as 4030, but with white "Schmidt / Lebkuchen / aus / Nürnberg" on each sliding door; white "4030" in upper side corner of body adjacent to brakeman's platform; sold with Set 20526. Price for set. **450**
4031: 1968-74 and 1980- , this number applies to the following cars.
(A) 1968-74, "Magnesium" boxcar with four wheels; unpainted body same as 4030, but in white color; Low-Arched LA1 roof (six seams, two roof vents); filigree roof supports; no frame markings. Late versions have E2 wheels and shading on roof. Some pieces may lack door decal (this should not dramatically change value). "MAGNESIUM" decal in black letters on sliding doors. **300**
(B) 1968-74, "MAGNESIT" decal on doors. **300**
(C) 1980- , white soft drink reefer car with four wheels. Same body as 4030, but with "PEPSI" logo covering panels on end opposite brakeman's platform; large blue snowflake above the Lehmann logo and "Getrankedienst"; miscellaneous black detail markings on first, second, third, and sixth panels from brakeman's platform; two black computer markings at each corner; Low-Arched LA1 roof (six seams, two vents); filigree roof supports; comes with three different brewery signs (Kulmbacher EKU, Weihenstephan, and Tucher) for conversion purposes; Type 1 or 2 frame markings. Some early cars were packaged in yellow 4032C Coca-Cola boxes. Length 300 mm. **Note:** Tucher label differs from 4032 in having smaller discs, facing toward the right rather than the left, with no "P.G.", blue background rather than white. **CP**

For those who like sterner drink, 4031 comes with three peel-and-stick beer company labels, including a variant on the "Tucher" label of 4032, discontinued in 1980. Only a small number of these cars were produced in the Coca-Cola version.

4031C: 1984, uncatalogued "Cluss Brauerei Cluss Heilbronn" beer reefer car; white body with same detail and dimension markings as 4031 Pepsi Car, but has Cluss billboard logo with company coat of arms above "Cluss" (in green and yellow) above "Brauerei Cluss Heilbronn" (in black) all surrounded by green and orange border; 100 produced. **500**

4031CC: 1980, Coca-Cola reefer car, very similar to 4031 Pepsi Car but has painted-on "Coca-Cola" logo in red and white on the red plastic billboards on sides of car. The body appears to be unpainted white with no black paint on the vent grate on the lower side of the body near the brakeman's platform. This is an extremely rare car; production was canceled due to licensing problems and most of the cars produced were apparently destroyed. Probably less than 25 reached the United States (also see 40832 in this chapter, and 4031CC in Chapter XII). **450**

4031HS: 1984, four-wheel red-painted boxcar, same body as 4031 ("4031" ID number), but with white "Freizeit Hobby Spiel" between door and brakeman's platform; two red, orange, and white stripes, one of which passes horizontally from the brakeman's platform and angles diagonally across door while the other angles up body panels opposite brakeman's platform; company logo in red and orange on white between door and end opposite brakeman's platform; charcoal gray Low-Arched LA1 roof (six seams, two vents), with black shading; sold with Set 20513.   **125**

4031L: 1987, Lutgenau Trainworld Company "First" Brewery boxcar; white-painted body with "FIRST" name and logos on each side (also see 4032L). This car was commissioned by Lutgenau Trainworld for their unnumbered set; 1000 produced.   **100**

4032: 1973-80 and 1985-87, two basic boxcars were offered with this catalogue number.
(A) 1973-78, Tucher Beer four-wheel reefer car (Tucher-Brauerei) with unpainted white-colored body, sliding doors, and brakeman's platform; Low-Arched LA1 roof (six seams, two vents), filigree roof supports; length 300 mm. Not to be confused with 4031 with "Tucher"

After a hiatus from 1981 through 1984, the number of the old "Tucher" beer car was reassigned to this "Nestle's Chocolate" Car 4032. Both white; both fattening products; but different railings.

The special issue Vedes Car, 4033V, seems out of place with the much older cars around it; its slogan translates more or less "We travel for play and holiday." Below it is the 4029, with its Medium-Arched roof, and the 4030, with its Low-Arched roof. At right, note the patriotic colors of two 4040As and a 4040E, all with the older long tank bodies. The handles at the end of the purge valve extension pipes show at left of the bottom two tankers as white and red circles, respectively, overlapping the profiles of the larger purge valves. A. Rudman Collection.

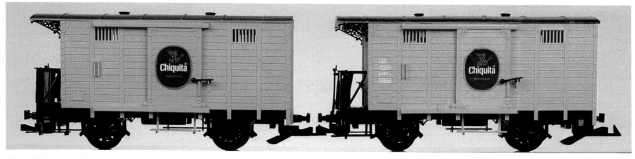

"I'm Chiquita Banana, and I've come to say," — The car on the left is variation (A) from 1973, and the car on the right is the more scarce variation (C) from 1974-1976. J. Hylva Collection.

label applied; (see 4031 note above, distinguishing labels). No markings on body except for large "Tucher Pils" sign covering body panels furthest from brakeman's platform; no frame markings.   **125**

(B) 1979-80, same as (A), but with black detail markings on body panel closest to brakeman's platform.   **100**

(C) 1979-80, same as (B), but with metal grab-irons between roof and brakeman's platform; Type 1 frame markings.   **100**

(D) 1985-86, Nestle Chocolate four-wheel boxcar painted white with a smooth, simulated metal sliding door on each side; markings on door include black "Chocolate" above "NESTLE" above red "PETER" above turquoise "Caillers" above dark blue "KOHLER". There are two black computer marks on the lower edges of each corner of the body; red dimension markings on first body panel next to brakeman's platform, as well as "LGB" over "4032" over "K3" on second body panel next to brakeman's platform; Medium-Arched MA3 roof (six seams, three vents). Edges of the upper (two per side) and lower (one per side) vent grills are painted black.   **100**

(E) 1986-87, edges of vent grills are not painted black.   **100**

4032BTO: See Chapter XII.

4032C: 1979, Coca-Cola soft drink four-wheel refrigerator car; two versions of this car exist, one produced for Primus (see 40832 on page 132), the other independently. Billboard plaques do not fit well on sides of car. Low-Arched LA1 roof (six seams, two vents). Car made for Primus has "Coca-Cola" graphics (in red and white) on billboard, but with Type 1 frame markings and black dimensional markings on one side only; no snowflake on door.   **400**

4032F: See Chapter XII.

4032L: 1980-84, Lowenbrau beer four-wheel reefer car; refrigerated wagon with brakeman's platform and two large vent fans on roof; white body with light blue "LOWENBRAU" over "MUNCHEN" on second and third panels from brakeman's platform and on sliding door; Lowenbrau lion logo covering panels furthest from brakeman's platform; other brewery decals available; Low-Arched LA1 roof (six seams, two vents), filigree roof support; length 300 mm; Type 1 or 2 frame markings; discontinued in 1984 (also see 4131).

(A) 1980-81, embossed "4031" identification number in upper left-hand corner of end body panel at brakeman's platform; unpainted body; usually came in a yellow box with window display; Type 1 or 2 frame markings. A painted version of (A) may also have been made; reader comments requested.   **150**

(B) 1981-84, "4032" identification number; unpainted body; no markings or decals; sold only in red boxes; Type 2 or 3 frame markings.   **85**

(C) 1984, same as (B), but with painted body. Door has a blue snowflake, Lehmann logo in red and white, and the word "Getrankedienst" is in blue.   **125**

4033: 1973-87, yellow "Chiquita" banana boxcar with sliding doors and brakeman's platform; yellow color may vary, some earlier pieces being light, faded yellow rather than the typical bright slightly orangish-yellow; positions of markings on car body may vary slightly from descriptions; Low-Arched LA1 roof (six seams, two vents), vents

Chiquita in 1988. G. Ryall Collection.

large (fans) or small; filigree roof supports; length 300 mm. The early versions with peel-and-stick "Chiquita" decals may lack these emblems since they can be easily removed. Sold separately and with Set 20401 until 1984; thereafter sold only with set.

(A) 1973, body markings limited to peel-and-stick door emblems with the "Chiquita" name in white; no frame markings.   **150**

(B) 1974-76, heat-stamped white dimension markings on body panel closest to brakeman's platform; same peel-and-stick "Chiquita" door emblems as (A); metal grab-irons link platform railings to roof on some pieces.   **125**

(C) 1977-79, same peel-and-stick "Chiquita" door emblems as (A); black heat-stamped dimension markings; "4033" and other markings added to the first panel next to brakeman's platform; one black computer marking at each corner of body; no metal grab-irons between roof and railings of brakeman's platform; Type 1 frame markings.   **100**

(D) 1982-87, similar to (C), but with silk-screened door emblem with the "Chiquita" name in yellow; Chiquita emblem slightly rounder at top and bottom; black-painted vent grate at base of first panel next to brakeman's platform (this was not painted on earlier versions) and two square-shaped computer markings at each corner of body; Type 1 or 2 frame markings.   **75**

4033B: 1983, uncatalogued; Brinkman boxcar; yellow body with same dimension and weight markings as 4033(G), but has blue and white billboard signs with the octagonal Brinkman Company logo and name attached to each side of body at end opposite brakeman's platform; originally sold with Set 20516.   **500**

4033V: 1984, uncatalogued; Vedes Company four-wheel boxcar; orange-yellow painted body; green "Wir fahren fur / Spiel & Freizeit" across the sliding door and a stationary door logo with "Vedes / Fachgeschafte" and black "4031 P" in upper side corner of body adjacent to brakeman's platform; other numbers and identification in black; Low-Arched LA1 roof (six seams, two vents); Type 3 frame markings; only about 800 produced.   **150**

The earliest version of this refrigerator car, made in 1984, with the embossed "4031" ID number, was only available with the Cardinal Beer Train Set 20512. When the car became available separately it was given a more personalized "4034" number. The large roof vents presumably represent fans; Cardinal, of course, is a beer.

4034: 1984-87, a 4031-series reefer having an unpainted yellow body with "CARDINAL" in large black letters across three panels next to brakeman's platform with black "2897p / HK-v / 9,ot / 6450kg"; large logo plaque on body panels opposite brakeman's platform has two red-painted figures outlined in black toasting one another over a beer barrel; Low-Arched LA1 roof (six seams, two vents), with filigree supports; solid ends, two sliding doors on sides.
(A) 1984, embossed "4031" identification number in upper left-hand corner of end body panel at brakeman's platform. Originally sold with Set 20512.   **125**
(B) 1985-87, same as (A), but with "4034" identification number. **60**

4035: 1980-88, boxcar originally of the Wurttemberg narrow gauge line for express freight of the Mosbach-Mudau Railway, which became part of the DB in more recent years. Sliding doors; black chalkboard on each side; no brakeman's platform; Low-Arched LA2 roof (no seams, no vents; textured); length 300 mm.
(A) 1980-88, markings as depicted in catalogues since 1980, and include one square white computer mark at each corner of body. **68**
(B) 1980, markings similar to (A), but no white dimension markings or computer marks. Factory prototype.   **NRS**

4036: 1985- , Circus boxcar with grillwork on sliding side doors; body is similar to the four-wheel 4035 Boxcar. The circus car is painted white with the word "CIRCUS" painted in blue, yellow, and red on each side to the right of the side door; black "Altenfurt / Fischbahn", blue "4036", and the black "message board" are on each side of the body to the left of door. Each body side has eleven five-pointed stars (five to the left of door and six to the right) in blue, red, and yellow. Although the chassis depicted in the 1984-85 catalogue is painted blue without painted markings, production versions have Type C frame markings; Low-Arched LA2 roof (no seams, no vents; textured). Includes animal loading ramp.   **CP**

4063: 1973- , eight-wheel boxcar (GGm/s type) with twin-axle trucks of the Pinzgau Local Railway. Brakeman's cab doors and four sliding doors actually open; Low-Arched LA3 roof (ten seams, rails for sliding doors); FA3 railing (Frame of Angle iron, half freestanding, half cast on brakeman's hut); length 430 mm.
(A) 1973, earliest version is straw brown-colored without markings on body or frame; FA3(A) railing (relief brake pipe and hose). **150**
(B) 1973-74, same as (A), but with four small body markings on the 11th through 14th slats of the panel closest to the brakeman's platform.   **100**
(C) 1975-78, same as (B), but in darker brown color.   **90**
(D) 1979-82, darker brown color with "OBB" over "GGm/S" over "16818", all on the lower half of the second body panel from the brakeman's platform; during this period FA3(A) railings (relief brake pipe and hose) changed to FA3(B) railings (freestanding brake pipe and hose).   **75**
(E) 1983- , similar to (D), but with markings on second panel from brakeman's platform slightly higher on panel and the addition of "4063LGB" above vent grate at center side of body; nine frame markings are added at eight intervals along the frame.   **CP**

4064: 1977-80, eight-wheel wooden-sided refrigerator car of the Denver & Rio Grande Western Railroad. Twin-axle, arch bar trucks; body has separately cast grab-irons and ice hatch latches; opening, double-leaf side doors; LA4 roof (peaks at center, 12 seams, catwalk); length 415 mm.
(A) 1977-78, bright yellow body sides; medium brown-painted ends and roof; ice hatches and catwalks around them are beige-colored; black markings on sides include "D & R G W" above "56" on left-hand portions and "REFRIGERATOR" above and slightly to the left of the detail markings in the lower right-hand corner region; the brown ends each have a small, white "D & R G W" over "56" in the upper right-hand corner. This version is shown in the 1977-78 catalogue, but confirmation is requested.   **NRS**

The 4036 Circus Animal Boxcar is only the first in the series of LGB Circus Cars. The more recently produced 3036 Circus Personnel Coach is a perfect compliment to the 4036, as will be subsequent circus models.

A companion to Gondola 4062, Boxcar 4063, like most Lehmann standard brown cars, has darkened somewhat in the several versions since its 1973 introduction. The separated pair of doors is an unusual feature of the prototype Pinzgau Railway cars.

(B) 1979-80, body is entirely bright yellow; gray roof, some may have black-shaded edges; white markings which include "D & R G W" over "4064" on left portion of body while the right-hand portion has a Denver & Rio Grande Western logo above and to the right of the word "REFRIGERATOR" which, in turn, is situated above and to the left of the detail markings in the lower right-hand corner; the ends of the body have specification markings at lower center and "D & R G W" above "4064" in the upper right-hand corner. J. Barton, B. Cage, and J. Hylva Collections. **375**

(C) 1979-80, uncatalogued; very similar to (B), but without white markings on ends of body. **375**

4067: 1974-88, eight-wheel wooden-sided boxcar with twin-axle arch bar trucks; sliding door on each side and catwalk and brakeman's wheel on roof; embossed grab-irons; LA4 roof (peaks at center, 12 seams, catwalk); length 415 mm. This car may have been produced in two body variations: the 1974-75 catalogue shows the vent cover

plates on the body sides with latches; the sliding vent doors on the ends have a horizontal strap across the middle. The large sliding doors are also shown to have an additional handle on the left-hand

The bright, new Union Pacific boxcar, 4067-AO1. G. Ryall Collection.

An assortment of American cars: 4067 is shown in two liveries, top left (C) and bottom right (D); the current version (E) is a darker brown and lettered "D. & R. G". 4064, top right, has its separately attached grab-irons contrasting to the relief grab-irons of the cars around it; the presence (rare) or absence (common) of white markings on the ends determines whether the car is 4064(B) or 4064(C). A very close look at a number on its open slats distinguishes this 4068(E), lower left, from the (C) of almost a decade earlier, for the newer cattle car's interior height ("I.H.") is "6 FT. 1 3/4 IN." rather than "6 FT. 1 1/4 IN."

The D. & R. G. Boxcar 4067 may have some unconfirmed body variation, but definitely was issued in three colors: yellow, medium brown, and a darker brown.

edge. The vent cover plates on the sides of the newer versions (1977 and later) are smaller, have simulated latches, and the sliding vent doors on the ends lack the horizontal strap. Discontinued in 1988.

(A) 1974-77, bright yellow-colored body same as 4064; gray roof and catwalk; brakewheel shaft is black all the way down the end of the body; black markings include "D & R G W" above "4067" on the left-hand portion of the body sides. This version is listed in the 1974-75 catalogue and may also have been produced with white markings. Confirmation is requested for both versions.   **NRS**

(B) 1974?, unpainted gray body without markings; unusual prototype version. J. Hylva Collection.   **NRS**

(C) 1977-78, same color as (A), but with black catwalk and black shading on roof; white "4067" above "CAPY 40000" above "LT. WT. 17900 KLR 4 34" on the side of the body to the left of the door; "SOUTHERN PACIFIC LINES" circular logo to the right of the door on the upper portion.   **375**

(D) 1979, unpainted medium brown body, no markings. J. Hylva Collection.   **350**

(E) 1979-81, unpainted medium brown body; same markings as (C), but with additional markings "NHM (9)" over "17 11 26.83" in the lower side corner to the right of the door.   **200**

Santa Fe Boxcar, 4067-DO3. G. Ryall Collection.

(F) 1982-83, similar to (E), but markings in lower right-hand corner are "NUM 910" above "17 11 2026". M. Richter Collection.   **200**

(G) 1984-85, D. & R. G. version, similar to (E), but with darker brown body; white "D. & R. G." to the left of the sliding door and "D. & R. G." above "4067" on the door itself.   **150**

(H) 1985-88, D. & R. G. version, color similar to (D) with markings similar to (G), but has additional plaque molded on body just left center of doors; plaque reads, "FLOUR SUGAR / AND BEAN / LOADING ONLY"; other markings added include "NEW ROOF" above

The open slats identify 4068's prototype as a stock car. Since 1974, it has appeared in three shades of green, and various letterings. Europeans, shipping their cattle shorter distances (such as to high meadows during summer), often use cars such as 4030, with its small closable vents on each side, rather than the porous slats of this American car.

The Budweiser Reefer, 4070, features a billboard side popular in the United States in the early part of this century, before the ICC's outlawing of such advertising (rescinded not long ago). The car was in production for only four years; variations are slight. Unlike 4067, 4070 has freestanding grab-irons.

"ALA-6-24" and door has "L" and "DO NOT CLEAT DOOR" at bottom. Roof is painted greenish-gray with black edging.   **90**

4067-AO1: 1988, Union Pacific wood-sided boxcar. Body is painted yellow with silver ends and roof; lettering and numbers are in black, with a red, white, and blue "UNION / PACIFIC" shield situated to the right of the sliding door; black catwalks on the roof. Cast boxcar body is similar to the 4067, but differs in the mounting of the brakewheel. On the standard 4067 the brakewheel shaft is cast as part of the body; on the 4067-AO1 the brakewheel shaft is a brass rod that runs through the original roof-mounted brakewheel pocket down to another pocket mounted on the chassis. Made for United States distribution only.   **165**

4067-DO1: 1988, Rio Grande (D & R G W) wood-sided boxcar. Body is painted yellow-orange and silver; the yellow-orange covers the roof and extends approximately two-thirds down the body, with silver covering the lower third of body and ends. Lettering and numbers are in black, with "Rio Grande" situated to the right of sliding door; black catwalks on roof. Cast boxcar body is the same as the 4067. Made for United States distribution only.   **165**

4067-DO3: 1988, Santa Fe wood-sided boxcar. Body and roof are painted medium brown with black catwalks; markings and logos are all in white. Cast boxcar body is similar to the 4067 but differs in the mounting of the brakewheel. On the standard 4067 the brakewheel shaft is cast as part of the body; on the 4067-DO3 the brakewheel shaft is a brass rod that runs through the original roof-mounted brakewheel

pocket down to another pocket mounted on the chassis. Made for United States distribution only.   **155**

4067-FO1: 1988, New York Central "Pacemaker" wood-sided boxcar. Body is painted red and gray; red covers roof, ends, and runs halfway down sides of body, with the lower half of body sides painted gray. Markings and logos are all in white; black catwalks. Cast boxcar body is the same as the 4067. Made for United States distribution only.   **155**

4068: 1974- , narrow gauge, eight-wheel stock car of the Denver & Rio Grande Western Railroad. Green-colored body with ventilated sides and sliding doors; catwalk and brakewheel are on a LA4 roof (peaks at center, 12 seams); length 415 mm.
(A) 1974, green body; bright gray unpainted roof and catwalk; the horizontal slat with white "D & R G W" is situated at the horizontal center of the box body (this is lower on more recent versions); the only other marking is "4068" beneath "D & R G W"; black brakewheel shaft is a separate piece attached to the end of the body. It is likely that this version was a prototype and not put into production in this exact form. However, a version may have been produced with similar markings using the commonly known body type with embossed brakewheel shaft and slat for "D &R G W" just below horizontal center of body (see (C)). Prototype model.   **NRS**
(B) 1974-?, unpainted gray body; without markings; lacks step rungs on end of body; unusual prototype version, only one is known. J. Hylva Collection.   **NRS**

Limited issue Railway Express Agency Refrigerator Car, one of approximately 2,000. G. Ryall Collection.

Like 4070, 4074 is based on the out-of-production 4064. Its ice hatches and center opening doors are typical of vintage American reefers.

(C) 1974-75, uncatalogued; unpainted medium green body; brakeshaft details are embossed below roof line; all markings are heat-stamped and include a white "D & R G W" on a horizontal slat just below the horizontal center of body; "4068" has a small "D" next to the upper portion of the "8"; white "Rio Grande" is on horizontal slat just above horizontal center of right-hand portion of body; "CAPY 50000", "LD.LMT.55000", and "LT. WT. 22700" on lower left-hand portion of body closest to door; "CU. FT. 1312", "I.L. 29 FT. 4 IN.", "I.W. 7 FT. 3 IN.", and "I.H. 6 FT. 1-3/4 IN." on right-hand portion of body beneath the "Rio Grande" lettering; black catwalk; gray roof with black shading at edges. J. H. Collection.   **400**
(D) 1975, similar to (C) with unpainted dark green body.   **400**
(E) 1975-76, unpainted dark green body; similar markings to (D), but are painted on and has a small letter "D" next to the upper portion of the "8" of the 4068 number; also has the markings "ALA. 12 49" beneath the "4068" number and "REBUILT 26" to the lower right of door beneath "Rio Grande". This car looks almost identical to the 1983-88 version (see (G)).   **250**
(F) 1979, medium green-painted body, no markings.   **350**
(G) 1977-82, medium green-painted body, almost same color as (B), with the same markings as (E).   **250**
(H) 1983- , uncatalogued; same markings as (E), with a dark green-painted body; deceptively similar to (E).   **CP**

4069G: See Chapter XII.

4070: 1982-87, Budweiser beer reefer car with same basic body as 4064; unpainted white plastic car body; brown-painted roof and ends; black "ANHEUSER-BUSCH" over red and white "BUDWEISER" logo above black "KING OF ALL BOTTLED BEERS" to the left of doors; black "STLR & CO" over "4070" on doors; yellow "ANHEUSER-BUSCH" over eagle logo above black "BEER CAR" to the right of doors; LA4 roof (peaks at center, 12 seams, catwalk); length 415 mm. Discontinued in 1987.
(A) 1981, plain white body without brown ends and markings. About 50 of these cars were left over from the assembly of the 4070BTO Boxcar and Al Lentz (their builder) sold them to several dealers and collectors.   **225**
(B) 1982, body has brown ends, yellow "ANHEUSER-BUSCH", and light-colored details on logo all to the right of doors; "A" in logo is red without black shadowing.   **120**
(C) 1983-87, goldenrod "ANHEUSER-BUSCH" and light-colored details on logo all to the right of doors; "A" in logo is red with black shadowing.   **100**

4070BTO: See Chapter XII.

4070NC: See Chapter XII.

4071: 1984, REA (Railway Express Agency) limited issue reefer; same basic body style as 4064; dark green-painted body; brown-painted LA4 roof (peaks at center, 12 seams, catwalk), with black edging; gold "REFRIGERATOR" sign glued on above a red and white diamond-shaped "RAILWAY / EXPRESS / AGENCY" sign glued on left-hand portion of body; gold "RAILWAY EXPRESS / AGENCY" and "REX 4071" signs glued on right-hand portion of body; gray side frames on

When Lehmann's plans for a 4031 Coca-Cola Car fell through, apparently for inability to reach a satisfactory arrangement on the use of the copyrighted name, American importer Lawton Jordon (Cimmaron Ltd.) was able to negotiate an eight-wheel American prototype Coca-Cola billboard reefer, 4072(A).

arch bar trucks. Only about 2000 produced and originally sold only in the United States.   **400**

4072: 1985- , two large refrigerator cars have been manufactured using this catalogue number.
(A) 1985, uncatalogued; eight-wheel Coca-Cola reefer car manufactured by Lehmann for Cimmaron, Ltd. of Atlanta, Georgia; same basic body and roof as 4064, but with glossy red-painted body; "Enjoy Coca-Cola" logo to the left of sliding doors and "Coke is it" to the right of doors; black door hinges on opening door, five black step rungs on right, one on lower middle left; came in gray sleeve with white "COKE / Model Train / Limited Edition" on Coke red background label; silver-painted roof; gray side frames on arch bar trucks. Only 2000 produced.   **375**
(B) 1987- , "Miller HIGH LIFE" beer refrigerator car; same type body as (A), but painted white with black markings and green, gold, and red Miller Brewery logo.   **CP**

4074: 1985-88, Pabst beer reefer with eight wheels; similar to 4064 Reefer; body is painted yellow with brown ends; roof painted brown; body markings include green "PABST" above black "MILWAUKEE" above black "U. R. T. Co. 91021" to the left of side doors; to the right of the side doors is a round-shaped logo with the words "PABST /

MILWAUKEE" on a red ring with a black outside edge, all of which surrounds a white center with a green leaf with a large, white letter "B" on it; black "Pabst-ette" above "MALT SYRUP / BEVERAGES" are to the right of the logo; below these markings are the following dimension markings in black: "CAPY 60000" above "LD. LMT. 788000" above "LT. WT. 57200" above "ICE CAPY. 8550". Discontinued in 1988. **100**

4074-BO2: 1988, Denver, South Park & Pacific Railroad (D., S. P. & P. R. R.) "Tiffany" reefer car. Body is painted white with black markings: "TIFFANY" above "SUMMER & WINTER" above "CAR" to the left of sliding doors; "D., S. P. & R. R." above "REFRIGERATOR" above "4074" to the right of sliding doors. Roof and catwalks are black. Made for United States distribution only. **175**

4074-ZO2: 1988, Schlitz Beer reefer as used by the Union Refrigerator Co. Body is painted yellow with brown roof and black catwalks. Markings are in black with the red, white, and blue Schlitz Co. logo to the right of side doors. Cast reefer body is similar to the 4070-series reefers, but differs in the mounting of the brakewheel. On the standard 4070 the brakewheel shaft is cast as part of the body; on the 4074-ZO2 the brakewheel shaft is a brass rod that runs through the

original roof-mounted brakewheel pocket down to another pocket mounted on the chassis. Made for United States distribution only. **165**

4128: 1989- , the "R. Blank Agricultural and Grain Co." reefer as used on the Montreux-Berner Overland Railway of France. Same body as used on the latest versions of the 4028 and 4029, but painted bright green with four-color paintings of vegetables and flowers above an irregularly outlined white field. Side doors are painted silver with white and black "R. Blank" logo. 335 mm chassis. **CP**

4131: 1988- , Lowenbrau refrigerator car similar to 4032L(C), but with embossed ID numbers and different door markings. The 4131 has blue and gold snowflake, Lehmann logo is black and yellow, and the word "Getrankedienst" is in black. Length is 300 mm. **CP**

40676: See Chapter XII.

40832: 1977-78, Coca-Cola refrigerator car produced for Primus, four-wheel chassis, unpainted white body with black dimension markings on one side only; plaque with "Coca-Cola" logo is entirely red with white lettering; embossed "4032"; no other painted body or frame markings than those mentioned; for comparison see 4031CC. **450**

IX
TANK CARS

Early and late tank car ends, the older ones in the center. The new and old at left are the valveless ends of a 4040E and a 4040S. Notice how much wider the old cars are, mounted as they are on standard flatcars, with their ladders angled out rather than vertical and, of course, their operating side valves reaching far out to clear the decks. At center right is the purge valve end of an old blue 4040A, with its long extension to the side; and at the far right is the equivalent end of a new 4040RZ, with its short tank. C. Colwell Collection.

LGB tank cars have been produced in two basic models: the 300 mm long, four-wheel (two axles) European type, and the 415 mm long, eight-wheel (four axles) American type. The 300 mm models were produced in two different versions. Those pieces produced from 1968 to 1978 have longer tanks, the caps at each end of the main tank body extend about 45 millimeters from the seam to the terminal bulge, and the purge drain at the end (not the side-mounted spout) has an additional pipe and valve jutting off to one side. These earlier tank versions are mounted on a flat similar to the black 4000 Flatcar. This early variation is designated as the ET type (for "early tank") in the descriptions below. The decals with company emblems and names for tanks were generally not put on at the factory, but were packed with each car to be put on by the purchaser. Therefore placement of decals may vary or they may be absent. The more recently produced tank cars have shorter

tanks, the cap at each end of the main body extends only about 25 millimeters from the seam to the terminal bulge, the purge drain lacks the additional pipe and valve, and hold-down lugs secure the dome tread plates. The tank is mounted on platform sections, one with brake handle and FA2 railing (Frame of Angle iron, two inverted "U"s with low cross members joined by a permanently raised tread plate; freestanding brake hose and pipe), specifically designed for this car which, in turn, is mounted on a typical 300 mm chassis. From 1979-1982 a single pair of lugs holds one end of the tread assembly to the tank top; since 1983 a second pair secures the other end as well. This more recent version, first catalogued in 1979, is designated as the LT type (for "late tank") in the descriptions. Company emblems are painted, in place of the earlier decals. Pieces to look for are possible transition cars that may have had the ET body with the more recent markings.

4040: 1968-70, 1984, oil car with "PETROLEUM" decal on each side of tank generally to the left of the fill dome; no other tank markings; ET type, gray-colored tank; no frame markings.
(A) 1968-70, gray-colored tank. **550**
(B) 1970, white-colored tank. **475**
(C) 1970, white-colored tank, "Dortmunder Hansa Bier" decals; this is a "one-of-a-kind" car that was produced as an experimental prototype. J. Hylva Collection. **NRS**
(D) 1984, unpainted white LT type car; no markings on tank. 500 sold to United States distributors for custom repainting, but many were retailed "as is" in blank form. Some were advertised for sale as "4040W". **125**

4040A: 1969-79, Aral tank car; several versions are known to have been produced from 1969 to 1978 only in the ET type.
(A) 1969-70, gray-colored tank, same as 4040, but with blue and white diamond-shaped ARAL emblem; no other tank markings; no frame markings. **550**
(B) 1971-76, same as (A), but with white-colored tank; black base, black spigot on tank, black ladder and walkway around cap on top. **450**

The four-wheel, European tank cars changed most obviously in tank length, which was shortened in 1978-1979. Above, the older style: 4040BP with 4040A (which also came in white and gray versions), and 4040S with 4040E. Other changes included a special open frame, replacing the flatcar body, with end railing on the platform permitted by the shorter tank: 4040S(E), the black Shell tank car made for Primus; two of the half dozen or so 4040Cs — the all-silver 4040C(A), and the wide-banded 4040C(E); and late version of the 4040, a limited American import intended for refinishing but often marketed unpainted and unlettered.

The new 4040BP, black rather than green. The end drain valve extension is missing from the LTs; a dummy valve is centered on the off side. Marker boards on the side, for which peel-and-stick colored labels are provided, are another difference between the older and newer tank cars.

(C) 1977-78, same as (A), but with light blue-colored tank.   **250**
(D) 1979, a four-axle version in medium blue; brakeman's platform, with fill dome off-center toward that end; a composite of two LT types. Has been identified as a prototype. R. Enners Collection.   **NRS**

4040B: 1971-74 and 1982- , BP (British Petroleum) Mineral Oil Company tank car; produced in at least three versions from 1971 to 1974, re-introduced in 1982. "BP" logo consists of yellow "BP" letters on a green shield in the center of a white square (peel-and-stick decal on early versions, painted-on in later versions); latest version lacks the white square.
(A) 1971-74, green-colored tank, ET type; peel-and-stick "BP" logo is usually placed on sides of tank to the left of the fill dome.   **550**
(B) 1973-74, same as (A), but tank is olive green. Limited number LT type car (see Chapter XII).   **575**

(C) 1982-83, flat black-painted tank, LT type; green BP shield with yellow "BP" on a large white square with rounded corners is situated to the right of the fill dome; may or may not have dual, white computer marks on ends of tank.   **300**
(D) 1983- , uncatalogued; same as (B), but without white, square field around BP shield. Some of these cars had a peel-and-stick logo decal similar to (C), but this is not a factory application.   **CP**

4040BTO: See Chapter XII.

4040C: 1978-88, BASF chemical tank car as used by the RhB; produced only in the LT type in at least six versions; black ladder and walkway, black base, black valve handle. Discontinued in 1988.
(A) 1978-79, silver-painted tank over gray plastic; small white-lettered "BASF" peel-and-stick decal, black rectangle with silver letters, generally situated to right of fill dome, gray plastic spout; no

4040C(B), distinguished by its very narrow black band. The new, narrow open frame for the LT types narrows the extremely wide loading gauge required by the working spigot on the old ET types, which had to reach far out to clear the wide decking of the flatcar base.

The end of the newer 4040E (and other LT types) is short enough for a platform and its special angle iron railing. All 4040s may be filled through the hinged cap on top and drained through the working spigot at the side.

other tank markings; detail markings present on display boards; Type 1 frame markings. **150**
(B) 1979-80, same as (A), but with 20 mm wide black band in the form of a peel-and-stick decal at vertical center of tank reaching from just below fill dome to lowest horizontal seam. **135**
(C) 1979-80, same as (B), but black band is painted on. **100**
(D) 1981-82, uncatalogued; similar to (A) and (B), but with slightly wider black band about 30 mm that reaches from about 20 mm below fill dome and to about 5 mm above lowest horizontal seam; small white and black rectangular warning sign in upper portion of black band; white-lettered "BASF" emblem is slightly larger than in (A) or (B). Type 1 or 2 frame markings. **65**
(E) 1982, uncatalogued, similar to (D), but without black band; has Type 3 frame markings. **65**
(F) Same as (E), but black rectangle is painted on with "BASF" letters in silver; computer markings on ends of tanks. **55**
(G) 1983-84, silver color on tank enhanced by clear, glossy finish; black band is very wide, covers area between the two vertical seams just beneath catwalks around fill dome; silver-lettered "BASF" emblem similar to (D); two black computer marks at each corner of tank, one rectangle over one pentangle. **100**
(H) 1985-86, same as (F), but without glossy finish. **75**
(I) 1986-88, same as (H), but with slightly darker, glossy finish. **75**

4040E: 1971- , Esso Oil Company tank car; produced in at least three versions.
(A) 1971-78, ET type in unpainted semi-gloss red color with blue, white, and red oval-shaped "Esso" emblem situated to the left of the fill dome; no additional tank markings or frame markings; black stairs and walkway around hatch, black fill spigot handle. **250**
(B) 1979-83, white LT type body with the same "Esso" oval emblem in the same position as in (A), but tank has a 25 x 100 mm red stripe at the horizontal center on the center and right sections of tank; Type 1 or 2 frame markings. **90**
(C) 1983- , uncatalogued; same as (B), but with two square computer marks at each corner of tank. **CP**

4040L: 1987, 1989- , two 300 mm LT tank cars carry this number.
(A) 1987, Kronen beer tanker, for Lutgenau "Dortmund" beer train, dark blue tank with "KRONEN" and Kronen Company logos in gold on each side. Originally sold with Set 20536L (Kronen Beer train set). **100**

(B) 1989- , Leuna Gas Company tanker; a tan-beige painted tank on black chassis. Markings include: "LEUNA" in red and black centered below fill dome with "DEUTSCHES" in red above "IG" logo in red and black, all to the left of "LEUNA" and "BENZIN" in red to the right. **CP**

4040RZ: 1984, uncatalogued, red-painted LT type body.
(A) Green and yellow "LGB" logo on white stripe to the left of fill dome; originally sold only with Set 20401RZ; however, some were broken up and sold separately. **75**
(B) Same as (A), but has "150th Nürnberg / Furth" decal lower right. **100**
(C) Same as (A), but "LGB" logo missing from stripe. **125**

4040S: 1971- , Shell Oil Company tank car; this yellow-colored tanker appears to have been produced in at least three variations.
(A) 1971-78, unpainted yellow ET type with a decal showing the company emblem comprised of the "SHELL" name in red letters across a yellow sea shell, surrounded by a square-shaped red field; this emblem is situated to the left of the fill dome; black stairs, walkaround, and valve handle, black simulated wooden base; steps at four corners on end sides. **165**

A tank car in transition, the gray 4040 Petroleum Car is on its way to becoming a white 4040A Aral Car. The typically long tank of this early ET type car came with "PETROLEUM" decals attached, and with "ARAL" peel-and-stick emblems loose in the box. C. Colwell Collection.

New Shell Tanker, 4080-YO4.

Water Car, 1989.

The 4080 Conoco Tanker, released in 1988, was the first American tank car made by the Lehmann factory.

(B) 1976-78, Shell tanker made for Primus; ET type car painted flat black with red and yellow Shell sticker; Primus number 40840. **200**

(C) 1979-80, black unpainted tank car, same decal as in (B), but LT type car made for Primus. **200**

(D) 1979-82, same yellow color as (A) in LT type; company emblem comprised of a yellow sea shell bordered in red which follows contour of shell and the "SHELL" name is in large red letters along horizontal middle in the center and right-hand tank sections; Type 1 or 2 frame markings; no square-shaped computer marks at each corner of tank. **85**

(E) 1983- , uncatalogued; same as (C), but with two square-shaped computer marks at each corner of tank. **CP**

4040SF: 1984, white-painted LT type car is lettered "Sudfunk" and was manufactured for a West German radio station. **NRS**

4080: 1988- , Conoco eight-wheel tank car. This is a faithfully detailed model of the tank cars used on virtually all American narrow gauge railroads. As with the actual tankers, this car is based on a flatcar with a tank cylinder set on lumber supports and secured with steel straps; fill dome is centered and has pressure relief valve and a brass grab-rail goes completely around tank. This car is painted satin black with white markings on tank and chassis. Total length is 415 mm. **CP**

4080-YO1: 1988, Transcontinental Oil Company eight-wheel tank car. Silver-painted tank on black chassis. Tank markings include "TRANSCONTINENTAL OIL COMPANY" above "T.R.O.X.799", all in red, outlined in black; all other tank markings are in black. Made for USA distribution only. **150**

4080-YO2: 1988, Gramps Oil Company eight-wheel tank car. Black-painted tank on black chassis. All markings on sides and ends of tank are in white. Made for USA distribution only. **150**

4080-YO3: 1988, Rio Grande Southern water car based on the eight-wheel tank car. Brownish-red painted tank on black chassis. All markings in white and include "RGS" above "4980" to the left of "WATER CAR". Made for USA distribution only. **150**

4080-YO4: 1988, Shell Oil Company eight-wheel tank car. Yellow-painted tank on black chassis. Markings include "SHELL" in red with black edging, with all other markings in black. Made for USA distribution only. **150**

40840: 1978, Shell Oil Company tank car made for Primus, similar to LGB 4040S(B), but is painted flat black with a red and yellow "SHELL" logo sticker similar to those used on the LGB 4040S(A). **550**

X
POWERED TRACK CARS, SHORT CARS (170 mm), SERVICE WAGONS, and CABLE CARS

Early catalogues list these very short cars as 150 mm long, but they are now more accurately identified as 170 mm. Typically, they are special purpose cars (cable, wine, excursion) and are found on very short prototype lines.

As the pump handles rise and fall, the workman's arms swing and he rocks back and forth. 2001 has no couplers or pickup slider; color of the deck has varied.

2001: 1971- , powered track inspection handcar, brown sides, yellow or tan bed, green toolbox; red wheels; color of the deck has varied; man pumps handle as car moves; no electrical pickup skates; length 140 mm.
(A) 1971-72, large toolbox, small wheels (visible through sides with running boards), no oil drums. This is a pre-production prototype; W. Richter comment. **NRS**
(B) 1973-86, small green toolbox, large wheels, two oil drums, tools (pick and shovel) on bed. Earlier versions had fewer painted parts

and the lever and its supports were in dull red. Other than minor paint color variations, these cars have been unchanged. **90**
(C) 1986- , similar to (B), but has red toolbox. **CP**

The 3041 Passenger Car's roof was darkened in 1979 and even more in 1981; the red body was darkened in 1984. The car has been featured in Set 300 with a battery-powered locomotive, Set 20701, and Set 20701T.

3041: 1974- , four-wheel summer-type, open passenger coach with grab-handles as used on tramway, park, exhibition, and beach railways. A flattened TA3 roof (tapered toward edges and ends, two roof vents); length 150 mm.
(A) 1974-78, no "3041" number painted on ends; embossed designs in ends unpainted; curtains painted white; very light whitish-gray roof. **75**
(B) 1979-80, similar to (A), but curtains more fully painted with black cross-hatchings; medium gray roof. **50**

(C) 1981-83, similar to (B), but with white and black "3041" on ends; embossed designs on ends painted white. **45**

(D) 1984- , similar to (C), but main body painted deep red. **CP**

3510: 1977-82, a short, open gondola for maintenance work; has red and white safety markings and brake crank; length 150 mm.

(A) 1977-78, bright yellow gondola body with red and white peel-and-stick safety markings pointing downward at corners. May be prototype. **NRS**

(B) 1978-79, lighter yellow gondola body than (A), with red- and white-painted safety markings pointing upward at corners. **50**

(C) 1979-82, same color body as (A), but with same safety markings as (B). **45**

The 3530 Tower Wagon with rotating platform, for servicing overhead wires, has gone through several changes in its browns and blacks and warning markings. One of the more conspicuous changes was the addition of the plaque on the side of tower opposite the ladder, in 1981.

3530: 1977- , tower wagon for servicing catenary systems; with pivot table work platform, tool chest, and ladders; length 170 mm.

(A) 1977-78, red and white safety markings cover lower edge of sides on pivot table work platform; no additional markings; light brown tower portion including work platform ladders and tool chest; tan bed and black chassis. **75**

(B) 1979-80, similar to (A), but with yellow and black safety markings limited only to lower corners of pivot table work platform; dark brown tower portion including work platform and tool chest; black ladder; orange-brown bed; came in yellow box. **50**

(C) 1981- , similar to (A), but with red and white safety markings with small rectangular moving sign on each side all the way around

lower edge of pivot table work platform; white-painted upper rail of work platform; large black rectangular sign with red, orange, yellow, white, and black lettering added to side of tower opposite the ladder. **CP**

4042: 1971- , four-wheel "Matra-Frankfurt" service crane car; crane cars were used by railways to clear blocked track, for rail or bridge construction, or for general loading. Yellow body and boom; operating boom and hook; crane base can be rotated 360 degrees; tool chest has opening, latching doors; length 300 mm.

(A) 1971-73, no marking other than red and white hazard stripes on end corners of tool chest; boom has early "snap-catch" for jib extension on end of boom. May be prototype. **NRS**

(B) 1974-78, red and white hazard stripes on all four corners of tool chest; boom has white markings just above hydraulic ram; Matra label in black letters on white rectangle on each side of car just below base of crane; frame markings limited to "ges. Tragfahigkeit 20t". **165**

(C) 1979-81, similar to (B), but with black markings on boom above hydraulic ram that include weight and angle charts; black and white arrows and triangles; doors of toolbox have black, red, and white markings; Matra label in blue letters on white rectangle on each side of car just below base of crane. **125**

(D) 1982-84, same as (C), but with "snap-catch" replaced by internal friction catch and a trigger support to secure boom in several upright positions. **100**

Tipping Bucket 4043 has remained virtually unchanged since a slight color variation in 1974. Like other short cars, it has appeared in low cost starter sets

The Rhaetian Railway operates a crane similar to 4042 (shown here), a fully hand-operable model with rotating extendable boom and crank-operated hook cable. The original in 1971 had no lettering; the type of extension boom lock has changed, and a boom support trigger has been added.

(E) 1984- , similar to (D), but with internal friction catch and a trigger support to secure boom in several positions; white markings on black portion of boom. **CP**

4043: 1971- , tipping bucket car that can be emptied by tipping the bucket to either side or bucket may be completely removed; length 170 mm.
(A) 1971-74, dull red plastic bucket, early couplers. **30**
(B) 1974- , shiny red plastic bucket; slightly lighter than (A), but some of the earlier pieces were produced in reddish-pink. **CP**

4044: 1974- , short, high-sided gondola or ore car; simulated wood-grained gondola sides; with brake crank; generally sold with three oil drums; chassis usually has small lead weight on underside; length 170 mm.
(A) 1974, unpainted straw brown gondola portion; white markings which include the "4044" on upper left end on each lateral side along with embossed "LGB" logo plate and "SULZBACH-ROSENBERG"; black chassis and brake handle. **50**
(B) 1974-75, similar to (A), but yellow; no ID number; sold with Set 20601. D. Doggett Collection. **NRS**
(C) 1976-84, same as (A), but with orange-brown gondola. **30**
(D) 1983-84, yellow gondola as in 3510 Service Wagon; without safety markings on corners; dark brown or black paint on simulated "LGB" plate logo, "SULZBACH-ROSENBERG" name, and "4044" number; originally sold with Starter Set 20602. **45**
(E) 1984- , orange-painted gondola with whitish-gray interior; yellow and red hazard stripes on corners pointing downward; black dimensional and detail markings. **CP**
(F) 1986- , same as (E), but white and red corner markings. **CP**
(G) 1986, similar to (E), but no corner markings and no gray interior. J. Barton Collection. **65**

Note: Around 1980 an unpainted red or yellow gondola was produced; no painted or embossed markings on gondolas. Has very thin metal axles, and no "LGB" logo. A non-Lehmann product that is a cheap imitation copying Lehmann models, but made in Thailand for the Ilco Company.

4045: 1973-76, 1979- , short stanchion wagon with bulkheads at each end and three stanchions, cast as part of body, on each side; originally sold with three to five blue or red oil drums; length 170 mm.
(A) Prior to 1974, uncatalogued, but visible in a photo scene of accessories for battery-powered Set 300 on page eight, 1979-80 catalogue, reprinted in the next three catalogues; gray stanchion body. **85**
(B) 1973, 1975, preproduction test run of 15 to 25: yellow stanchions and body. C. Colwell Collection. **NRS**
(C) 1974, similar to 4045 shown above, but in dark green, unpainted plastic. H. Betruger Collection. **100**
(D) 1975-76, straw brown stanchions and body. **45**
(E) 1979- , medium brown stanchions and body. **CP**

4046: 1974-85, short flatcar with reel (sometimes called a cable jimmy) with a single cable reel, rotatable on support stand; spool and/or stand can be removed from bed; discontinued in 1985; length 170 mm.
(A) 1974-75, very dark green reel (has embossed "LGB" and "4046" on spool side) on light tan support; dark brown bed; no markings. **75**
(B) 1974-75, same as (A), but with black support. **75**
(C) 1976-82, medium green reel; black support; orange-brown bed. **65**
(D) 1982, same as (C), but with white and black markings on green reel. **65**
(E) 1983, similar to (D), but markings on plaques glued on reel read "For shipment to Australia only". **90**
(F) 1985, yellow reel with same white and black markings as (D); medium brown bed. **45**

4047: 1974- , short flatcar with barrel for providing water at construction sites; cask can be filled and tap utilized; length 170 mm.

(A) 1974-78, medium dark green cask top cap, drain plug, and cask supports; yellow tap; black-painted barrel hoops around cask; dark brown bed; may be prototype. **NRS**
(B) 1979-80, cask very dark green (nearly olive green); black top cap, drain plug, and cask supports on an orange-brown bed; unpainted hoops. **85**
(C) 1980, light tan-colored cask; dark brown tap, fill plug, and barrel hoops; black cask supports; rectangular white signs with black eagle and shield; red and black lettering on white placed with "Ferninand" over "Pieroth GM" with "BH" under "GM", over "Weingut-Weinkellerei"; to the right of the shield, "Burg Layen" over "bei Bingen" over "am Rhein-Nahe Eck" added to each side of cask; medium brown bed. **75**
(D) 1980-86, same as (C), but with dark orange-brown cask; eagle is filled in gold, shield in blue. **40**
(E) 1987- , rectangular white signs on cask have green markings of a wine company. **CP**

4047BTO: See Chapter XII.

A very big, bright light on the 4049 Searchlight and Repair Car can be hand operated by children as well as adults. G. Ryall Collection.

4049: 1986- , four-wheel searchlight and repair car "Hilfszuge-Wagon"; has small workshop on one end with hand-operated searchlight on the other; Low-Arched LA6 roof, a rotating work platform on a tower similar to the 3530 Tower Wagon is situated in the middle of the bed. Light rotates 180 degrees and can be raised and lowered.
(A) 1986, workshop housing is unpainted medium brown; toolbox next to light is also brown; rotating platform has yellow and black hazard markings; sign on platform stanchions has "4049" below "WAGON"; prototype. **NRS**
(B) 1986- , same as (A), but workshop housing is unpainted orange with white markings. **CP**

4075: Prototype made in 1984, but no production date set. Searchlight and workshop wagon catalogued in 1984-85, 1986-87; a railway service car with open platforms, a gray-colored service compartment and guardrails; bridge with four searchlights and a scaffold; High-Arched HA3 roof with smokestack has flashing warning lamp, service compartment has internal lighting; voltage supply can be taken directly from the track or from an independent battery system; has work bench and tool details. This car was to be built on the basic 4060 Flatcar chassis in black, however, dramatic changes may be made in the actual production model if and when it is produced. **NA**

Note: This number (4075) has also been assigned to a caboose; see Chapter VII.

Cable cars typify the mountainous regions of Europe in which narrow gauge trains thrive. Set 9000S is the two-cabin electrified version of Lehmann's cable cars, named for Mount Rigi, its top accessible from one side by narrow gauge cog railway, from the other by cable cars larger than but similar to these; the summit offers a 180 degree panorama of snowcapped Alps. Earlier sets were lithographed tinware, like many of Lehmann's older toys, rather than plastic.

CABLE CARS

The Rigi cable cars came in two basic versions, both with a sliding side door; all-around glazing, three benches, foldable escape ladder, and trap door in floor. Early cars (1978-1979) are of metal construction with rather sharp corners giving them a very boxy shape and are painted red and white with black LGB letters. The more recent versions (1980 on) are of molded red plastic with white-painted detail. The body corners and edges are more rounded. The single units (i.e. 900 and 900E) were discontinued in 1986. The 9000S was first offered in 1983 and is still available though it has a limited production.

900 has a single gondola and manual hand crank.   **CP**

900E is the same as 900 with a battery-operated drive unit in plastic box.   **CP**

9000 is the same as 900 with two gondolas and four figures.   **CP**

9000E is the same as 9000 with a battery-operated drive unit with cardboard building to cover drive unit; also has tickets, ticket punch, and four figures.   **CP**

9000S is similar to 9000E with green-painted wooden-covered electric (220v) drive unit, but lacks figures and other accessories.   **150**

The metal gondola sets are valued at approximately twice the current retail value of their plastic gondola counterparts.

XI
CATALOGUES, PUBLICATIONS, VIDEOS, TRACK, and ACCESSORIES

CATALOGUES AND OTHER LITERATURE

Catalogues were generally published every two years; however, several catalogue-like brochures were printed at different intervals. Lehmann publications are high quality in material and design, their catalogues (except for the early "menus") being heavy, glossy paper, with well laid out photographs and blocks of text. As the collector market has become more cognizant, interest is growing in this somewhat neglected aspect of the line.

1968: Single-sheet flyer, first literature describing product: "Premiere 10-16 Februar 1968 auf der Internationalen Spielwarenmesse in Nürnberg! Stand 2001" German text, black and white with some green lettering and a green track plan; photos show a 2020-type steam locomotive with flaring stack and pale cab, but number "4" on cab as if 2040; 3010 and 3000 (no number listed); also the Richter children playing with those items, with what looks like a 3011, with some track; a silhouette drawing on the reverse includes a 4020 or 4021. Five of the nine photographs and five of the seven paragraphs, slightly edited, appear as page three of 1968-69 catalogue. C. Colwell Collection.
NRS

Circa 1968-69: Catalogue, eight pages, no date, and has very few items in it; prices in German. Cover depicts the 2010 Locomotive. Cover and pages are black and white and has patches of orange color throughout.
(A) In right-hand lower corner are the words "original size" in black.
100
(B) "Lehmann" in right-hand lower corner, replacement motor and other spare parts are listed in this version only. J. Hylva Collection.
300

1969-70 Catalogue cover. J. Ottley Collection.

1969-70: A 13-page color catalogue with the cover depicting an early 2010 Locomotive pulling four cars (3000, 3010, 3015, and 3020), also has the "LGB" logo and "Lehmann Gross-Bahn 1969-70" in black on front cover; rear cover depicts a 3000 Coach in blue, however this is due to the color separations and is not an unusual variation of this car. English, French, or German; 210 x 270 mm.
75

1970: A 58-page color catalogue, undated (date identified by W. Richter), with a tight overhead scene on the cover of a 2060, 2020, 4040S, 4041, 3010, 3009, 2050, and 4040E on several parallel tracks with a station and freight house between; "Lehmann" in upper right corner, "Die Welt der L.G.B." (green letters, beige logo) in lower right corner. Rear cover is a head-on shot of a 2010 pulling 3011, 3010, 3012, and 3040; beside it, a 2060G pulls a 4040S, a blue 4040A (which does not appear inside; only the gray 4040A is catalogued), and 4040E. 31 inside pages in color. 210 x 150 mm. C. Colwell Collection. **90**

1970-71: A black and white single page, folded six ways; date is not shown on cover. Cover shows 2010 pulling two freight cars, 2030 pulling one freight car, 2050 pulling two coaches, two 2060s pulling three freight cars, 2020 pulling two and one-half coaches, all from an overhead view on four sidings; rear cover depicts different sets; in German. J. Hylva Collection. **50**

1971: Four-page black and white folder showing new items and price changes for 1969-70 catalogue. New pieces listed include Locomotives 2030, 2070, etc.; in English. D. Weiler Collection. **NRS**

1971-72 Catalogue.

1971-72: A black and white single page, 885 x 420 mm unfolded, with three folds making six sheets; date is not shown; cover shows a 2060Y Diesel, a 2020 Locomotive, an early 2001 Track Inspection Car, and a 2030 Steeple-cab Electric; a young boy and girl are in the background. German or English; 210 x 296 mm folded. **40**

1971-72: "Lots of Fun w/LGB" booklet. 24 pages with 2010 Locomotive on cover. Bottom half of cover is orange, 15 x 21 cm size, early 1970s. Sort of an instruction manual printed in seven languages. J. Hylva Collection. **NRS**

1972: Orange cover supplement catalogue, lists accessories for LGB trains from companies like Mossmer, Lindberg, Fischer, Herpa, etc. J. Hylva Collection. **20**

1972-73: Similar to 1971-72 (black and white single page, 885 x 420 mm unfolded, with three folds making six sheets), but with "Auf LGB umsteigen-einsteigen-abfahren!" in green; "Programm 72-73" in green in lower right corner; LGB logo, white on green, upper right corner. Cover shows 2010 pulling into station, with people sitting on bench under a covered platform. Rear cover depicts various sets. 210 x 296 mm folded. J. Hylva and D. Weiler Collections. **40**

1972-73: A poster board folded twice with glossy finish depicting all of the 1972-73 catalogue. J. Hylva Collection. **NRS**

1973-74: Similar to 1972-73 (black and white single page with green highlights, 885 x 420 mm unfolded, with three folds making six sheets), but with date in upper right corner; "The giant Railway with the Guarantee for Great Fun" in green letters upper left corner; LGB logo, white on green, lower right. Cover shows 3080 pulling 4063 and 4066, and 2095 pulling 4062; 5065 and 5029 also shown. Printed in both English and German. Folded, 210 x 296 mm. **35**

1974: Single sheet in color; "Die Grosse Bahn für Haus und Garten" on front, with pictures of 4043, 2010, 2030, 3050, 4040E (ET), and 4042; 2030 pulling two 3011s and two 3012s on back; German text; 210 x 297 mm. B. Roth Collection. **NRS**

1974: Similar to preceding (single sheet, color, 210 x 297 mm), but with "Die Grosse Bahn Fahrt in der Kleinsten Hutte" on cover; indoor layout on back. **NRS**

1974-75 Catalogue.

1974-75: A color, single-folded page, 260 x 1775 mm unfolded, with seven vertical creases; date is shown in the lower right-hand corner of the front cover; cover depicts anterior aspects of 2070 Steam Locomotive and 2095 Diesel Locomotives; English or German; 185 x 260 mm folded. **40**

1975: Single sheet, in German, printed in black and white; 2080S and 2015 (prototype model) on front; various cars on back; 210 x 290 mm. B. Roth Collection **NRS**

1975-76: A color catalogue of twelve pages including covers, which folded in half is 185 x 260 mm; unfolded but not opened, 365 x 260 mm; opened, 725 x 260 mm. Cover shows side view of 2080; "Die Grosse Bahn. 75-76" in red with an arrow in place of the hyphen; "Das LGB- Programm" above the date in black; green shield around yellow "LGB". English and German. J. Hylva Collection. **50**

1976: New items sheet; single sheet folded; color and black and white; prototype model of 2035 shown on cover, German only. W. Gallagher Collection. **NRS**

1977: Trifold color flyer with, inside, larger than life-sized photo of 2017; on front: "Hobby, Fun and Recreation", "LGB", and collage photos; English; 310 x 650 mm. B. Roth Collection. **NRS**

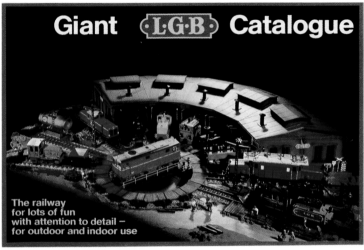

1977-78 Catalogue cover. J. Ottley Collection.

1977-78: An 18-page color catalogue with the cover depicting the same roundhouse scene utilized on the early 0020 458 x 610 mm color poster; English or German; 240 x 344 mm unopened.   **30**

1977-78 (circa): Four-page, brown matte-type brochure depicting American prototypes. Possibly issued by LGB National Sales Office, Milwaukee, Wisconsin. J. Hylva Collection.   **NRS**

1977-78: Primus Catalogue with 20872 Locomotive and 20860 Diesel on cover; yellow background; "The Super Railway" in upper left-hand corner; "PRIMUS Die Superbahn" in upper middle; "Le super-train" in upper right-hand corner; all lettering is in black; 20 pages in color; English and German. J. Hylva Collection.   **100**

1978: Black and white supplement, six pages, shows new items for 1978 like 2040, 2036 and 3600, 4040C, etc. J. Hylva Collection.   **20**

1979-80 Catalogue.

1979-80: First of the big color catalogues. Cover has two horizontal yellow stripes with the "LGB" logo and a round photograph of an 0-4-0T locomotive with the Lehmann plant in the background. 96 numbered pages plus cover pages; 210 x 302 mm.
(A) German version has a semi-glossy black cover.   **20**
(B) English version has a semi-glossy red cover.   **20**

1980: Black and white supplement, four pages; shows new items for 1980 like 2065, 2051S, 2060H (new horn location), new catenary, etc.; J. Hylva comment.   **15**

1981: Catalogue for handmade locomotives; has color pictures of each piece and a brief description of the prototype and the load capabilities and model specifications. English only.   **25**

1981-82: The Jubilee catalogue to commemorate "100 Years of Lehmann", very glossy black cover, 128 numbered pages plus cover pages.
(A) German version with "100 JAHRE" lettered in green; inside rear cover depicts scenes with well-known German personalities enjoying LGB. Page 78 shows very early prototypes of the 3080 and 3081 Coaches without markings and with unpainted roofs.   **20**
(B) English version with "100 YEARS" lettered in red on upper right of cover; inside rear cover depicts a group of Lehmann factory personnel.   **20**
(C) Same as (B), with standard production models of the 3080 and 3081 Coaches depicted on page 78; 5009 and 5010 deleted from page 105.   **10**

1982: Unnumbered — condensed catalogue in English. Spiral-bound with same cover as Main Jubilee Catalogue "100 Years of Lehmann", but containing only the summary pages: "Advantages of the LGB", "Locomotives at a Glance", and "LGB Track Range" and several pages depict Lehmann toys and Rigi Cable Cars.   **30**

1982: No number, a single 215 x 280 mm page folded three times to form a small brochure; blue front; in German.   **NRS**

1983-84: Very glossy, deep maroon-red cover; two stripes and large "LGB" logo, 160 numbered pages plus covers.
(A) German version has gold stripes on maroon red and "LGB" logo only on the front cover.   **15**
(B) English version has silver stripes on maroon red, "LGB" logo, and the words "The Big Train" all in silver on the front cover.   **15**

1984: Brochure, six pages folded twice with 2010 Locomotive on color cover. Opens up to three pages wide which shows all the LGB displayed on the floor with admiring people in the background. J. Hylva Collection.   **10**

1984-85: Same as the 1983-84 version, except the stripes are white with a green stripe in the middle with the "LGB" logo and "The Big Train" in white print.   **15**

1985: English or German versions with white engine on maroon cover with green stripe; an updated version of 1983-84 catalogue; 160 numbered pages plus cover.   **12**

0011N Catalogue Supplement introducing new items for 1985.

1985: Supplemental Catalogue 0011N; 1985 in red letters on white background with 150 red Jubilee anniversary engine on front cover; eight pages.   **5**

1986-87: Cover has photo of 2045 Electric Locomotive, back cover has aerial photograph of Lehmann factory. 112 pages. Produced in English and German. According to factory personnel, this will be the last of the bi-annual catalogues; beginning 1987 a new catalogue will be produced each year to keep up with new items.   **10**

1987: United States Early American train set brochure, cover has photograph of 2017(B) Locomotive; brochure is a single, folded sheet making four pages; not dated.   **4**

1987: Cover has photo of 2074 Spreewald Steam Locomotive with "Neuheiten 1987—Novelties 1987" in gold in upper left-hand corner of front cover; "0011 N" in black underneath; two maroon circles in upper right-hand corner; one with Lehmann trademark in white lettering; one with white LGB train with maroon-lettered "LGB" logo in center, this circle overlaps the other one; both circles have a white band around circle; 12 pages in color; English and German. J. Hylva Collection.   **3**

1987-88: Cover has photo of 2018D Locomotive with "The World of LGB" in upper left-hand corner of front cover, back cover has aerial photograph of Lehmann factory. 112 pages, English.   **10**

1988-89: A large format catalogue that is approximately 300 mm square rather than rectangular as in earlier editions. Glossy black cover with a golden circle containing a black LGB locomotive silhouette with the LGB logo. Available in German and English versions; 147 pages.

(A) German version, cover as described above with white "Die Welt der LGB" above gold logo with "20 Jahre LGB Gesamtkatalog 88/89" below logo.   **CP**

(B) English version, cover as described above with white "The World of LGB" above gold logo with "20 Years of LGB".   **CP**

001989E: Brochure listing new items; rectangular black cover similar to the 1988-89 Catalogue, but with " — New Items —/ The World Off LGB '89" (sic); 14 pages.   **CP**

OTHER PUBLICATIONS

0010: 1971- , **Depesche** magazine, a publication by the Lehmann Company about new items, articles on large scale trains, modeling, and kit bashing; originally published twice a year, now published three times a year, in German language (W. Richter comment); 21 x 30 cm; enameled paper; pages vary from issue to issue. About $12 for annual subscription, although price varies with currency fluctuations.

0010E: 1989- , **LGB Telegram** magazine. This is the English version of **Depesche**; reportedly to be published twice during 1989.   **CP**

0010M: 1971-?, miniature **Depesche** magazine; cover is subscription form. Four pages.   **10**

0011: See catalogue section.

0011N: 1985-87, a catalogue supplement which lists new LGB items. Comes in both English and German.

(A) 1985, 11-page supplement with Set 20150 on cover.   **3**

(B) 1986, no number on cover; the list of discontinued items in the 1986 full catalogue includes the number 0011N.   **3**

(C) 1987, cover depicts 2074D Locomotive, 12 pages of both English and German text.   **3**

0012: 1974-78, operating instruction manual; 36-page, seven-color booklet in several languages providing basic information on LGB. Some black and white photos, many diagrams, some track plans. Three-page listing of narrow gauge railroads in Europe. One-page listing of model railroad and fan clubs in Germany. Rear cover says "FM5-027-1977". Front cover shows price of booklet in 22 countries. One dated 7/2/76 and one dated 5/2/77. J. Hylva Collection.   **NRS**

0012: 1986- , counter book with full catalogue line.   **CP**

0014: 1978, track planning manual.   **NRS**

0021: 1979-82, parts sheet in German, black-colored cover.   **NRS**

0021EPL: 1981-87, EPL directions and use guide; in German with foreign language translations, 24 pages; size 21 x 30 cm.

(A) 1981-87, cover depicts outdoor scene with 2066 Railbus.   **12**

(B) 1988- , cover depicts railyard scene with 2096S Diesel and 2074D Steam Locomotives pulling trains.   **CP**

0023: 1979-87, manual for operating battery-powered LGB trains.
                                                                                                    3

0024: 1979- , manual for operating electric LGB trains, in German with foreign language translations; two versions; 38 pages, size 15 x 21 cm.

(A) 1979-84, small version, approximately 15 x 20 cm.   **15**

(B) 1985- , larger version, 21 x 30 cm.   **15**

0025: 1979-80, track planning book; softcover, in German.   **25**

0026: 1980-85, track planning book; hardcover, in German; format 21 x 30 cm, 260 photographs; two tables, 152 pages, 340 illustrations.
                                                                                                   16

Early Operating Instruction Manual, 0012. J. Hylva Collection.

Track Planning book, 0025.

0026N: 1985-86, LGB track planning and information book; has 192 pages with 700 photos, plans, and layout diagrams; available in German or English. **30**

0027: 1981- , **Lehmann Toys — The History of E. P. Lehmann — 1881-1981**; 220 pages; in German. **45**

0027E: 1983- , same as 0027, in English. **45**

0028: 1987- , LGB Track Plan Book; 256 pages, German text with English and French translated pages. **CP**

0028E: 1989- , same as 0028, but with English text. **CP**

0041: 1986, **Greenberg's Guide to LGB Trains**, though not published by Lehmann, it was catalogued and offered by the Company; 96 pages, first edition; English version only. **25**

0042: 1989, **Greenberg's Grosser LGB Almanach**; German version of **Greenberg's Guide to LGB Trains**, second edition. **30**

0042E: 1989, **Greenberg's Guide to LGB Trains**, second edition; English version. **30**

0088: 1988-89, LGB Model Railroad Calendar, 12 color photos of beautiful LGB layouts; German text. **CP**

0088E: 1988-89, same as 0088, but with English text. **CP**

0199: LGB full-color calendar. Not available until 1990. **NA**

VIDEOS

0030: 1986- , "The World of LGB Video", a 25-minute tour of the factory and interviews with Lehmann personnel and LGB operators; VHS, German version. **CP**

0031: 1986- , same as 0030, but in English. **CP**

0032: 1986- , same as 0030, but BETA in German. **CP**

0033: 1986- , same as 0030, but VIDEO 2000 in German. **CP**

0034: 1986- , same as 0030, but 8 mm in German. **CP**

0035: 1986- , same as 0030, but VHS in NTSC system in English. **CP**

0036: 1986- , same as 0030, but BETA in English. **CP**

NOVELTY ITEMS

0013: 1978, large glossy photograph poster depicting steeple-cab locomotive with coaches on outdoor layout. **20**

0015: 1977-87, 135 mm diameter, round sticker for autos (in German). **4**

0015E: 1983-87, same as 0015, but in English. **4**

0016: 1983-87, illuminated counter or window sign; shows locomotive and three cars; 220V; length one meter. **200**

0017/1: 1989- , LGB Slogan Stickers in German; pack of eight. **CP**

0017/1E: 1989- , LGB Slogan Stickers in English; pack of eight. **CP**

0018: 1985-87, LGB plastic bag, red, white, and green, with "LGB" logo, "LEHMANN-GROSS-BAHN" and "The Big Train" at top; will hold train set box; 60 x 72 cm.
(A) 1985, simple slot handle. **4**
(B) 1986-87, improved carrying bag for train set. **4**

0019: 1979-85, metal and baked enamel LGB lapel pin.
(A) 1979-80, red with crude "LGB" logo in black; wheels in black and white. **12**
(B) 1980-85, red, yellow, and black with well-formed "LGB" logo in yellow; 40 x 27 mm. **9**

0020: 1979-86, LGB 62 x 44 cm color poster.
(A) 1979-82, shows roundhouse scene. **20**
(B) 1983-84, shows 1981 Anniversary train with all anniversary cars. **12**
(C) 1985-86, shows 2096S Locomotive opened up to expose electronics. **10**

8001: 1987- , white T-shirt, solid red 2020 Locomotive inside a red circle with a white "LGB" logo superimposed on locomotive. 100 percent cotton, size small. **CP**

8002: 1987- , white T-shirt, same as 8001. Size medium. **CP**

8003: 1987- , white T-shirt, same as 8001. Size large. **CP**

8015: 1982-83, 1987- , LGB key ring. **CP**
(A) 1982-83, silver-colored metal with black LGB locomotive silhouette on medallion. H. Langer Collection. **7**
(B) 1987- , silver-colored metal, LGB locomotive silhouette logo on five-color medallion. Three yellow and two red five-petal flowers scattered below locomotive; circular green band with "Zuhause fahre ich mit ver LGB" (At home I travel LGB) surrounding locomotive. **CP**

8016: 1987- , triangular orange-red plastic luggage tag with black 2020 Locomotive inside a thin black circle with the "LGB" logo superimposed on the locomotive, with "FAN" in bold black sans-serif capital letters on a white triangular-shaped background. **CP**

8017: 1987- , orange heavy-duty bottle opener with a black 2020 Locomotive and an orange "LGB" logo superimposed on the locomotive. **CP**

8020: 1987- , traditional-style ceramic beer mug, with pewter lid, cream-colored with five red bands. Bands one, two, four, and five are thin. The center band is wide and has a cream-colored train printed on it. **CP**

8025: 1987- , red and white baseball-style cap, with black drawing of a 2020 Locomotive and black "LGB" logo below locomotive on a white background. **CP**

8030: 1987- , pewter wall plate with a silhouette of a 2020 Locomotive superimposed with the "LGB" logo on a textured background in the center of the plate. **CP**

8035: 1987- , walking stick, dark red, eight-ribbed umbrella, with gold-colored 2020 Locomotive inside a gold circle with a red "LGB" logo superimposed on locomotive on every other section (four), and two gold stripes near bottom of umbrella. **CP**

8036: 1989- , LGB coffee service; three pieces, red and white ceramic set commissioned from the Hutschenreuther Company of West Germany. **CP**

TRACK

In the early 1970s Lehmann manufactured track with aluminum as well as brass rail. The catalogue numbers of these track sections were basically the same; but the brass track originally had the letter "W" for weatherproof added to its number, i.e. early brass 300 mm track sections had the catalogue number "1000W". Lehmann dropped the "W" designation when they ceased production of the aluminum track about 1977-1978; to avoid confusion, the "W" designation has not been used in this book.

100: 300 mm plastic straight track. **CP**

110: 60 cm radius, plastic curved track. **CP**

120: Plastic Y-switch track. **CP**

1000: 1969- , straight track section; length 300 mm.
(A) 1971-78, aluminum rails. **20**
(B) 1974-76, chrome-plated aluminum rails. **20**
(C) 1969- , brass rails. **CP**

1000K (1000KW): 1971-82, reverse loop kit in two sections for polarity reversal; rectifying diodes concealed under simulated grade crossing; length 2 x 300 mm.
(A) 1971-78, no green dot on diode section. **30**

(B) 1979-82, has green dot on diode section.   **30**

1000/T: 1969-82, isolation track interrupts current flow to both rails of track; length 300 mm.   **NRS**

1000/U: 1971-82, isolation track interrupts current flow to both rails of track; length 300 mm.   **NRS**

1000/1: 1978- , pack of ten brass rail joiners.   **CP**

1000/2: 1978- , assortment of 100 self-tapping screws in four sizes and assorted knurled nuts.   **CP**

1000/3: 1981- , flexible sleeper bed section, pack of five; can be used as replacement or for 1.5 m track sections.   **CP**

1000/5: 1981- , 1.5 m brass rail sections.   **CP**

1001: 1974-79, 1986-87, track planning template.
(A) 1974-79, clear plastic; no section for 1400 Turntable.   **NRS**
(B) 1986-87, similar to 1001N, but in green plastic.   **20**

1001N: 1980-84, clear orange plastic track planning template which includes 1400 Turntable.   **20**

1002: 1986- , wheel guide for placing locomotives or rolling stock on track; made of orange plastic.   **CP**

1004: 1979- , brass track section; length 41 mm.   **CP**

1005: 1979- , brass track section; length 52 mm.   **CP**

1006: 1986- , 150 mm plastic adaptor track for joining regular brass track sections with the plastic track sections of the battery-operated trains.   **CP**

1007: 1984- , brass track section; length 75 mm.   **CP**

1008: 1971- , brass track section; length 82 mm.   **CP**

1009: 1979- , expandable brass track section; variable length 88-120 mm.   **CP**

1015: 1983- , brass track section; length 150 mm.   **CP**

1015K: 1983- , reverse loop kit in two sections designed for use with EPL system; length 2 x 150 mm.   **CP**

1015T: 1983- , isolation track, both rails; length 150 mm. **CP**

1015U: 1983- , isolation track, one rail; length 150 mm.   **CP**

1021: 1986- , 300 mm rack section for use with 2046 rack Electric Locomotive.   **CP**

1022: 1986- , rack section lock pieces for securing 1021 to track.
                                                                 CP

1030: 1969-85, standard terminal track buffer (not illuminated).   **4**

1031: 1981- , same as 1030, but with illuminated warning light; buffer stop with "stop" (dead-end) signal.   **CP**

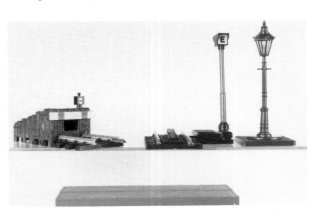

Illuminated track-end Buffer 1031, at left, simulates a sturdy construction of timbers filled with gravel. To its right, electrically-operated Uncoupler 1056, with indicator light so the operator may read the ramp position from a distance. At far right is Light 5050, after an old-fashioned prototype; and in front, a section of Platform 5034, which fits between and beside straight tracks for pedestrian crossing.

1050: 1969-82, brass manual uncoupling track; length 300 mm. **16**

1052: 1971- , standard permanent uncoupler.
(A) 1971-80, larger size, red-colored parts; coil spring, button action.
                                                                 NRS
(B) 1981- , slightly slimmer, black-colored parts; leaf spring, lever action.   **CP**

1055: 1974-83, remote electromagnetic uncoupler; length 300 mm.
                                                                 35

1056: 1984- , electromagnetic uncoupler similar to 1055, but suited for use with EPL equipment.
(A) 1984-85, length 300 mm.   **35**
(B) 1985- , length 150 mm.   **CP**

1060: Brass track section; 600 mm.   **CP**

1100: 1969- , 120 cm diameter curved 30 degree track section.
(A) 1971-78, aluminum rails.   **20**
(B) 1969- , brass rails.   **CP**

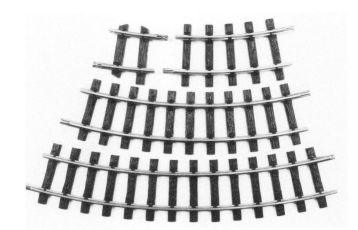

1102, 1100, and 1500 Track Sections.

1102: 1984- , half curved brass track.   **CP**

1104: 1981- , short curved 7.5 degree brass make-up track section.
                                                                 CP

1150: 1969- , track clips for securing track on temporary layouts; set of 28.   **CP**

1200: 1969-82, right-hand manual switch track; same radius as 1100 Curved Track.
(A) 1969-75, early housing with pivoting throw arm; attached directly to track; switch machine not removable.   **10**
(B) 1976-82, later housing with sliding actuating arm.   **20**

1200N: 1983- , right-hand electric switch track.
(A) 1983-85, same as 1200, but with latest actuating box, which is smaller than those of previous units and square-shaped; length 300 mm.   **CP**
(B) 1985- , same as (A), but with unjointed point rails, continuous from plastic frog to point blade, pivoted at the frog itself, rather than halfway from frog to blade as (A) is.   **CP**

1201: 1983- , EPL points drive mechanism.   **CP**

1203: 1983- , additional switch for EPL drive mechanism; used in conjunction with 1201.   **CP**

1204: 1983- , rotatable switch lantern; for use with 1201. **CP**

1205: 1971-82, right-hand, remote switch track with 1206 Electromagnetic Switching Actuator; same radius as 1100.   **26**

1205N: 1983- , left-hand remote switch track.
(A) 1983-85, same as 1205, but with 1201 EPL Switch Drive Mechanism; length 300 mm.   **CP**

(B) 1985- , same as (A), but with unjointed point rails, continuous from plastic frog to point blade, pivoted at the frog itself, rather than halfway from frog to blade as (A) is.   **CP**

1206: 1974-82, early electromagnetic switch actuator.   **8**

1207: 1974-82, rotatable switch lantern for use with 1206; non-illuminated.   **3**

1208: 1981-82, electric drive mechanism for actuating switches. This unit was rarely used and may have only been used on the 1235 Three-way Switch.   **NRS**

1209: 1982-85, electric drive motor and mechanism for 1225 Slip Switch.   **25**

1210: 1969-82, left-hand manual switch track; same radius as 1100 curved track; similar to 1200(A).

(A) 1969-75, early housing with pivoting throw arm.   **NRS**

(B) 1976-82, later housing with sliding actuating arm.   **20**

1210N: 1983- , left-hand manual switch track.

(A) 1983-85, same as 1210, but with latest actuating box which is smaller than those of previous units and square-shaped; length 300 mm.   **CP**

(B) 1985- , same as (A), but with unjointed point rails, continuous from plastic frog to point blade, pivoted at the frog itself, rather than halfway from frog to blade as (A) is.   **CP**

1211: 1981-82, rotatable illuminated switch lantern for use with 1206.   **6**

1215: 1971-82, left-hand, remote switch track with 1206 Electromagnetic Switching Actuator.   **26**

1215N: 1983- , left-hand remote switch track.

(A) 1983-85, same as 1215, but with 1201 EPL Switch Mechanism; length 300 mm.   **CP**

(B) 1985- , same as (A), but with unjointed switch rails, continuous from plastic frog to switch blade, pivoted at the frog itself, rather than halfway from frog to blade as (A) is.   **CP**

1225: 1979-85, 22.5 degree double-slip switch driven by electric motor mechanism 1209; length 2 x 375 mm.   **65**

1226: 1985- , double-slip switch with two electromagnetic operating mechanisms; for use with 22.5 degree curves (1600 Curved Track); total length 375 mm.   **CP**

1235: 1980-??, three-way switch driven by two separate drive mechanisms; has same radius as 1600 curved track.

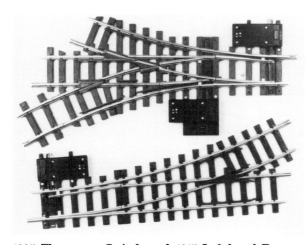

1235 Three-way Switch and 1615 Left-hand Remote Switch Track.

(A) 1981-??, has 1208 Electric Drive Mechanisms.   **NRS**

(B) 1980-82, has 1206 Electromagnetic Switch Actuator.   **65**

1235N: 1983-85, same as 1235, but with 1201 EPL Switch Drive Mechanism.   **65**

1236: 1985- , three-way switch with two electromagnetic operating mechanisms for use with 30 degree curved track (1100 curved track); total length 375 mm.   **CP**

1300: 1971- , 30 degree brass crossing track; length 300 and 341 mm.   **CP**

1320: 1982- , 22.5 degree brass crossing track; length 2 x 375 mm.   **CP**

1225 Double-Slip Switch and 1320 Crossing.

1400: 1979- , manual turntable with 65 cm diameter; handmade, not weather proof.   **CP**

1500: 1971- , 155 cm diameter curved 30 degree brass track.   **CP**

1600: 1975, 235 cm diameter curved 22.5 degree brass track.   **CP**

1605: 1975-85, right-hand, remote switch track with the same radius as the 1600 Curved Track; 1206 Electronic Switch Actuator.   **35**

1605N: 1983- , same as 1605, but with 1201 EPL Points Drive Mechanism.   **CP**

1615: 1975-82, left-hand version of the 1605.   **35**

1615N: 1983- , left-hand version of 1605N; length 440 mm.   **CP**

1700: 1983- , contact switch for automatic switching operations; actuated by 1701 Switching Magnet. The first version of this unit is depicted in the 1981-82 catalogue. It is an "H"-shaped mechanism with a brass shoe and a single-wire version which was never produced. The unit which finally saw production is shown in the 1983-84 and more recent catalogues and is more elongated with two small boxes: one for the switch mechanism and one for the connecting wires.   **CP**

1701: 1983- , switching magnet for attaching on the bottom of the locomotives to automatically actuate 1700 Contact Switch.   **CP**

1705: 1988- , magnetic sound activator switch for sound locomotives.   **CP**

1900: 1981-85, toporama layout (242 x 395 cm).   **600**

2060/3: 1978- , contact strip for triggering horn on 2051S, 2060H, and 2096S Diesel Locomotives, and whistle and bell on 2080S Locomotive; length 300 mm.   **CP**

2060H/3: 1975-78, early number for 2060/3 Contact Strip.   **CP**

10800: 1978, 300 mm long straight track section for Primus.   **CP**

11800: 1978, curved track section for Primus.   **CP**

12800: 1978, manual right-hand switch track for Primus.   **28**

12810: 1978, manual left-hand switch track for Primus.   **28**

20901: 1977- , buffers track pack set; includes six 1000s, one 1100, one 1200 or 1200N, one 1030.   **CP**

20902: 1979- , station track pack set; includes nine 1000s, two 1100s, one 1200 or 1200N, one 1210 or 1210N.   **CP**

50800: 1978, Primus 220-volt transformer.   **15**

208901: 1978, Primus track extension pack.   CP
208902: 1978, Primus track extension pack.   CP

ACCESSORIES

0090: 1971- , reversing unit for display.
(A) 1971-79, early unit, length 240 cm.   **200**
(B) 1980- , late model, length 120 cm.   CP
130: Train direction controller for battery-powered locomotives. CP
Note: When locomotive wheels were changed from "solid" wheels with plastic "disks" to metal rims with plastic centers, the crank pin was changed from a machine screw to a self-tapping sheet metal-type screw. Thus new wheels cannot be used as replacements for engines with solid wheels unless the crank pin screws are replaced as well.
2010/1: Four-piece set of red solid locomotive drive wheels, with non-skid tire.   CP
2010/2: One set of coupling with metal spring and coupling bracket for all twin-axle locomotives.   CP
2010/3: Standard smokestack.   CP
2010/4: Ten spare non-skid tires.   CP
2010/5: Chassis for 2010, 2020, and 2040 Locomotives.   CP
2010/7: One set of standard locomotive couplings with plastic spring and coupling bracket.   CP
2010/27: Ten locomotive buffers, new version with rounded corners and white outlining.   CP
2015/1: Four-piece set of red-spoked locomotive drive wheels with non-skid tire.   CP
2015/3: Smokestack with spark arrestor.   CP
2015/5: Chassis for 2015 Locomotive.   CP
2015/6: 1975- , two-axle powered black tender; same as unit sold with 2015D; became available as a separate item from 1980 until 1985; not available separately after 1985.
(A) 1975, black body with coal load; red chassis; unpowered; not sold separately.   **NSS**
(B) 1976, black body, brown coal load; powered; not sold separately.   **NSS**
(C) 1977-78, medium green body, black coal load; powered; not sold separately.   **NSS**
(D) 1979- , similar to (C), but with black body; some early versions lack KPEV eagle emblem.   CP
2017/1: Four-piece set of black-spoked locomotive drive wheels with traction tire.   CP
2017/5: Chassis for 2015 Locomotive.   CP
2017/6: 1975- , two-axle, powered green tender; same unit sold with 2017D; became available as a separate item in 1980.
(A) 1975-76, medium green body with yellow stripes; black and yellow "LGB" logo; black chassis; unpowered, sold only with 2017. **NSS**
(B) 1977- , same as (A), but powered; sold with 2017 and 2017D; also sold separately from 1980-85.   CP
2018/1: Locomotive driving wheels, 46 mm diameter, for 2018D. CP
2018/4: Traction tires, 46 mm.   CP
2018/5: Pilot truck for 2018.   CP
2019/2: 1989- , operating knuckle coupler that can be attached to the talgo of LGB cars manufactured from 1980 to date.   CP
2030/1: Four-piece set of black solid locomotive drive wheels with non-skid tire.   CP
2030/3: Red pantograph for 2030 E-Lok Electric Locomotive, 2035 Trolley, or early 2040 Crocodiles.   CP
2030/5: Motor block without frame for newer 2030 and 2033 Electric Locomotives, and 2035 and 2036 Trolleys.   CP
2035/1: Four-piece set of black solid locomotive drive wheels with non-skid tire.   CP

2036/3: Electric current collector bow for 2036 Trolley. CP
2040/1: Four-piece set of black-spoked locomotive drive wheels, with non-skid tire.   CP
2040/2: One set of coupling with plastic spring and pin. CP
2040/3: Silver pantograph for 2040 and 2045 Electric Locomotives.   CP
2040/5: Set of motor bogies.   CP
2040/7: One set of standard locomotive couplings with plastic spring and coupling brackets for all rolling stock.   CP
2040/8: Set of 17 insulators, large and small, for 2040 Electric; came in brown, green, or red.   CP
2040/9: Eight pieces of plastic springs for universal coupling. CP
2040/11: A new lighting module for 2040 Crocodile Locomotive, can be installed in older versions.   CP
2051/5: One set of motor bogies for 2051 and 2051S.   CP
2060/5: Motor block without frame for 2050, 2060, 2060H, 2017 Tender.   CP
2065/1: Four-piece set of late model black solid locomotive drive wheels, without non-skid tire.   CP
2065/2: Two steering axle gears.   CP
2070/0-N: Locomotive truck with lead for 2071D and 2073D; trailing. CP
2070/1: Six-piece set of red-spoked locomotive drive wheels, with non-skid tire.   CP
2070/2: One set of coupling with metal spring and coupling bracket for 2071D and 2073D.   CP
2070/3: Smokestack with spark arrestor.   CP
2070/5: Chassis, complete with linkage, for 2071D and 2073D. CP
2070/7: One set of standard locomotive couplings with plastic spring and coupling bracket for 2071D and 2073D.   CP
2072/3: Standard smokestack.   CP
2075/5: Chassis, complete with linkage, for 2075.   CP
2080/0-N: Locomotive trailing truck with electrical pickup for 2080D and 2080S.   CP
2080/0-V: Locomotive leading truck for 2080D and 2080S. CP
2080/1: Six-piece set of red-spoked locomotive drive wheels, with non-skid tire.   CP
2080/2: One set of coupling with metal spring and coupling bracket for 2080D and 2080S.   CP
2080/3: Smokestack insert for early 2080D or 2080S.   **15**
2080/5: Chassis, complete with linkage, for 2080D.   CP
2085/1: Six-piece set of red-spoked locomotive drive wheels, with non-skid tire.   CP
2085/3: Smokestack insert; 5 volt for 2018D, 2076D, 2080D, 2080S, and 2085D.   CP
2085/5: One set of Mallet motor bogies, with linkage for 2085D. CP
2090/1: Four-piece set of red-spoked locomotive drive wheels, with non-skid tire.   CP
2090/5: Motor block, without frame, with coupling rods, for 2090 and 2090N.   CP
2090/5: One set of motor bogies, with coupling rods and hall-type crank, for 2095.   CP
2100: Replacement motor for grinders, one spur-gear on motor; last catalogued in 1974-75.   **NRS**
2110: Four current pickup carbon brushes.   CP
2117-6: 1989- , tender with four wheels, painted in Russian Iron color for use with 2117 Locomotives; motorized with rear lighting and coach light plug receptacles. Also see 2015/6 and 2017/6.   CP
2200: Universal DC motor worm-drive with ball bearings for most railcars.   CP

2200/6: Gear set for all two- and three-axle motor blocks, except 2001 Track Car. **CP**

2204: DC motor for 2018D and 2045 Locomotives. **CP**

2206: DC motor for 2065 Streetcar and 2066 Wismar Bus. **CP**

2210: Two sliding contacts (pickup shoes) for all locomotives that came with such contacts or pickup skates except 2040. **CP**

2214: Two sliding contacts for 2040 only. **CP**

2218: Two sliding contacts for 2018D and 2045 Locomotives. **CP**

2300: Replacement motor with ball bearings for 2001 Track Car. **CP**

3000/1: Two wheel sets with spoked wheels. **CP**

3000/2: Two wheel bearings for all twin-axle passenger coaches and goods wagons. **CP**

3000/3: Two bogies for 3061, 3062, 3063, and 3064 Coaches. **CP**

3000/9: Metalized door handle set. **CP**

3019/1: Two metal, solid-wheel sets. **CP**

3019/2: Two metal, spoke-wheel sets. **CP**

3019/3: Two sets electrical contacts for additional coach lighting. **CP**

3030: 1973- , interior coach lighting; earliest bulbs were 4-6 volt, for use with batteries, then 12-14 volt, now 18 volt. **CP**

3031: 1983- , taillighting set. **CP**

3070/2: Two bogies for 3070 and 3071 Coaches. **CP**

3080/2: Two bogies for 3080 and 3081 Coaches. **CP**

4000/1: Two wheel sets with disc wheels. **CP**

4000/2: Two bogies for all four-axle goods wagons. **CP**

5000: 1978- , 220v, variable transformer; 30 volt amps. **15**

5000/110: Same as 5000 for 110v service. **15**

5001: 1971-73, 110v, 1 amp. transformer. **NRS**

5001: 1976- , LGB smoke and cleaning fluid in 1/4 L container with fill nozzle. **CP**

5001/9: 1986- , lubrication and cleaning needle pen, for reaching small holes or tight spots in need of oil. **CP**

5002: 1971-73, 220v, 1 amp. transformer. **NRS**

5002: 1983- , five-piece tool set consisting of two screwdrivers, two nut drivers, and a wire stripper. **CP**

5003: 1971-82, 220v, 1 amp. variable transformer. **NRS**

5003/110: 1971-82, same as 5003 in 110v. **NRS**

5003/110: 1985- , new USA version in gray plastic; sold separately and with 1985-87 sets. **CP**

5004: 1969- , track cleaning block with 20 grade sandpaper. **5**

5005: 1971- , automatic rail cleaning unit for attachment to 300 mm cars. Improved in 1986 by replacing sandpaper pieces with pieces of abrasive sponge. **CP**

5006: 1981- , 220v, 2 amp. transformer for use with 5007 Speed Controller. **NRS**

5006/110v: 1986, 110v, same as 5006. Catalogued but never produced. **NA**

5007: 1984- , electronic speed controller with cruise-control, brake, accelerator, etc.; can be used on AC or DC transformers. **65**

5008: 1971-80, high performance 220v, 2 amp. transformer for use with 5012 Speed Controller. **NRS**

5009: 1971, electronic cockpit control with transformer, 220v, 2 amp. **NRS**

5009: 1986- , power booster for power packs; will double amperage. **CP**

5010: 1969-72, speed controller with brown protective housing, black roof. **NRS**

5012: 1971-82, outdoor speed controller with similar housing as 5010, but in green; carries up to 1.5 amps. **45**

5012/1: 1988- , speed control replacement mechanism for 5012. **CP**

5012N: 1983- , speed controller in signal box. **CP**

5013: 1983- , double-strand roll of wire, orange and white; length 20 m; twin-core lead. **CP**

5013/1: 1983- , wire terminal plugs for crimping on wire ends; pack of 50. **CP**

5014: 1983- , double-strand roll of wire, black and white; length 20 cm; twin-core lead. **CP**

5015: 1979-85, cable to link transformer to speed controller; length 500 cm; connecting and extension cable with terminals. **12**

5015/1: 1979-87, electrical eyelet connectors for use on threaded poles; pack of ten. **6**

5016: 1969- , cable with clamp lugs linking speed controller and transformer to track; early versions have small all-metal track clamps, while later versions have larger plastic track clamps with metal lining and bolt. Although the newer clamp is catalogued separately as item 1600 as early as 1979-80, catalogue pictures of 5016 continue to show the older metal lugs until 1985. Connecting lead, length 150 cm.
(A) 1969-79, with older all-metal lugs. **NRS**
(B) 1980- , with newer plastic mounted clamps and thumbscrews. **CP**

5016/1: 1979- , two track terminals for clamping electrical feed wires to track, without wires; originally these were small all-metal pieces attached to lead wires and were never available as separate pieces; those that are sold separately have large plastic bodies with metal lining and screws. **CP**

5016/5000: 1981-86, wire lead with static suppressor, heavy duty; length 150 cm. **12**

5016/5000N: 1977-78, early version of 5016/5000; length 150 cm. **NRS**

5016/5003: 1977-82, high performance cable with static suppressor; length 150 cm; heavy-duty connecting cable. **12**

5016/5012: 1977-85, high performance cable with static suppressor; length 150 cm; heavy-duty connecting cable. **12**

5017: 1971-85, cable linking 5075 Control Box to remote switch track. **6**

5018: 1971-86, similar to 5017 with double-strand wire; control box cable, length 200 cm. **8**

5019: 1973-85, single-strand cable linking 5080 Control Box to transformer; control box cable 200 cm. **8**

5020: 1973-85, similar to 5019, but links control box to track. **8**

5021: 1973-86, single-strand cable linking track to track; jumper lead, length 300 cm. **8**

5022: 1979- , roll of single-strand gray wire; single-core lead; length 40 m. **CP**

5023: 1981- , roll of double-strand wire, blue and red; twin-core lead; length 20 m. **CP**

5024: 1981-85, roll of triple-strand wire, green, white, and yellow; three-core lead; length 20 m. **12**

5025: 1974- , wheel stop blocks for rails; pack of 12. **CP**

5026: 1974- , yellow plastic rail joiners for isolation, pack of four; rail isolating clips. **CP**

5027: 1985- , circus animals and trainer; includes seven standing figures: chimpanzee, lion, elephant, camel, rhinocerous, polar bear, and a trainer wearing a red turban and blue vest. **CP**

5028: 1988- , four seated figures of American "Old West", includes child, woman, gentleman, and farmer; also sleeping dog and travel case. **CP**

5029: 1973-82, electromagnetic semaphore signal with lighting. **30**

5029: 1986- , baggage and crates. **CP**

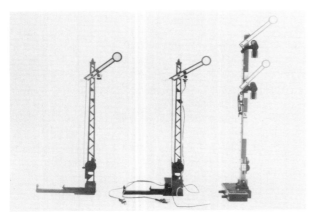

The two older signals, 5030 manual at left and 5029, lighted with electric throw, in center; both have the original snap-on base for attaching to track rather than the later slide-on piece, and both are in the "proceed" position. At right is signal 5094, with wires concealed in mast; its lights show green over yellow in the "proceed" position which, like the two arms, means proceed slowly. When the arms move to "stop" they rotate in opposite directions, so that one aligns invisibly with the mast and the other drops to horizontal. The "stop" signal thus is the same as for a one-arm signal, rather than confusingly different; both lights then show red.

5030: 1971-87, same as 5029 signal, but manual control. Early version has friction snap to track but later issues had less fragile movable snap lock.   **40**

5030/1: 1971-87, replacement arm for Prussian semaphore.   **8**

5031: 1983- , set of 27 different subsidiary signals.   **NRS**

5031/1: 1973-87, replacement arm for Bavarian semaphore.   **8**

5032: 1973- , warning signs; set of 16.   **CP**

5033: 1977-78, two tram stop posts.   **NRS**

5033: 1983- , tram stop set; eight pieces.   **CP**

5034: 1979- , street level station platform; 12 pieces consisting of eight broad and four narrow.   **CP**

5035: 1973- , telephone pole with no supports, used on straight track; telephone poles are not necessarily designed to run along side of track.   **NRS**

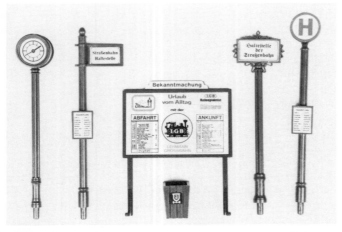

The four signs of Tram Stop Set 5033 may represent different historical periods, and presumably should not be mounted on the same platform.

5036: 1973- , telephone pole with single side support; used on curves.   **CP**

5038: 1979- , advertising column.
(A) 1979- , outdoor advertising pillar with various period and modern posters.   **CP**
(B) 1986, red advertising column, with decal applied. Decal proclaims LGB open house, July 12, 1986.   **30**

5039: 1988- , six seated figures, includes man reading LGB catalogue, mother and daughter, young couple hugging, and backpacker.   **CP**

Three sets of people are hand-painted in the Nuremberg area as a cottage industry. Over the years, colors have changed somewhat. From left to right: TOP SHELF: 5040 Station Figures, including two passengers and two trainmen, one with ticket bag and the other with train signal on a movable arm; and 5042 Seated Passengers. CENTER SHELF: 5043, more Station Figures, including a porter, a paper vendor, a track worker, and an oiler; and 5044, more Station Figures, including a passenger with poodle, a nurse, a porter with cart of bags, and a track worker. BOTTOM SHELF: 5045, more Station Figures, including a waiter, a sandwich vendor, a trainman with lantern, and an engineer with wrench; and 5047, four Seated Figures, including a hobo, a teenager, and a black couple.

5040: 1969- , four station figures, Set I: station master with signal disc, conductor, man and woman passengers.
(A) 1969-73, man is wearing hat and woman is carrying umbrella.   **NRS**
(B) 1974- , man not wearing hat and woman is carrying suitcases.   **CP**

5041: 1969- , six figures in traditional dress of the Black Forest.   **CP**

5042: 1969- , four seated figures in business and traditional dress.
(A) 1969-73, two men in Alpine attire, identical except one with black vest, gray hat and one with green vest and hat, and two women, identical except one with red dress and one with blue dress.   **NRS**
(B) 1974- , two different couples, one woman in blue dress and one man in Alpine attire with black vest, gray hat; new couple added and introduced as 2035/3500 Trolley Passengers.   **CP**

5043: 1971- , four-figure station personnel set: engine oiler, porter, newspaper man, and track workman.   **CP**

5044: 1973- , four station figures, Set II: porter with hand-cart, Red Cross worker, waving girl with dog, and track worker with shovel.   **CP**

5045: 1971-74, battery-operated signal baton as used by station master.   **75**

5045: 1977- , four station figures, Set III: engine fitter with wrench, conductor with lamp, waiter, and Bratwurst vendor.   **CP**

5046: 1979- , six-figure tourist group: two hikers with backpacks, man with camera, three skiers.   **CP**

5047: 1980- , four seated figures, Set I: black couple, teenager, hobo.   **CP**

5048: 1980- , four standing passengers; includes man and woman greeting each other, motorcyclist with helmet, woman with moped cycle.   **CP**

5049: 1985- , United States figures of the 19th century; includes six standing figures: well-dressed traveling couple, sheriff, hobo, railroad conductor, and telegraph operator.   **CP**

5050: 1969- , station lamp; height 210 mm.   **CP**

5050/1: 1975- , universal screw-in replacement bulbs; set of 25; yellow lens.   **CP**

5050/2: 1983- , two bulb sockets and wire lead.   **CP**

5051/1: 1981- , white plug-in micro bulbs for locomotives and cars; set of ten.   **CP**

5051/2: 1981- , same as 5051/1, but in red.   **CP**

5052: 1983- , illuminated warning light for terminal track buffers.   **CP**

5055: 1984- , single-arm station lamp with shade and bulb; height 335 mm.   **CP**

5056: 1984- , double-arm station lamp with shades and bulbs; height 335 mm.   **CP**

5060: 1969- , railway trestle bridge; length 450 mm.   **CP**

Very large 5061 Bridge. G. Ryall Collection.

5061: 1986- , 1200 Trestle Bridge (outside height 300 mm, inside height 224 mm); comes with supports to provide track with gradual incline.   **CP**

5061/1: 1988- , supports for 5061 Girder Bridge for expandable trestle set; two pieces.   **CP**

5061/2: Single-tier trestle piece for expandable trestle set.   **CP**

5061/3: Triple-tier trestle piece for expandable trestle set.   **CP**

Railroad Crossing 5065 includes road grading to fit over the track, which sits on spring levers that lower the gates when depressed by the weight of a passing train.

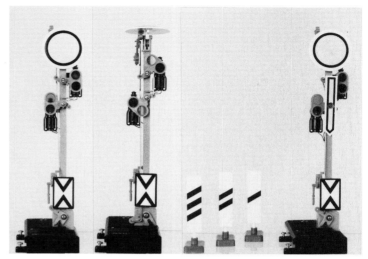

Pictured from left to right: Distant Signal; the same distant signal, with disk up; three "signal ahead" boards that come with each signal; and 5093 Distant Signal with rotating arrow.

5061/4: Trestle cap with slot to secure crosstie for expandable trestle set.   **CP**

5065: 1973- , level crossing barrier with mechanical arms; length 250 mm; width 310 mm.   **CP**

5070: 1969-82, multi-pole wiring terminal plate; distributor strip.
(A) 1969-76, gray plate with two poles.   **NRS**
(B) 1977-80, yellow plate with three poles.   **NRS**
(C) 1981-82, gray plate with three poles.   **3**

5071: 1979- , track side cable holders; pack of five.   **CP**

5072: 1983- , two-pole wiring terminal block; distribution box.   **CP**

5073: 1983- , twelve-pole wiring terminal block; connecting block.   **CP**

5075: 1971-82, switch control box for operating track switches and other electromagnetic mechanisms.   **25**

5075N: 1983- , same as 5075, for use with EPL mechanisms.   **CP**

5075/1: 1973- , 5075 or 5075N decal sheet of control box signs.   **CP**

5080: 1981-82, control box with protective lid for lights and other connect/disconnect mechanisms.   **25**

5080N: 1983- , same as 5080, for use with EPL mechanisms.   **CP**

5080/1: 1971- , 5080 or 5080N decal sheet of control box signs.   **CP**

5090: 1981-88, electromagnetic mechanism for actuating semaphore signals.   **22**

5091: 1981- , distant warning signal with movable signal disc; light changes from yellow to green; height 230 mm.   **CP**

5092: 1981- , home stop signal with single arm and light change; height 350 mm.   **CP**

5093: 1981-87, two-form distant warning signal with fixed disc, movable arm, and light change; height 230 mm. Discontinued in 1987.   **48**

5094: 1983- , two-form home stop signal with two arms and double lights, height 350 mm.   **CP**

5127: 1989- , Longhorn cattle set (three pieces).   **CP**

5143: 1989- , USA railroad and track personnel (six figures).   **CP**

CATENARY SYSTEM

6000: 1971-85, catenary mast; early masts only snapped to track (the catch often broke); later masts have a movable snap lock.   **15**

6000/2: 1971-85, catenary mast support arm; mast bracket arm.   **8**

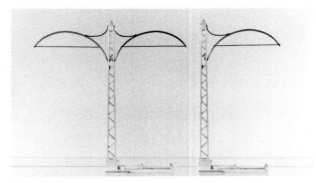

Catenary support 6000 can be fitted with single or double arms to hold overhead wires which can function as electric feeds through engine pantographs, making independent control of two trains possible; one rail of track is common to both control circuits. Models of electric engines have a switch for selection of overhead, rather than track, power.

6001: 1971-85, catenary mast connection; feeder mast, similar to 6000.   **18**

6009: 1979-85, catenary wires to change direction of current collector bow; pack of two.   **6**

6010: 1971-85, catenary wire for 1000 track section; length 300 mm.   **10**

6011: 1971-85, catenary wire for 1100 track section; length 315 mm.   **10**

6015: 1979-85, catenary wire for 1500 track section; length 400 mm.   **10**

6016: 1979-85, catenary wire for 1600 track section; length 470 mm.   **10**

6060: 1979-85, catenary wire for 1060 track section; length 600 mm.   **10**

6100: 1981-85, aluminum catenary mast; maximum height 365 mm.   **25**

6100/2: 1981-85, contact wire support arms.   **8**

6100/4: 1981-85, metal connectors for catenary (pack of 12); these are sold separately as well as in boxed sets.   **8**

6100/5: 1981-85, plastic connectors for catenary (pack of 12); these are sold separately as well as in boxed sets.   **6**

6101: 1981-85, contact wire support arm for catenary; cable length 1 m each.   **6**

6102: 1981-85, gantry supports for catenary, pack of three.   **5**

6160: 1981-85, 12-piece contact wire kit with 600 mm wire for catenary.   **10**

6190: 1981-85, 12-piece contact wire kit with 900 mm wire for catenary.   **10**

6200: 1988- , catenary pole made of aluminum for use with catenary wiring with support cable and hangers (6201 and 6202, etc.); replaces 6100.   **CP**

6201: 1987- , catenary wire set, 12 pieces, 680 mm long; replaces 6106.   **CP**

6202: 1987- , support wires and hangers for 6201 wires; 12 pieces.   **CP**

6204: 1987- , insulated wire snaps for joining 6201 wires; 12 pieces.   **CP**

6300: 1987- , tilting catenary posts for inclines, to operate 2046 Electric Cog Locomotive.   **CP**

6400: 1988- , single track catenary pole for making 6400 or 6401 masts dual track catenary.   **CP**

6400/2: 1988- , metal catenary arm; replaces 6000/2.   **CP**

6401: 1988- , catenary pole for single track with electrical lead; 305 mm high. Replaces 6001.   **CP**

XII
NON-FACTORY PRODUCTION

Items described in this chapter were either modified in some way after they left the Lehmann factory, or are unusual items whose status is questionable since their manufacture cannot be confirmed by Lehmann. The most common changes to equipment were new paint or the addition of decals. Some changes were undertaken by American dealers or distributors who contracted with independent companies (as in the case of the 4070NC), some by European manufacturers, or they were handled by a private party (as in the case of BTO convention cars). Though it is sometimes difficult to know where to draw the line between one-of-a-kind and other non-factory finished items, this chapter is generally devoted to those pieces that were mass-produced and have either become popular with collectors or have some historical value. Listed catalogue numbers may or may not be "official."

Collectors should be forewarned that non-factory-finished items are in a realm of their own and should be considered borderline collectibles at best. Exercise caution when purchasing non-factory collectibles that have little or no historical import. Also, be aware that some items have not only been modified after they left the factory, but they have been passed off as unusual factory "mistakes" and have sold for considerably more money than their more common, authentic counterparts. Caveat emptor or "let the buyer beware" is an important collector rule!

TRAIN SETS

1980BTO: Raffle set, custom-painted for LGB Model Railroad Club's Second Anniversary (not painted by Lehmann); consists of 2095 Diesel Locomotive painted orange with black stripe and "LGB" on sides; one green 3062 Coach converted to an observation car, and two 3063 Coaches also with body painted orange with black stripe; black roofs

and chassis. The set was raffled in a suitcase-like box with a handle and foam-cushioned pockets for protection. J. Hylva Collection.

NRS

20515: 1984, this is a non-factory set put together by a distributor in California. The only consistent item in the set was a 2020(E) Locomotive supplied with a cowcatcher (from the 2017 Locomotive) to be attached by the customer; the cars for the set could be chosen by the customer on the basis of 300 mm rolling stock that would fit in the box. The 20515 label on the box was printed separately and glued on over the factory-printed number.

NRS

20528: 1985, uncatalogued, "150 Jahre Deutsche Eisenbahnen", Modelleisenbahn Schweiger (Schweiger Model Train Shop) anniversary passenger set. The version listed in Chapter I (with gold boiler front) is the only one authenticated by the Lehmann factory.

1980BTO Raffle Set. J. Hylva Collection.

A collection of special livery cars prepared for participants in the annual conventions of the American LGB Club, publisher of the "B.T.O. Newsletter." "B.T.O." stands for "Big Train Operator's." The club was organized by Al Lentz, who originated the idea of these post-factory, special occasion liveries. Since typically no more than 100 of each car were run, they are rare. TOP SHELF: 4040BTO (75 issued) and 4011BTO. SECOND SHELF: 4070BTO (100). THIRD SHELF: 4003BTO (about 50, but only six for Chateau Louise because of a site change) and 3063BTO (75). BOTTOM SHELF: 4065BTO and 3080BTO (100). Reader comments requested on the number of 4011BTOs and 4065BTOs produced.

(A) 2020SB Locomotive has silver-painted boiler front; other aspects of set are the same as in Chapter I.   450
(B) 2020SG Locomotive with black boiler front that matches the rest of boiler.   475

20531A: 1985, uncatalogued, Abele Company limited edition train set; includes 2010D(F) Locomotive and two silver 4003A Container Cars; 25 sets produced.   475

20531B: 1985, uncatalogued, Breuninger Company limited edition train set; includes 2010D(F) Locomotive and two chocolate brown 4003B Container Cars; 100 sets produced. **475**

20531CS: 1985, uncatalogued, Capri-Sonne limited edition train set; includes 2010D(F) Locomotive and two royal blue 4003CS Container Cars; 100 sets produced. **475**

20531DV: 1985, uncatalogued, Dauth Company limited edition train set; includes 2010D(F) Locomotive and two silver 4003DV Container Cars; 25 sets produced. **500**

20531K: 1985, uncatalogued, Kurtz Company (of Stuttgart, West Germany) limited edition train set; includes 2010D(F) Locomotive and two yellow 4003K Container Cars; 75 sets produced. **485**

20531KT: 1985, uncatalogued, Kenner Trinken Wurtemberger limited edition train set; includes a 2010D(G) Locomotive and two silver 4003KT Container Cars; 100 sets produced. **475**

20531L: 1985, uncatalogued, Lindau limited edition train set; includes 2010D(F) Locomotive and two silver 4003L Container Cars; 25 sets produced. **500**

20531MC: 1985, uncatalogued, Modellbahn-Center (Schuler Company) limited edition train set; includes 2010D(F) Locomotive and two royal blue 4003MC Container Cars; 60 sets produced. **485**

20531P: 1985, uncatalogued, Panne Company limited edition train set; includes 2010D(F) Locomotive and two silver 4003 Container Cars; 25 sets produced. **500**

20531S: 1985, uncatalogued, Schinacher Company limited edition train set; includes 2010D(F) Locomotive and two silver 4003S Container Cars; 50 sets produced. **485**

20531SF: 1985, uncatalogued, Schnabel Company limited edition train set; includes 2010D(F) Locomotive and two silver 4003SF Container Cars; 25 sets produced. **500**

20531SLM: 1986, uncatalogued, SLM Company train set; includes 2010D(F) Locomotive and two silver 4003SLM Container Cars. **450**

20531TS: 1985, uncatalogued, Sindel Company limited edition train set; includes 2010D(F) Locomotive and two silver 4003TS Container Cars; 75 sets produced. **475**

20531Z: 1985, uncatalogued, Zinthafner Company limited edition train set; includes 2010D(F) Locomotive and two silver 4003Z Container Cars; 50 sets produced. **485**

21988N: 1988, uncatalogued; "Nürnberger Bierzug", the only limited edition set manufactured by LGB for 1988, distributed by Train World. Engine is black 2020 Steam Locomotive with white cab and red roof, next to which are the words "Nürnberger Bierzug". The three 4040 Tank Cars, named for famous Nuremberg breweries, are Lederer, Tucher, and Patrizier Brau, each with its crest (decal). The sets are numbered from 1 to 1,000; ten handmade sets are unnumbered.
(A) Black nose locomotive, 650 sets. **300**
(B) Gold nose locomotive, 350 sets. **385**
(C) Unnumbered, handmade sets. **1000**

25000: 1985, Pennsylvania train set with 2060 Diesel and two 4003 Container Cars; North Coast Distributors of Ohio repainted and relettered about 150 of the 380.7030 Phillips Video Train Sets; two separate versions were produced.
(A) Diesel and containers are repainted dull dark red; Pennsylvania lettering is in gold. **250**
(B) Same as (A), but repainted in dark green. **250**

1988 white LGB Model Railroad Club's 10th Anniversary Set, custom produced by Alfred Lentz. 344 sets made. In addition, 20 black versions, serially-numbered, were manufactured. J. Hylva Collection.

PASSENGER COACHES AND BAGGAGE CARS

3007BTO: 1986, Bci/s four-wheel coach produced for LGB Model Railroad Clubs' Eighth Anniversary; royal blue Simulated Metal SM2(B) body (unraised boards or plaques; corner seams and one horizontal seam), black Medium-Arched MA3 roof (six seams, three vents) with filigree roof supports, orange-yellow window frames; markings are gold-painted and include "GOLDEN STATE RAILWAY" over windows, "B", "T", "O" between windows, "EIGHTH YEAR" over "1986" bottom left, LGB Model Railroad Club logo in center "SANTA ROSA" over "CALIFORNIA" bottom right; 157 produced.   **125**

3062BTO: 1980, made for LGB Model Railroad Club's raffle; custom-painted orange body with black pin stripes; flat black-painted roof; passage bellows added; only two produced and included with set numbered 1980BTO. Not painted by Lehmann. J. Hylva Collection.   **NRS**

3063BTO: 1980, special version of 3063(A) Coach produced for LGB Model Railroad Clubs' Second Anniversary, held in Orlando, Florida; special orange-painted body with black lettering; 75 produced.   **165**

3080BTO: 1983, special version of 3080(C) Coach produced for LGB Model Railroad Clubs' Fifth Anniversary; yellow body with special black dry transfer decals to commemorate meet at Strasburg, Pennsylvania, with clear lettering and markings to allow the standard yellow color to show through on the black sides; 100 produced.   **175**

FLATCARS, GONDOLAS, HOPPERS, CONTAINER CARS, CONTAINERS, AND CABOOSES

4003BTO: 1984, car produced for the LGB Model Railroader Clubs' Sixth Anniversary, held in Rockford, Illinois; same basic bed as 4003 Flatcar; 56 produced in two versions.
(A) With 4069/1BTO(A) Container; dry transfer decals which read "PORT OF CHICAGO" upper left, "1984" in the center, and "CHATEAU LOUISE" in upper right; "BIG TRAIN OPERATOR'S" in black runs across the middle over a blue stripe, "LGB" logo on bottom left, and "6TH ANNUAL CONVENTION" along bottom center and right. The Chateau Louise Hotel closed due to financial difficulties prior to the convention; production had begun and six were produced.   **150**
(B) With 4069/1BTO(B) Container; similar to (A), but "Clock Tower Inn" is in place of "Chateau Louise"; approximately 50 produced.   **85**

4003A: 1985, uncatalogued; Abele Company container car, commissioned by same company of Aalen, West Germany; on standard 4003 Flatcar with 4069/1A Container painted silver with "ABELE" in heavy black lettering, with Vedes logo to its left and "SPIEL & FREIZEIT" to its right, also in black; originally sold with Set 20531A; 50 produced, some boxed separately.   **200**

4003B: 1985, uncatalogued; Breuninger Company container car, commissioned by same company of Stuttgart, West Germany; on standard 4003 Flatcar with 4069/1B Container painted chocolate brown (same brown as 4003SB) with "BREUNINGER" in large gold letters above "Stutttgart...& Spielwaren" also in gold; originally sold with Set 20531B; 200 produced, some boxed separately.   **175**

4003CS: 1985, uncatalogued; Capri-Sonne container car; on standard 4003 Flatcar with 4069/1CS Container painted royal blue with "Capri-Sonne" in white and orange lettering on each side above the words "Oberall. Fruchtig Kuhl und Fruchtig prall." in white; originally sold with Set 20531CS; 200 produced, some boxed separately.   **185**

4003CSK: 1988, Christmann Sammler Katalog container car. Standard black 4003 Flatcar carrying a yellow-painted container with the LGB silhouette logo of an 0-4-0T locomotive on track and the words

"SAMMLER KATALOG CHRISTMANN" in black on each side of container. Only 100 produced; each with its own serial number.   **85**

4003DV: 1985, uncatalogued; Dauth Company container car, commissioned by same company of Tubingen, West Germany (Dauth is part of the Vedes Company); on standard 4003 Flatcar with 4069/1DV Container painted silver with "Vedes...Fageschaft" logo to the right of the Dauth logo on each side; the Dauth logo is a rectangle containing the words "Spiel & Freizeit" above "Dauth" (with rocking horse to its left) above "Tubingen", and the words "...immer ein guter Rot mehr" outside and just above rectangle; lettering and logos in black; originally sold with Set 20531DV; 50 produced, some boxed separately.   **225**

4003GB: 1986, "Gummi-Bears" container car commissioned by the Heidi Candy Company; container is brown with a five-color production of a Gummi-Bear, mountains, and Heidi Candy company logo.   **NRS**

4003K: 1985, uncatalogued; Kurtz container car, on standard 4003 Flatcar with 4069/1K Container painted yellow with "Spielwaren Kurtz" with a toy soldier on horseback logo and "Stuttgart. Leonberg. Kirshheim/Teck"; markings in black; originally sold with Set 20531K; 150 produced, some boxed separately.   **175**

4003KT: 1985, uncatalogued; Kenner Trinken Wurtemberger container car on standard 4003 Flatcar with 4069/1KT Container painted silver with company logo depicting man sipping glass of wine, in black and red; company coat-of-arms in black, red, and brown, with "Genossenschaftskellerei" above it and "Heilbronn-Erlenbach-Weinsberge G." below it; 200 produced; sold only with Set 20531KT.   **190**

4003L: 1985, uncatalogued Lindau container car of the Thommes Company, Lindau, West Germany, on standard 4003 Flatcar with 4069/IL Container painted silver with the entrance to the Lindau harbor and "Lindau" to its right; all markings in black; originally sold with Set 20531L; 50 produced, some boxed separately.   **185**

4003MC: 1985, uncatalogued; Modellbahn-Center (MC) container car of Modelleisenbahn Center Schuler, Stuttgart, West Germany, on standard 4003 Flatcar with 4069/1MC Container painted royal blue with red "MC" logo and words "Modellbahn-Center" above "Container-Service"; originally sold with Set 20531MC; 120 produced, some boxed separately.   **175**

4003N: 1988, Spur II Nachrichten/LGB Model Railroad Club container car. Standard black 4003 Flatcar with painted container and decals to honor these clubs.   **NSS**

4003P: 1985, uncatalogued; Panne Company container car of the Panne Company of Reutlingen, West Germany, on standard 4003 Flatcar with 4069/1P Container painted silver with "Treibwagons" and "Modellbahnstation" in black lettering adjacent to logo; originally sold with Set 20531P; 50 produced, some boxed separately.   **225**

4003PH: 1986, Paul Hinsche container car painted silver with "PAUL HINSCHE" in black across each side of car; 50 produced; may have been sold with a black 4003 Flatcar or boxed separately.   **150**

4003S: 1985, uncatalogued; Schinacher Company container car of the Schinacher Company of Friedrichshafen, West Germany; on standard 4003 Flatcar with 4069/1S Container painted silver with black rectangle with "Schinacher" in silver letters inside it; to the right is "SPIEL & FREIZEIT" in black lettering; 100 produced; sold only with Set 20531S.   **225**

4003SB: 1984, uncatalogued; Schmidt Bakery container car, on standard 4003 Flatcar with 4069/1SB Container painted chocolate brown with white and red markings; sold only with Set 20526.   **NSS**

4003SF: 1985, uncatalogued; Schnabel Company container car of the Schnabel Company of Schwabisch-Gemund, West Germany, on standard 4003 Flatcar with 4069/1SF Container painted silver with "Schnabel" logo and teddy bear head, with "Spiel & Freizeit" above it; "Schwab.Gmund Ledergasse 63-65" to the right of the logo; markings in black; originally sold with Set 20531SF; 50 produced, some boxed separately.   **175**

4003SLM: 1986, SLM container car painted silver with 4069/1SLM Container with black lettering; originally sold with Set 20531SLM. **165**

4003SSB: 1988, Schwaben Brau Brewery container car. The standard black 4003 Flatcar with a white-painted container with the brewery's coat-of-arms composed on a gold and red shield with the words "STUTTGARTEN, SCHWABEN BRAU" in green on it; all other markings in black; only 150 produced, each with its own serial number. **100**

4003TS: 1985, uncatalogued; Sindel Company container car of the Sindel Company, Ulm, West Germany, on standard 4003 Flatcar with 4069/1TS Container painted silver with "TECHNIC SINDEL" across top of each side with "Donaustrasse 2 Ulm" below and a figure of a model airplane, remote-control car, model boat, remote-control radio, and steam locomotive along lower portion of each side; markings in black; originally sold with Set 20531TS; 150 produced, some boxed separately. **165**

4003Z: 1985, uncatalogued; Zinthafner Company container car of the Zinthafner Company of Ludwigsburg, West Germany, on standard 4003 Flatcar with 4069/1Z Container painted silver with company logo and "Spiel & Freizeit Zinthafner"; markings in black; originally sold with Set 20531Z; 100 produced, some boxed separately. **175**

4011BTO: 1982, produced for LGB Model Railroad Club's Fourth Anniversary, held at Coleman Nursery in Portsmouth, Virginia; standard 4011(DS) hinged-hatched Service Wagon; repainted bright red with white silk-screened lettering on doors to commemorate convention; Type 1 frame markings. **125**

4011O: 1986, commemorative car produced for the 75th anniversary of OEG; essentially the same car as the orange, hinged-hatch OEG Service Wagon 4011(B), but the sloped hatches on one side of the car have the following black, heat-stamped markings: "1911" (on left hatch), "75" inside a circle above "Jahre OEG" (on middle hatch), and "1986" (on right hatch); the sides of the bed have the "OEG 4011" markings typical of the current production 4011; 200 produced. H. Kahl Collection. **125**

4011SD: 1986, commemorative car produced for the 100th anniversary of Strassenbahn Darmstadt. This car is very similar to the 4011O, but lacks the "OEG" letters on the sides of the bed and has the following black, heat-stamped markings: "1886-" above "1986" (on left hatch), "100" inside a circle above "Jahre" (on middle hatch), and "Straßenbahn" above "Darmstadt" (on right hatch); 200 produced. H. Kahl Collection. **125**

4065BTO: 1985, produced for LGB Model Railroad Club's Seventh Anniversary, held at Suffolk, Virginia; painted brownish-red body has a series of white decals to commemorate the event. **150**

4065F: 1982, caboose similar to 4065(E), but with Florsheim decal over standard body markings. Decals were added by the LGB National Sales Office of Milwaukee, Wisconsin. Sold separately and with Set 20501F; 500 produced. **125**

4069/1A: 1985, Abele Company container commissioned by same company of Aalen, West Germany; container is painted silver with "ABELE" in heavy black lettering, with Vedes logo to its left and "SPIEL & FREIZEIT" to its right, also in black; came with 4003A Container Car; 50 produced. Price includes flatcar. **200**

4069/1B: 1985, Breuninger Company container commissioned by same company of Stuttgart, West Germany; container is painted chocolate brown with "BREUNINGER" in large yellow letters above "Stuttgart ... & Spielwaren", also in yellow; originally came with 4003B Container Car in Set 20531B; 200 produced. Price includes flatcar. **175**

4069/1BTO: 1984, uncatalogued; LGB Model Railroad Club's Sixth Anniversary car; two versions produced by Al Lentz; price is for container and 4003 Container Car.

(A) Container has Chicago freight logo and a pronouncement of the 1984 LGB Model Railroad Club at the Chateau Louise, Chicago, Illinois. Only six of these pieces were made due to the closing of that hotel just prior to the convention. Chateau Louise was the original site picked by the Chicago Chapter; however due to the hotel's financial problems the site was changed to the Clock Tower Inn at Rockford, Illinois. The Chateau Louise containers were made prior to cancellation notice. The meeting was relocated at the "Clock Tower" hotel. Entire side of container done with a peel-and-stick decal. Upper left side says "PORT OF CHICAGO", center "1984", upper right "CHATEAU LOUISE". Across middle in black letters on blue stripe, "BIG TRAIN OPERATOR'S"; bottom left is LGB logo. Bottom center and right, "6TH ANNUAL CONVENTION"; six produced. Price includes flatcar. **150**

(B) Similar to (A), but with wording to commemorate 1984 LGB Model Railroad Club's Convention at Clock Tower Inn in Rockford, Illinois (the location of the actual convention); 50 produced. **85**

4069/1CS: 1985, uncatalogued; Capri-Sonne container painted royal blue with "Capri-Sonne" in white and orange on each side above the words "Oberall. Fruchtig Kuhl und fruchtig prall." in white; originally came with 4003CS Container Car in Set 20531CS; 200 produced. Price includes flatcar. **185**

4069/1DV: 1985, uncatalogued; Dauth Company container commissioned by same company of Tubingen, West Germany (Dauth is part of the Vedes chain of stores); container is painted silver with "Vedes...Fachgeschaft" logo to the right of the Dauth logo on each side; the Dauth logo is a rectangle with the words "Spiel & Freizeit" above "Dauth" (with a rocking horse to its left) above "Tubingen" inside and the words "...immer ein guter Rot mehr" outside and just above the rectangle, all in black printing; originally came with 4003DV Container Car in Set 20531DV; 50 pieces produced. Price includes flatcar. **190**

4069/1GB: 1986, Gummi-Bear container; brown with five-color production of a Gummi-Bear, mountains, and Heidi Candy Company logo. **NRS**

4069/1K: 1985, uncatalogued; Kurtz Company container, yellow-painted container with black-lettered "Spielwaren Kurtz" with a toy soldier on horseback logo; other black lettering includes the words "Stuttgart. Leonberg. Kirshheim/Teck"; originally came with 4003K Container Car in Set 20531K; 150 pieces produced. Price includes flatcar. **175**

4069/1KT: 1985, uncatalogued; Kenner Trinken Wurtemberger container; painted silver with company logo depicting a man sipping a glass of wine in black and red and the company's coat of arms in black, red, and brown, with "Genossenschaftskellerei" above it and the words "Heilbronn-Erlenbach-Weinsberge G." below it; originally sold with 4003KT Container Car in Set 20531KT; 200 pieces produced. Price includes flatcar. **190**

4069/1L: 1985, uncatalogued; Lindau Container commissioned by the Thommes Company, Lindau, West Germany; container is painted silver with entrance to the Lindau harbor depicted in black and "Lindau" to its right; originally sold with 4003L Container Car in Set 20531L; 50 pieces produced. Price includes flatcar. **185**

4069/1MC: 1985, uncatalogued; Modellbahn-Center (MC) container commissioned by Modelleisenbahn Center Schuler, Stuttgart, West Germany; container is painted royal blue with red "MC" logo and the words "Modellbahn-Center" above "Container-Service" also in red; originally came with 4003MC Container Car in Set 20531MC; 120 produced. Price includes flatcar. **175**

The LGB Model Railroad Club's 1986 and 1987 Convention Cars. G. Ryall Collection.

4069/1P: 1985, uncatalogued; Panne Company container commissioned by Panne, Reutlingen, West Germany; container is painted silver with the Panne logo and name in black; the words "Triebwagons" and "Modellbahnstation" are adjacent to logo also in black print; originally sold with 4003P Container Car in Set 20531P; 50 produced. Price includes flatcar.   **185**

4069/1PH: uncatalogued; Paul Hinsche container with "PAUL HINSCHE" across each side; painted silver with black lettering.   **175**

4069/1S: 1985, uncatalogued; Schinacher Company container commissioned by Schinacher, Friedrichshafen, West Germany; container is painted silver and has a black rectangle with "Schinacher" in silver letters inside it; to the right of rectangle are the words "SPIEL & FREIZEIT" in black; originally came with 4003S Container Car in Set 20531S; 100 produced. Price includes flatcar.   **175**

4069/1SF: 1985, uncatalogued; Schnabel Company container car commissioned by Schnabel, Schwabisch-Gemund, West Germany; container is painted silver and has the "Schnabel" logo with a teddy bear head and the words "Spiel & Freizeit" above it, also has the address "Schwabisch-Gemund Ledergasse 63-65" to the right of logo, all in black print; originally sold with 4003SF Container Car in Set 20531SF; 50 produced. Price includes flatcar.   **175**

4069/1TS: 1985, uncatalogued; Sindel Company container commissioned by Sindel, Ulm, West Germany; container is painted silver with "TECHNIC SINDEL" across top of each side with "Donaustrasse 2 Ulm" below and figure of a model airplane, remote-control car, model boat, remote-control radio, and steam locomotive along lower portion of each side, all in black; originally sold with 4003TS Container Car in Set 20531TS; 150 pieces produced. Price includes flatcar.   **165**

4069/1Z: 1985, uncatalogued; Zinthafner Company container commissioned by Zinthafner, Ludwigsburg, West Germany; container is painted silver with company logo and the words "Spiel & Freizeit Zinthafner" all in black; originally came with 4003Z Container Car in Set 20531Z; 150 pieces produced. Price includes flatcar.   **175**

BOXCARS AND REFRIGERATOR CARS

4032: 1980, very similar to 4031 Pepsi Car but has silk-screened "Coca-Cola" logos on sides at end opposite brakeman's platform; no frame markings.   **85**

4032BTO: 1987, boxcar produced for the LGB Model Railroad Club's Ninth Anniversary held at Helena, Georgia; white car with billboard on side reads "NINTH YEAR" above "19 87" with circled LGB logo between the "9" and "8", all in black; "B.T.O." The door is simulated metal with the markings "PEACH STATE / RAILWAY" above "HELENA / GEORGIA". Lettering is black, flag is in gold, and door is outlined in red. Dimension and computer markings in reduced block.   **100**

4032F: 1983, four-wheel Florsheim boxcar, similar to 4032 Refrigerator Car but has small rectangular decal with gold lettering on doors, no other markings on body, Low-Arched LA1 roof; sold originally with Set 20501F put together by the National Sales Office, Milwaukee, Wisconsin. These cars were packaged with set in 20401 boxes or separately in 4032 Tucher beer boxes, B. Cage Collection; or in red boxes stamped "4032F", M. Richter Collection.
(A) Florsheim decal in gold and white on both sides of body and "Florsheim Shoe" decal, also in gold and white, on each sliding door.   **75**

(B) Similar to (A), but Florsheim decal attached to slightly larger red plaque on side doors; simulated door on body end at brakeman's platform in the form of a decal; may be prototype. J. Hylva Collection.   **NRS**

4067G: 1988, Golden Gate Bridge boxcar. Yellow-painted 4067 Boxcar with black markings that include the silhouette of the Golden Gate Bridge of San Francisco, California, surrounded with a wreath and the lettering "50 YEAR GOLDEN GATE BRIDGE". Number of pieces made is unknown to author.   **120**

4069G: 1988, Gloria Fire Extinguisher double container car. Black-painted 4069 Flatcar with no markings. Containers are painted glossy red with white markings which are in English on one side of each container and in German on the other side.   **200**

4070BTO: 1981, produced for LGB Model Railroad Club's Third Anniversay held at the Red Caboose Lodge, Strasburg, Pennsylvania. Same basic body as 4070, but unpainted white with red, black, and yellow commemorative decals. 100 blank (unlettered) 4070 Reefer Cars were received by Al Lentz, but only around 50 had decals. **225**

LGB cars have been customized for many years. These two, customized in Germany, are a very long Ruhr-Gas tanker and a short R4208 RhB Uce 8075 Tanker. G. Ryall Collection.

4070NC: 1984, Tiffany eight-wheel reefer car finished for North Coast Distributors of Medina, Ohio; custom-painted white with brown ends, roof is brown with black edges; lettering on sides of car is brown and reads as follows: to the left of the doors are the words "TIFFANY" in an arc above "SUMMER & WINTER" above "CAR", to the right of the doors is "D.S.P. & P.R.R." in an arc above "REFRIGERATOR" above "1062"; the markings on each end are white and read "D.S.P. & P.R.R." above "1062"; 200 produced.   **200**

TANK CARS

Circa 1981, Al Lentz offered a limited number of LT cars painted a deep, glossy bluish-green with "BP" stickers, yellow letters on a green shield on a white background, through the BTO Newsletter of the LGB Club; not a Lehmann finish.   **55**

4040BTO: 1979, produced for LGB Model Railroad Club's First Anniversary held in Strasburg, Pennsylvania. Similar to 4040C(D), but has black "BASF" label replaced with special decals for the event; cars were personalized with each club member's membership number; 50 produced.   **135**

POWERED RAILCARS, SHORT CARS, SERVICE WAGONS, AND CABLE CARS

4047BTO: 1984, produced for LGB Model Railroad Club's Sixth Anniversary (also see 4003BTO). This car was not the official commemorative car, but was offered as an additional memento. Same as 4047(C), but with silver cask; side boards proclaiming "1984-LGB Chicago" on side of cask. J. Hylva, J. Henderson, and R. Rench Collections; 40 produced.   **200**

Appendix
PRIMUS

Train Set

8000: 1977-78, black and dark green 20875 0-4-0T Locomotive, pinkish-red 30800 Coach, blue 40821 high-sided Gondola. Included twelve pieces of LGB 1100 Curved Track, 5000 (Primus number 50800) 220-volt Transformer, 5016 Connector Cables, 5040 Figures, etc. Set came packaged in a compartmentalized, styrofoam box with a windowless, yellow lid and the "8000" set number printed on it. **1400**

Locomotives

20860: 1977-78, blue four-wheel Schoema diesel locomotive; horn on roof may be black or gold. **550**

20872: 1978, 0-6-2T steam locomotive. **275**

20875: 1977-78, 0-4-0T locomotive, semi-glossy dark green water tanks with a "LEHMANN" label in the middle (on each side) while the rest of the body is flat black. Disc type drivers, slotted wheels. **875**

Passenger Coaches

30800: 1977-78, unpainted, pinkish-red, Bi/s type, four-wheel coach. SW1 body marked with Arabic second or third class numbers, no "LGB" logo plaque. "3000" ID number, LA1 roof, yellow window frames, and no frame markings. **185**

30801: 1977-78, same as the 30800, but dark green. **200**

30819: 1978, postal and baggage car with unpainted, medium brown body, Low-arched LA3 roof, and four-wheel chassis. The few body markings are heat-stamped in white. Has factory-mounted LGB 3019/1 Metal Wheels with LGB 3019/3 Carbon Brush Holders on the trucks and two red LGB 3031 Taillights on rear of body.
(A) White, heat-stamped markings on the same end of car on both sides. **325**

(B) White, heat-stamped markings are "kitty-corner" from one another. **325**

Freight Cars

40821: 1977-78, high-sided "Ow" type gondola.
(A) Medium blue gondola body with embossed "4021" ID number, no painted detail markings on body and frame. **275**
(B) Yellow gondola body, Type 1 frame markings. **275**

40832: 1977-78, Coca-Cola refrigerator car, four-wheel chassis. Unpainted white body with black dimension markings on one side only; plaque with "Coca-Cola" logo is red with white lettering; embossed "4032" ID number. **400**

40840: 1978, Shell Oil Company tank car, painted flat black with a red and yellow "Shell" logo sticker. **150**

40841: 1978, O.E.G. hopper car; identical to the LGB 4041G. **275**

40861: 1978, Southern Pacific "S.P." low-sided gondola on eight-wheel chassis; unpainted, dark green gondola sides, white numbers and dimension markings on black bed. **650**

Track and Transformer

10800: 1978, 300 mm long straight track section. **CP**

11800: 1978, curved track section. **CP**

12800: 1978, manual right-hand switch track. **28**

12810: 1978, manual left-hand switch track. **28**

208901: 1978, track extension pack. **CP**

208902: 1978, track extension pack. **CP**

50800: 1978, 220-volt 30 va transformer. **15**

INDEX

C indicates a color photograph.

Code	Pg	Code	Pg	Code	Pg	Code	Pg	Code	Pg	Code	Pg	Code	Pg	Code	Pg
4023	86	4040E	107	4067-DO3	101	4076-DO2	92	5026	121	5080N	123	11800	119	20531L	127
4025	86	4040E-C	96	4067-DO3-C	100	4076-XO1	92	5027	121	5080/1	123	12800	119	20531MC	127
4026	94	4040E-C	105	4067-FO1	101	4080	108	5028	121	5090	123	12810	119	20531P	127
4026	86	4040E-C	107	4067G	130	4080-C	108	5029	121	5091	123	20087	20	20531S	127
4027	94	4040L	107	4068	101	4080-YO1	108	5029	122	5092	123	20150	20	20531SF	127
4028	94	4040RZ	107	4068-C	99	4080-YO2	108	5030	122	5093	123	20277	20	20531SLM	127
4029	94	4040S	107	4068-C	100	4080-YO3	108	5030/1	122	5094	122	20301	20	20531TS	127
4029	95	4040S-C	105	4069	91	4080-YO3-C	108	5031	122	5094	123	20301-C	20	20531Z	127
4029-C	96	4040SF	108	4069-C	90	4080-YO4	108	5031/1	122	5127	123	20301BP	21	20532	24
4030	95	4041	87	4069G	130	4080-YO4-C	108	5032	122	5143	123	20301BP-C	26	20532-C	26
4030-C	24	4041-C	86	4069/1	93	4103	93	5033	122	6000	123	20301BZ	21	20534	25
4030-C	95	4041G	87	4069/1A	129	4128	103	5034	118	6000	124	20301BZ-C	21	20536L	25
4030-C	96	4042	87	4069/1B	129	4131	103	5034	122	6000/2	123	20301MF	21	20536L-C	27
4030SB	95	4042	110	4069/1BTO	129	4141	92	5035	122	6001	124	20301MF-C	24	20575	25
4031	95	4042-C	22	4069/1CS	129	4169	92	5036	122	6009	124	20302	21	20601	25
4031-C	95	4042-C	110	4069/1D	93	5000	121	5038	122	6010	124	20401	21	20601B	25
4031C	95	4043	111	4069/1DV	129	5000/110	121	5039	122	6011	124	20401RZ	21	20601B-C	25
4031CC	95	4043-C	110	4069/1F	93	5001	121	5040	122	6015	124	20401RZ-C	21	20601T	25
4031HS	95	4044	111	4069/1GB	129	5001/9	121	5041	122	6016	124	20500	22	20602	25
4031L	96	4045	111	4069/1K	129	5002	121	5042	122	6060	124	20501	22	20636L-C	27
4032	96	4046	111	4069/1KT	129	5003	121	5043	122	6100	124	20501-C	22	20675	25
4032	130	4047	111	4069/1L	129	5003/110	121	5044	122	6100/2	124	20501-C	27	20701	25
4032-C	96	4047BTO	131	4069/1MC	129	5004	121	5045	122	6100/4	124	20501F	22	20701DC	25
4032BTO	130	4049	111	4069/1P	130	5005	121	5045	123	6100/5	124	20501F-C	23	20701DC-C	24
4032C	97	4049-C	111	4069/1PH	130	5006	121	5046	123	6101	124	20501JR	22	20701T	25
4032F	130	4059	87	4069/1PV	93	5006/110V	121	5047	122	6102	124	20502	23	20872	39
4032L	97	4059-C	87	4069/1RZ	93	5007	121	5047	123	6160	124	20512	23	20875	39
4033	97	4060	87	4069/1S	130	5008	121	5048	123	6190	124	20512-C	22	20901	119
4033-C	97	4060-C	88	4069/1SB	93	5009	121	5049	123	6200	124	20513	23	20902	119
4033B	97	4061	88	4069/1SF	130	5010	121	5050	118	6201	124	20513-C	24	21401	26
4033V	97	4061-C	85	4069/1SR	93	5012	121	5050	123	6202	124	20514	23	21980-C	19
4033V-C	96	4061-C	88	4069/1TS	130	5012N	121	5050/1	123	6204	124	20514-C	25	21980B	26
4034	98	4062	89	4069/1Z	130	5012/1	121	5050/2	123	6300	124	20515	125	21981	26
4034-C	22	4062-C	89	4070	102	5013	121	5051/1	123	6400	124	20516	23	21988N	127
4034-C	98	4063	98	4070-C	101	5013/1	121	5051/2	123	6400/2	124	20518	23	21988US	26
4035	98	4063-C	99	4070BTO	130	5014	121	5052	123	6401	124	20519	23	22301US	26
4036	98	4064	98	4070BTO-C	126	5015	121	5055	123	8000	20	20519-C	25	22401US	26
4036-C	98	4064-C	99	4070NC	131	5015/1	121	5056	123	8001	117	20520	23	25000	127
4037	86	4065	90	4071	102	5016	121	5060	123	8002	117	20520-C	21	30800	83
4040	104	4065-C	89	4071-C	101	5016/1	121	5061	123	8003	117	20522	23	30801	83
4040	107	4065BTO	129	4072	102	5016/5000	121	5061/1	123	8015	117	20526	23	30819	83
4040-C	105	4065BTO-C	126	4072-C	102	5016/5000N	121	5061/2	123	8016	117	20526-C	25	40821	92
4040A	104	4065F	129	4073	92	5016/5003	121	5061/3	123	8017	117	20528	23	40832	103
4040A-C	96	4065LG&B	90	4073-C	91	5016/5012	121	5061/4	123	8020	117	20528	125	40840	108
4040A-C	105	4065-GO1	90	4073-CO3	92	5017	121	5065	123	8025	117	20528-C	26	40841	92
4040B	106	4066	90	4074	102	5018	121	5070	123	8030	117	20529	24	40861	92
4040BP-C	105	4066-C	90	4074-C	102	5019	121	5071	123	8035	117	20530	24	50800	120
4040BP-C	106	4067	99	4074-BO2	103	5020	121	5072	123	8036	117	20531A	126	208901	119
4040BTO	131	4067-C	99	4074-ZO2	103	5021	121	5073	123	9000	112	20531B	127	208902	120
4040BTO-C	126	4067-C	100	4075	92	5022	121	5075	123	9000E	112	20531CS	127	380.7030	27
4040C	106	4067-AO1	101	4075	111	5023	121	5075N	123	9000S	112	20531DV	127	380.7030-C	22
4040C-C	105	4067-AO1-C	99	4075-C	91	5024	121	5075/1	123	9000S-C	112	20531K	127		
4040C-C	106	4067-DO1	101	4076	92	5025	121	5080	123	10800	119	20531KT	127		

-C indicates a color photograph.